europeanisation and party politics

how the eu affects domestic actors, patterns and systems

Edited by

Erol Külahci

ecpr PRESS

First published by the ECPR Press in 2012

The ECPR Press is the publishing imprint of the European Consortium for Political Research (ECPR), a scholarly association, which supports and encourages the training, research and cross-national cooperation of political scientists in institutions throughout Europe and beyond. ECPR Press, ECPR Central Services, University of Essex, Wivenhoe Park, Colchester, CO4 3SQ, UK

Typeset by AnVi Composers
Printed and bound by Lightning Source

British Library Cataloguing in Publication Data
A catalogue record for this book is available from the British Library

Hardback ISBN: 978-1-907301-22-3

www.ecprnet.eu/ecprpress

ECPR – Studies in European Political Science

Series Editors:
Dario Castiglione (University of Exeter)
Peter Kennealy (European University Institute)
Alexandra Segerberg (Stockholm University)
Peter Triantafillou (Roskilde University)

ECPR – Studies in European Political Science is a series of high-quality edited volumes on topics at the cutting edge of current political science and political thought. All volumes are research-based offering new perspectives in the study of politics with contributions from leading scholars working in the relevant fields. Most of the volumes originate from ECPR events including the Joint Sessions of Workshops, the Research Sessions, and the General Conferences.

Books in this series

Interactive Policy Making, Metagovernance and Democracy
ISBN: 9781907301131
Edited by Jacob Torfing and Peter Triantafillou

A Comparative Sociology of European Attitudes
ISBN: 9781907301155
Edited by Daniel Gaxie, Jay Rowell and Nicolas Hubé

Personal Representation: The Neglected Dimension of Electoral Systems
ISBN: 9781907301162
Edited by Josep Colomer

Political Trust: Why Context Matters
ISBN: 9781907301230
Edited by Sonja Zmerli and Marc Hooghe

Please visit www.ecprnet.eu/ecprpress for up-to-date information about new publications.

| contents

| list of figures and tables

Figures

Tables

| contributors

STEFANO BARTOLINI is Professor of Comparative Politics and Director of the Robert Schuman Centre for Advanced Studies at the European University Institute in Florence. His academic interests cover the field of European comparative politics, electoral history, and European Integration.

DAVID S. BELL is Professor of French Government and Politics and teaches at the University of Leeds in Politics and International Studies. His research is on political parties in Western Europe and on political leadership in the Western world. His publications include articles on the recent elections in France and on the parties of the extreme left in Europe.

IOSIF BOTETZAGIAS is Assistant Professor at the Department of Environment, University of the Aegean, Greece. His academic interests include Environmental Politics and Policies, Environment Sociology and New Social Movements.

NICOLÒ CONTI is Assistant Professor of Political Science at the University Unitelma Sapienza of Rome. He has recently edited "Which Europe do Parties Want? A View from France, Italy, Portugal and Spain" (special issue of *Perspectives on European Politics and Society* vol. 1 (2), 2010).

JEAN-MICHEL DE WAELE is Professor of Political Science at the Université libre de Bruxelles. He is also the Dean of the Faculty of Social and Political Science. His research centres on political parties and interest groups, Central and Eastern Europe, and comparative European politics. His publications include recent books on Central and Eastern Europe.

DAVID HANLEY is Emeritus Professor of European Studies and former Head of the School of European Studies at Cardiff University. His research centres on comparative European politics, especially political parties and transnationalism. He is currently Visiting Professor at the Centre for International Studies Research, University of Portsmouth, where he is continuing his work on European political parties.

ISABELLE HERTNER is a Ph.D candidate and research assistant at the Department of Politics and International Relations, Royal Holloway, University of London. Her Ph.D focuses on the Europeanisation of social democratic party organisation. Her wider research interests include British, German and French EU policies and policy making.

EROL KÜLAHCI is member of the Centre d'étude de la vie politique (CEVIPOL, Université libre de Bruxelles). He co-created and chairs the standing group Young ECPR Network on Europeanisation. His research centres on comparative European politics, especially domestic and European political parties. His publications include recent books and articles on multi-level party politics.

JOHN LOUGHLIN is Fellow of Edmund's College, Cambridge and Affiliated Lecturer in Politics in the Department of Politics and International Studies, University of Cambridge. He was Professor of European Politics at Cardiff University and Visiting Professor at the Institut d'Etudes Politiques, Aix-en-Provence. He has published extensively on issues of territorial governance in Europe and elsewhere, and has acted as an adviser on these issues to the UK Government, the Council of Europe, the European Union and the United Nations. He founded and edited for eleven years *Regional and Federal Studies* (Routledge) and created the ECPR Standing Group on Regionalism.

ANNA PACZEŚNIAK holds a Ph.D and she is currently at the Department of European Studies, Institute of Political Science of Wroclaw University. Her research is on European integration, political parties and patriotism. Her publications include articles on issues related to the integration of Poland to the European Union from the angle of party politics.

JAMES SLOAM is Senior Lecturer in Politics and International Relations at Royal Holloway, University of London, where he is also co-director of the Centre for European Politics. His research interests include German party politics, European social democracy, youth participation in democracy, and citizenship education. His most recent publication is *Germany's Gathering Crisis: the 2005 Federal Election and the Grand Coalition* (Palgrave, 2008).

SORINA SOARE holds a Ph.D from the Université libre de Bruxelles (ULB). She is member of the CEVIPOL, ULB. She also teaches a course in Political Science at the University of Palermo (Italy). She has published numerous works in the field of the democratisation process and post-communist political parties. Her current work analyses the post-communist patterns of party organisation and the communist legacies.

RAFAEL VÁZQUEZ-GARCÍA is Lecturer in the Department of Political Science and Public Administration at University of Granada (Spain). He has focused on the study of civil society and political leadership and elites. He was awarded the Spanish National Prize of Political Science and Administration (2001).

CHRISTOFOROS VERNARDAKIS is Assistant Professor at Aristotle University of Thessaloniki, Department of Political Science. His academic interests are: the study of political parties, electoral sociology and the methodology of political research. He has recently published (2011) *Political Parties, Elections and Party Systems; the transformation of political representation 1990–2010* (Editions Sakoulas).

LUCA VERZICHELLI is Professor of Political Science at the Centre for the Study of Political Change (CIRCaP, University of Siena). His academic interests cover the field of comparative political institutions, political elite and budgetary politics.

| acknowledgements

This edited book would not have been possible without the support of a large number of people and organisations. Among the latter, I need to single out the CEVIPOL/ULB (*Centre d'étude de la vie politique, Université libre de Bruxelles*) and the European Consortium for Political Research (ECPR) as well as the standing group on the Young ECPR Network on Europeanisation (YEN).

In addition to institutions, there are the individuals. To begin with, I would like to remember my dad and give my thanks to him, and thank my mum for her extraordinary commitment of time and resources. Most especially, I am grateful for my education and research opportunities.

Next, I thank very much Professor Pascal Delwit for his excellent support throughout this research project.

This book could not have been produced without the enthusiasm of the many contributors (professors and researchers), including well-known specialists in party politics and European affairs. I thank all of them for following patiently the project guidelines.

I would like to express my deepest gratitude to the editors – Professors Dario Castiglione and Peter Kennealy – for giving full consideration to this book within the ECPR's Studies in Political Science series and for bringing this project to completion. In addition, I thank also very much the external referee for their insightful contributions in revising chapters of this volume. Moreover, I thank colleagues for their respective and very important contributions: the copy editors – Michael Woodmansey and Ildi Clarke – the Marketing Executve – Pippa Kerry and the ECPR Press Manager – Mark Kench.

For fruitful exchanges, I am grateful to Professors David S. Bell, David Hanley, Simon Lightfoot and John Loughlin, as well as to Mr Russel Miller and Professor Peter Mair who is already very much missed.

I am very indebted to Lect. Ana Maria Dobre for helping me bring this edited project to a conclusion, since the very beginning.

Finally, I owe my thanks to baby Alexandra Dina Sezen as she inspired me and was quite patient (sometimes less!) when daddy was working. I dedicate this book to her and hope that she will grow up in a democratic, effective and more humane Europe.

Erol Külahci
Brussels, 12 February 2012

chapter one | introduction to european integration, party systems and political parties[1]

Erol Külahci

In European liberal democracies, political parties have played a key role in representing citizens by conceiving political projects in competitive party systems and by trying to deliver them when in government. With the growing development of multilevel European politics, the impact of the European Union (EU) on these key political actors and their party systems is a pertinent issue. However, the influence of the EU on the member states' party systems and political parties is under-researched. The aim of this book is to contribute by filling in this gap in comparative literature.

Before presenting the general argument, the literature on Europeanisation in relation to party politics will be reviewed in order to single out the relevant dimensions for this book's research purposes: the concept's definition, the two-way adaptation/influence process, the outcomes, the indirect/direct effects, the intervening variables and one important paradox of the Europeanisation of party politics.

Europeanisation and party politics

For several decades, the Europeanisation of party politics[2] has been a subject of increasing academic debate, theorisation and empirical research. This interest is attributable to the intricacies of the topic and the diversity of the dimensions of party politics.[3] Indeed, academics have singled out different analytical aspects, including ideology and the manifestos (as well as programmatic change),[4] the patterns of party competition,[5] the electoral campaigns,[6] the policies of the party in government,[7] the relationship between citizens and the elected politicians,[8] relations beyond the national party system[9] and, recently, adaptation in terms of power and organisation.[10] In contrast, academics have paid less attention to the Europeanisation of party systems.[11]

The objective is to analyse the ways in which, and the extent to which, domestic party systems and the policy stances of political parties have adapted to European integration, and this book focuses mainly on the top-down dimension of Europeanisation. The analytical framework draws on Ladrech's definition of Europeanisation, which is understood as a process in which, 'European integration influences the operating arenas, or environments, of national political parties, and the Europeanisation of parties is consequently a dependent variable'.[12] This definition is adapted in order to analyse the Europeanisation of domestic parties' policy stances and the party systems (political cleavages and party competition, including format and mechanics).

This is not to neglect the fact that Europeanisation is characterised by a two-way process.[13] On the one hand, the literature focuses on the impact of EU decisions on domestic political parties, Europarties and Euro-parliamentary groups. In this volume, contributors analysing country cases concentrate on the top-down process, without neglecting – when necessary – the bottom-up process. On the other hand, political scientists have examined the impact of domestic parties, Europarties and Euro-parliamentary groups on European integration. Chapters Ten and Eleven reflect and consider the bottom-up aspects of party politics' Europeanisation.

As emphasised in the literature, there are differences in the Europeanisation outcomes. Indeed:

> Europeanisation fully acknowledges that the impact of European integration on domestic actors and the extent to which these actors may or may not engage in any adaptation is likely to be non-uniform, within countries, across countries, and over time.[14]

Drawing on these findings, this book brings an extra contribution to the current literature by singling out three *patterns* of party system responses to European integration:

- the Europhile party system;
- the divided party system; and
- the party system with significant Eurosceptic parties.

The literature points out that party systems, individual parties and the interaction between the European and national levels could be affected by the *direct* and *indirect* effects of European integration. *Direct* effects are defined as visible national changes or consequences in response to European integration (such as anti-European movement, party split, etc.). Note that Bartolini has warned that *indirect* effects, though less visible, may be much more important than direct changes. For instance, European integration could empower and open up opportunities for some groups of actors while marginalising others.[15] This book, however, focuses on the direct effects of European integration without neglecting, when necessary, the indirect effects such as the question of 'depoliticisation'.

The complexity of domestic and external systems, where political parties and party systems operate, and the multiplicity of actors involved in this process of Europeanisation and domestic adaptation, make it useful to refer to additional theories and concepts. As Featherstone so synthetically argues, it 'would be misleading [...] to suggest that "Europeanisation" has been widely used as a standalone conceptual framework.'[16] Different authors suggest integrating the concept of Europeanisation within the methods and theories deriving from comparative analysis and politics. Several intervening variables are identified in the literature: institutional, systems of policy beliefs, values, discourses, identities, the political preferences of actors, and the emergence (and mobilisation) of political and partisan competition.[17]

This book proposes a multi-variable framework of analysis by linking the

Europeanisation concept with country-specific factors and explanatory variables deriving from theories of party change and development. In doing so, one of the aims is to position ourselves vis-à-vis an important paradox in the literature,[18] namely the non-Europeanisation of party systems (Mair postulate) and the Europeanisation of political parties and their policies (Ladrech's postulate). Ladrech has already shown that Europeanisation has an impact on five areas, among which is the policy/programmatic content of parties.[19] Even though he shares Ladrech's finding on the impact of EU integration on domestic political parties' policy stances, Mair argues that European integration has little (if any) impact on the party systems. He distinguishes between the *direct* and *indirect* effects of European integration and finds *little evidence of any major direct effects* on the *format* and *mechanics* of Western European national party systems. Furthermore, Mair assumes that Europe reinforces the domestic trend of depoliticisation.[20] In contrast, Hooghe and Marks consider that the politicisation of an issue occurs whenever the issue 'enters mass politics' and this depends on whether party leaders 'see electoral advantage in doing so'.[21]

In testing this paradox, the purpose is to present a framework for the analysis of party systems and political parties in EU member states by looking at the European and state-wide levels and, if significant from an institutional and policy point of view, at the sub-national level (regions, communities and local). This research also aims to contribute and further develop the tradition of comparative analysis of party Europeanisation. However, unlike most previous work, this book explores the Europeanisation of both party systems and individual parties. In addition, this analysis aims at studying the connection between EU and domestic partisan factors and the way parties are shaped in each country. Each chapter focuses on a country and examines how Europeanisation has taken shape and the extent to which it is linked to various intervening variables such as those that are country-specific.

The theoretical arguments

The aim of this book is to describe and explain the cross-national variation of responses of domestic party systems and the policy stance of individual parties in relation to the European integration process. To do so, it addresses the following research questions:

1. What explains the outcome (disjunction or conjunction) of both the party systems and the domestic parties' Europeanisation? More specifically, is the domestic party system Europeanised or not? To what extent has there been an impact on political cleavages and party competition? Through which main partisan *mechanism* is Europeanisation promoted? Is it through European elections and/or Europarties (party groups and party federations)?

2. Given conjunction or disjunction, what factors explain the Europeanisation of individual domestic parties' policy stances?

3. Given the Europeanisation of domestic parties, what variables explain the

different patterns of co-operation/competition in domestic party systems in the EU? Are the party systems Europhile, divided or characterised by significant Eurosceptic parties?

These questions are addressed, when relevant, by distinguishing 'state-wide' parties/party systems from 'peripheral' ones.

General argument

The general argument is that a tripartite explanation – the European integration processes, the country-specific factors and the factors from theories of party change and development – accounts for the Europeanisation of party politics. The following independent and intervening variables have key explanatory power:

- *The independent variable:* European integration processes that include, in particular, European elections and European parties (both parliamentary groups and party federations).
- *The intervening variables:* these include country-specific factors (intervening variables I) and the transversal factors pointed out by theories of party change and development (intervening variables II).

The consequences of the independent and the intervening variables are explored with reference to the dependent variable, which is the Europeanisation (or non-Europeanisation) both of the party systems (political cleavages and party competition, including the format and the mechanics) and of the political parties (policy stances).

Disjunction or conjunction?

Disjunction or conjunction of both party systems and domestic parties in the context of Europeanisation vary from one country to another. From this, two competing hypotheses are proposed:

First Hypothesis (H I): European integration may lead to a disjunction between a 'non-Europeanised party system' and 'Europeanised political parties'.

Second Hypothesis (H II): European integration may result in a shift not only of individual parties, but also of party systems. In other words, a conjunction may emerge between a 'Europeanised party system' and 'Europeanised political parties'.

Policy stances of domestic parties

The second theoretical question concerns the Europeanisation of domestic parties' policy stances. Following Stefano Bartolini, this book distinguishes three types of European issues:

1. the negative or positive general orientation towards the European Union;

2. the constitutive issues (membership, competences, decision-making rules); and

3. the isomorphic issues (neo-liberalism versus economic interventionism, rights of citizens, immigration and welfare issues, etc.).[22]

At the individual party level, the authors will analyse key policies on these issues and investigate the main intervening variables explaining the domestic policy stances of major parties (social democratic, liberal, Christian democratic and conservative)[23] as well as those of parties from different political families (radical left, radical right and right-populist, green and regionalist).[24] The concluding chapter will explicate the link between the country studies and these political families.

Patterns of party systems

The third theoretical question focuses on the Europeanisation of patterns and variations of domestic party competition/co-operation. The present analysis acknowledges this variation and puts forward three patterns of co-operation/competition in domestic party systems (see below). The typology proposed by this book differs in crucial respects from the three patterns of party competition proposed by Taggart and Szczerbiak. Our typology proposes a different terminology and definition of the three patterns[25] and it is based on a comparison of selected countries, focusing on the Europeanisation of party systems and the policy stances of domestic parties. In Chapter Eleven, the testing and refinement of this typology is another contribution that this book brings to the literature by proposing the following distinctions and definitions:

– The *Europhile party system* is not characterised by an opposition between pro- and anti-Europe mainstream domestic parties; in this setting, the mainstream parties are Europhile. However, the Eurosceptic parties are not necessarily absent,[26] but their political weight is limited since they win less than 10 per cent of the seats in the national assemblies (X<10%). However, referendums[27] and even European Parliamentary elections might reinforce Eurosceptic parties (X>10%) and Eurosceptic voters (X>50%) in one or another country case.

– The *divided party system* is animated by the European cleavage between Eurosceptics and integrationists. In this case, there is opposition between (and/or within) pro- and anti-Europe mainstream parties on isomorphic and constitutive issues as well as on EU orientation. The Eurosceptic parties' political weight is very significant since they win more than 30 per cent (X>30%) of the seats in the national assemblies. In some cases, Eurosceptic parties are even governing the country (e.g., Hungary).

– The *party system with significant Eurosceptic parties* tends to oppose pro-Europe mainstream parties and anti-Europe 'non-mainstream' parties. Usually, the former represents 'governing' parties and the latter is more typical of opposition parties[28] debating EU orientation as well as constitutive or isomorphic issues. In this setting, the Eurosceptic parties are again inevitably present. The political weight of Eurosceptics is significant since they win between 10 and 30 per cent ($10\% < X < 30\%$) of the seats in the national assemblies. Some of them even have the potential to give outside support to the government (the Netherlands) or may be part of a government coalition. Accordingly, referendums on European integration issues might reinforce Eurosceptic parties and Eurosceptic voters ($X > 50\%$).

Dependent, intervening and independent variables

Dependent variables – party systems and political parties' policy stances

At the level of *party systems*, the focus is on the Europeanisation of political cleavages and party competition. The analysis of *political cleavages*[29] is structured along the following lines:

- the description of specific domestic types of party systems;
- the illustration of political party representation of social groups or classes; and
- the evolution of the main political cleavages.

Regarding the Europeanisation of partisan cleavages, the following two indicators are considered:

1. 'when' and 'how' the EU intervenes in the party systems; and
2. the likely new cleavage between Eurosceptics and Integrationists.

The analysis of *party competition* Europeanisation[30] is structured along certain key lines:

- the possible changes induced by Europe on the format and the mechanics of party systems; and
- the probable change in the pattern of party system mechanics (Europhile, divided, or party systems with significant Eurosceptic parties).

There is also an indicator related to European elections: the extent of the impact of the European parliamentary elections on the voting patterns at domestic level. However, these elections continue to have a second-order character,[31] which is interpreted by Hooghe and Marks as being 'popularity tests for national governments'.[32]

In addition and closely linked to the systemic and macro level, the focus is on the Europeanisation of *individual parties*. Each contributor will analyse the Europeanisation of 'policy stances'[33] by focusing on the key changes in party positions on issues of European integration (positive or negative general orientation toward the EU as well as constitutive and isomorphic issues) and eventually on the consequences of these changes within political parties.

It is important to note that both party positions and alliances are often based on pragmatic considerations rather than political commitment. In defining 'left' or 'right of centre', it is evident that the position of 'centre' varies according to the nation state and historical period. For this book, the positioning of each national party on the scale of left to right is based upon that nation's contemporary perception of what is the political 'centre'. The span of parties runs from the radical left,[34] social democrats,[35] Greens,[36] agrarian,[37] regionalists,[38] liberals[39] and Christian democrats to conservatives[40] and radical right-populist parties.[41]

Independent variable – European integration

European integration has changed the environment of national parties and therefore it is useful to analyse how European integration relates to party politics and what mechanisms are at stake in the process. As Featherstone and Radaelli argue, Europeanisation 'raises the important question of how political equilibrium is altered by the mechanisms triggered by EU integration.'[42] Vertical Europeanisation mechanisms 'seem to demarcate clearly the EU level (where policy is defined) and the domestic level, where policy has to be metabolised'.[43] The European elections constitute one of the main sources of 'partisan' vertical mechanisms. In comparison, horizontal mechanisms:

> involve a different form of adjustment to Europe based on the market or on patterns of socialization. In horizontal Europeanization, the process is not one of conforming to EU policy which 'descends' into the domestic policy arena as in a hierarchical chain of command. Horizontal Europeanization is a process of change triggered [...] by the diffusion of ideas and discourses about the notion of good policy and best practice.[44]

Regarding political parties, the linkage with Europarties (both European parliamentary political groups and European party federations) is potentially an important source of change.[45]

Intervening variables I – country-specific factors

Domestic change may be explained by a number of *international factors* such as globalisation[46] in the form of economic and financial 'neo-liberalism', the IMF and action by the World Bank. Acknowledging these factors, we will mainly focus on testing country-specific explanations and transversal factors pointed out by theories of party change and development. The comparative literature on party Europeanisation emphasises the explanatory power of a number of country-specific factors[47] such as:

- the institutional framework (parliamentary, semi-presidential or presidential executives, unitary versus federal systems);
- the cabinets (the single-party or coalition character, the duration in office);
- policy making (the fields and types);
- the effectiveness of the structures set up to scrutinise EU affairs;

- the length of a country's EU membership;
- public opinion on the EU;
- the existence (or not) of a Eurosceptic party and the politics of Euroscepticism; and
- the nature of national discourse on EU-related matters.

Moreover, the geopolitical model 'assumes that support/opposition is mainly determined by national specific features or geopolitical interests'[48] related, for instance, to Atlanticism (or not) and to additional European organisations (the Council of Europe or the Organisation for Security and Co-operation in Europe). In addition, one key element of the interaction between the EU and the domestic regimes is the way political parties use (or do not use) certain national democratic mechanisms such as referendums[49] and the 'popular initiative'. Contributors will take into account these factors as long as they prove to be relevant.

Intervening variables II – explanatory factors of party change and development

The literature points to various explanatory factors[50] with regard to the position of political parties. Bartolini proposes three 'non' country-specific models[51]:

1. the *institutional* model 'explains attitudes to the EU as a function of parties being in government or opposition at the national (and therefore European) level';

2. the *partisan* model 'interprets orientation to the EU of national parties on the basis of the main dimension of competition prevalent at the national level, such as left-right, libertarian-authoritarian, materialist-post-materialists'; and

3. the *genetic* model 'interprets party orientation towards European integration as shaped by or related to their original national cleavage'.

Carter, Luther and Poguntke put forward two additional, potentially important, factors:[52]

- the level of internal party consensus or division over EU-related issues; and
- party organisational size.

Moreover, Hooghe, Marks and Wilson point out the importance of the political parties' ideologies and strategic responses.[53] Last but not least, the changes in political party policy have been attributed by Blondel and Cotta to party characteristics such as structure, ideology and leadership.[54]

In comparison with the above, there are explanatory factors for the domestic inertia/changes at the level of the party systems.[55] Accordingly, the literature emphasises several factors that influence *political cleavages and party competition*:

- the elites' insulation from electoral constraints and public opinion as they perceive no electoral advantage in politicising Europe at the domestic level, except in cases of referendum and direct democracy[56];

- the similarities/differences between domestic parties in terms of policy stances[57] on European issues;
- the electoral system[58] in the member states may also, to some degree, explain the extent of change in domestic partisan arenas, including both party systems and individual parties.

There are different electoral systems in member states for both national and European elections such as the Droop quota, the d'Hondt system, the Single Transferable Vote or the constituency unit (regional or national). These electoral systems have different properties and these influence the way political parties frame their tactics, affect the chances of success and the results measured by seats won.

Selecting and comparing cases

This book is a collection of qualitative country studies. This approach 'attempts to approximate experimental rigour by identifying comparable instances of a phenomenon of interest and then analysing the theoretically important similarities and differences among them'.[59] The contributors develop *in-depth* studies on individual political parties and party system continuity, and changes in response to the European Union. The comparative method here involves the selection of cases and the analysis and refinement of the findings. Thus:

> the object is to test a relationship by discovering whether it can be observed in a range of different countries. If so, our confidence that the relationship is real, and not due to both factors depending on an unmeasured third variable, will increase.[60]

We have selected eight country cases on the basis of three criteria. The first criterion is the representativeness of the cases, taking into account the three patterns of party competition over European integration (the Europhile and divided party systems, as well as those with significant Eurosceptic parties). Secondly, particular attention is devoted to Member States in terms of geographical coverage, economic and/or political size (France, Germany, Greece, Italy, Poland, Romania, Spain and the United Kingdom). Thirdly, the selection and presentation of cases takes into account their history of EU membership. We begin with the founding member states (France, Italy and Germany), followed by a subsequent member of the Economic Community (UK), then member countries after the downfall of right-wing authoritarian systems of government (Greece and Spain) and, finally, the new EU member states following the collapse of the Soviet bloc (Poland and Romania). Authors use various types of data to answer the research questions, including party documents (Germany, UK, Poland, Romania), domestic newspapers (France) and EU documents such as the Eurobarometer (Greece). Contributors also extensively use the country-specific academic literature on political parties and party systems.

The country-specific chapters include four main sections:

- the introduction;
- the party system's Europeanisation (the questions of cleavage and party competition, including the main type of party system and evolution);
- the main individual parties' Europeanisation (policy stances); and
- the conclusion (the implications of each empirical case for the paradox of Europeanisation and the likelihood of politicisation versus depoliticisation of national politics).

Chapter Ten provides a general – but key – contribution that focuses on the Europarties themselves in relation to the deficit of EU representation.

Chapter Eleven is a comparative analysis of similarities and differences across countries, party systems and political parties. In addition, this final chapter includes synthesised information on the additional nineteen remaining EU member states not studied in depth in this book. Moreover, it examines the relationship between Europeanisation, party politics and multilevel representation. Overall, this publication will contribute to a better understanding of the Europeanisation of both party systems and individual parties, as well as the way in which European integration issues are 'framed' *within* the party systems and *by* political parties involved in the act of national and European representation and democracy.

Notes

1   I would like to express my gratitude to Prof. Dario Castiglione and to the anonymous reader of the ECPR Press for their advice and insightful contribution in revising this chapter. In addition, I thank Prof. David S. Bell, Prof. David Hanley and Prof. John Loughlin for their suggestions. I thank especially Lect. Ana-Maria Dobre for the excellent exchanges on the Europeanisation concept and for proofreading this chapter.

2   P. Delwit, *Les partis socialistes et l'intégration européenne: France, Grande-Bretagne, Belgique*, Brussels, Editions de l'Université de Bruxelles, 1995, pp. 282–3.

3   R. Ladrech, 'Europeanization and political parties: towards a framework for analysis', 2002, *Party Politics*, vol. 8, no. 4, pp. 389–403.

4   K. Ka-Lok Chan, 'Strands of conservative politics in post-communist transition: adapting to Europeanization and democratization', in P. G. Lewis (ed.), *Party Development and Democratic Change in Post-Communist Europe: The first decade*, London, Frank Cass, 2001, pp. 152–78; E. Bomberg, 'The Europeanization of Green Parties: exploring the EU's impact', *West European Politics*, 2002, vol. 25, no. 3, pp. 29–50.

5   P. Daniels, 'From hostility to constructive engagement: the Europeanisation of the Labour Party', *West European Politics*, 1998, vol. 21, no. 1, pp. 72–96; Ladrech, pp. 396–8; A. Ágh, 'The dual challenge and the reform of the Hungarian socialist party', *Communist and Post-Communist Studies*, 2002, no. 35, pp.269–88.

6   P. Delwit, 'Le processus d'européisation et la crise du socialisme miterrandien', in M. Telo (ed.), *De la Nation à l'Europe: Paradoxes et Dilemmes de la Social-Démocratie*, 1993, Brussels, Bruylant, pp. 261–99; J. Gerstlé, H. A. Semetko, K. Schoenbach and M. Villa, 'L'européanisation défaillante des campagnes nationales', in G. Grunberg, P. Perrineau and C. Ysmal (eds), *Le Vote des Quinze: Les élections européennes du 13 juin 1999*, 2000, Paris, Presses de Science Po, pp. 95–118.

7   Delwit, 'Le processus...', pp. 261–99; A. Cole, 'National and partisan contexts of Europeanization: the case of the French Socialists', 2001, *Journal of Common Market Studies*, vol. 39, no. 1, pp. 15–36; E. Külahci, 'EU political conditionality and parties in government: human rights and the quest for Turkish transformation', in I. Botetzagias (ed.), 'Europeanising Southern Europe', *Journal of Southern Europe and the Balkans*, 2005, vol. 7, no. 3, pp. 387–402.

8   S. Bartolini, 'Political representation in loosely bounded territories: between Europe and the nation-state', paper presented at conference organised by S. Bartolini, *Multi-level Party Systems: Europeanization and the Reshaping of National Political Representation*, Florence, European University Institute, 16–18 December 1999, 55 pp.

9   Delwit, pp. 282–4; D. Hanley, 'Christian Democracy and the Paradoxes of Europeanization: Flexibility, Competition and Collusion', *Party Politics*, 2002, vol. 8, no. 4, pp. 463–81; S. Lightfoot, *Europeanising Social Democracy: the rise of the Party of European Socialists?*, 2005, Oxford, Routledge; E. Külahci, *La social-démocratie et le chômage*, Brussels, Editions de l'Université de Bruxelles, 2008, pp. 173–4.

10 T. Poguntke, N. Aylott, E. Carter, R. Ladrech and K. R. Luther (eds), *The Europeanization of National Political Parties: Power and organizational adaptation*, London and New York, Routledge, 2007; R. Ladrech, 'National political parties and European governance: the consequences of missing in action', *West European Politics*, 1997, vol. 30, no. 5, pp. 945–60.

11 See some exceptions such as P. Mair, 'The limited impact of Europe on national party systems', *West European Politics*, 2000, vol. 23, no. 4, pp. 27–9; G. Pridham, 'Patterns of Europeanization and transnational party co-operation: party development in Central and Eastern Europe', in P. G. Lewis (ed.), pp. 179–98; S. Bartolini, 'La structure des clivages nationaux et la question de l'intégration dans l'Union européenne', in D. Chabanet (ed.), 'Mobilisations et clivages socio-politiques en Europe', 2001, *Politique Européenne*, no. 4, pp. 15–45.

12 Ladrech, 'Europeanization and political parties...', pp. 394–95.

13 Delwit, pp. 282–3; K. Deschouwer, 'What Is Europe Doing To Political Parties? What Parties Do With Europe?', paper presented at the Third Summer School in Comparative Politics 'Europeanisation of National Politics: Challenges and Opportunities for European Institutions and National Political Systems', Università degli Studi di Siena, July 10–22, 2000, 19 pp.; S. Hix and K. H. Goetz, 'Introduction: European Integration and national political systems', *West European Politics*, 2000, vol. 23, no. 4, pp. 1–3; E. Carter, K. R. Luther and T. Poguntke, 'European integration and internal party dynamics', in Poguntke, Aylott, Carter, Ladrech and Luther (eds), *The Europeanization...*, p. 5.

14 Carter, Luther and Poguntke, 'European integration...', p. 5.

15 Bartolini, 'Political representation...', pp. 3–10.

16 K. Featherstone, 'Introduction: In the name of Europe', in K. Featherstone and C. Radaelli (eds), *The Politics of Europeanization*, Oxford, Oxford University Press, 2003, p. 12. See for instance an application by A.-M. Dobre, 'Europeanization and new patterns of multi-level governance in Romania', in I. Bache and G. Andreou (eds), *Cohesion Policy and Multi-level Governance in South East Europe*, Oxford, Routledge, 2010; A.-M. Dobre, 'Romania: from historical regions to local decentralization via the unitary state', in J. Loughlin, F. Hendriks and A. Lidström (eds), *The Oxford Handbook of Local and Regional Democracy in Europe*, Oxford, Oxford University Press, 2011, pp. 684–712.

17 See the literature review by Carter, Luther and Poguntke, pp. 5–6.

18 For an initial impression, see E. Külahci, 'European Integration, party systems and individual parties: comparative Politics Approach and the Assumption of Variations', *Revue d'études européennes*, 2007, no. 1, pp. 8–11.

19 Ladrech, 'Europeanization and political parties...', p. 396.

20 Mair, 'The limited impact...', pp. 27–9: the format of party system 'is the number of relevant parties in contention in national electoral arenas' (p. 27) and the mechanics of party system 'is the way in which parties interact with one another in the national electoral arenas, either by modifying the ideological distance separating the relevant parties or by encouraging the emergence of wholly new European-centred dimensions of competition' (p. 28). See also P. Mair, 'Political parties and party systems', in P. Graziano and M. P. Vink

(eds) *Europeanization: new research agendas*, London, Palgrave Macmillan, 2007, p. 159, p. 162, pp. 164–5.

21 L. Hooghe and G. Marks, 'A postfunctionalist theory of European Integration: from permissive consensus to constraining dissensus', *British Journal of Political Science*, 2009, 39, pp. 18–9.

22 S. Bartolini, *Re-Structuring Europe: centre formation, system building and political structuring between the nation state and the European Union*, Oxford, Oxford University Press, 2005, p. 310.

23 G. Marks and C. J. Wilson, 'The past in the present: a cleavage theory of party response to European Integration', *British Journal of Political Science*, 2000, vol. 30, no. 3, p. 442.

24 Marks and Wilson, 'The past...', pp. 438–9 and L. Hooghe, G. Marks and C. J. Wilson, 'Does left/right structure party positions on European integration', in G. Marks and M. R. Steenbergen (eds), *European Integration and Political Conflict*, Cambridge, Cambridge University Press, 2004, pp. 123–4.

25 This typology is different from the one proposed by Taggart and Szczerbiak (p. 350, p. 354 and p. 358) who focus mainly on Eurosceptic parties:
   • limited contestation grouping instances of limited Euroscepticism (France, Germany, Italy, Belgium, The Netherlands, Luxembourg Spain, Portugal, Finland, Ireland, Slovenia),
   • the open contestation characterised by the spectacular nature of Euroscepticism (UK, Greece, Sweden, Austria, Malta, Czech Republic, Denmark and Norway) and
   • the constrained contestation bringing together sensitive post-communist candidate states (Poland, Hungary, Slovakia, Latvia, Lithuania, Estonia).
   See A. Szczerbiak and P. Taggart, 'Conclusion: opposing Europe? Three patterns of party competition over Europe', in A. Szczerbiak and P. Taggart (eds), *Opposing Europe? The Comparative Party Politics of Euroscepticism*, Vol. 1, *Case Studies and Country Surveys*, Oxford, Oxford University Press, 2008, pp. 348–63.

26 Regarding the nature of 'Euroscepticism', see the distinction between 'Hard Euroscepticism' and 'Soft Euroscepticism' proposed by A. Szczerbiak and P. Taggart, 'Introduction: opposing Europe? The politics of Euroscepticism in Europe', in Szczerbiak and Taggart (eds) *Opposing Europe?*, pp. 7–8:
   • 'Hard Euroscepticism is where there is a principled opposition to the EU and European integration and therefore can be seen in parties who think that their countries should withdraw from membership, or whose policies towards the EU are tantamount to being opposed to the whole project of European integration as it is currently conceived.'
   • 'Soft Euroscepticism is where there is not a principled objection to European integration or EU membership but where concerns on one (or a number) of policy areas lead to the expression of qualified opposition to the EU, or where there is a sense that "national interest" is currently at odds with the EU's trajectory.'

27 Mair, 'The limited impact...'; J.-M. De Waele (eds), *European Union Accession Referendums*, Brussels, Editions de l'Université de Bruxelles, 2005.

28 Mair, Political parties...', p. 165.

29 Bartolini, 'Political representation...', pp. 26–53.

30 Mair, 'The limited impact...', pp. 27–9.

31 K. H. Reif and H. Schmitt, 'Nine second-order national elections: a conceptual framework for the analysis of European election results', *European Journal of Political Research*, 1980, vol. 8, pp. 3–44.

32 Hooghe and Marks,'A postfunctionalist theory...', p. 6. See also Mair, 'The limited impact...', p. 38.

33 Ladrech, 'Europeanization and political parties...', pp. 396–7.

34 P. Delwit, J.-M. De Waele and J. Gotovitch, *L'Europe des communistes*, Brussels, Editions Complexe, 1992; D. S. Bell (ed.), *Western European Communists and the Collapse of Communism, Oxford, Berg, 1993*.

35 S. Bartolini, 'The membership of mass parties: the Social Democratic Experience, 1889–1978', in H. Daalder and P. Mair (eds), *Western European Party Systems: continuity and change*, London, Sage, 1983, pp. 177–220; M. Lazar (ed.), *La gauche en Europe depuis 1945: Invariants et mutations du socialisme européen*, Paris, PUF, 1996; G. Moschonas, *In the Name of Social Democracy*, London, Verso, 2002; P. Delwit (ed.), *Social Democracy in Europe*, Brussels, Editions de l'Université de Bruxelles, 2005.

36 P. Delwit and J.-M. De Waele (eds), *Les partis verts en Europe*, Brussels, Editions Complexe, 1999; F. Müller-Rommel and T. Poguntke (eds), *Green Parties in National Governments*, London, Frank Cass, 2002; B. Rihoux, 'Governmental participation and the organisational adaptation of Green Parties: on access, slack, overload and distress', *European Journal of Political Research*, 2006, vol. 45, pp. 69–98.

37 J.-M. De Waele and D.-L. Seiler (eds), *Les partis agrariens et paysans en Europe*, Brussels, Editions de l'Université de Bruxelles, 2009.

38 L. De Winter and H. Tursan (eds), *Regionalist Parties in Western Europe*, London and New York, Routledge, 1998; L. Morlino, 'Europeanization and Representation in Two Europes: Local Institutions and National Parties', conference organised by S. Bartolini, *Multi-level Party Systems: Europeanization and the Reshaping of National Political Representation*, Florence, European University Institute, 16–18 December 1999, 29 pp.; P. Delwit (ed.), *Les partis régionalistes en Europe: Des acteurs en développement?*, Brussels, Editions de l'Université de Bruxelles, 2005.

39 E. Kirchner (ed.), *Liberal Parties in Western Europe*, Cambridge, Cambridge University Press, 1988; N. Rousselier, *L'Europe des Libéraux*, Brussels, Editions Complexe, 1991; P. Delwit (ed.), *Libéralisme et partis libéraux en Europe*, Brussels, Editions de l'Université de Bruxelles, 2002.

40 D. Hanley (ed.), *Christian Democracy in Europe: a comparative perspective*, London, Pinter, 1994; P. Delwit (ed.), *Démocraties chrétiennes et conservatisme en Europe: Une nouvelle convergence?*, Brussels, Editions de l'Université de Bruxelles, 2003.

41 P. Delwit, J.-M. De Waele and A. Rea (eds), *L'extrême droite en France et en Belgique*, Brussels, Editions Complexe, 1998; P. Delwit and P. Poirier (eds), *Extrême droite et pouvoir en Europe, [The Extreme Right Parties and Power in Europe*, Brussels, Editions de l'Université de Bruxelles, 2007; P. Ignazi, *Extreme Right Parties in Western Europe*, Oxford, Oxford University Press, 2006.

42 K Featherstone and C. Radaelli, 'A conversant research agenda', in Feather-stone and Radaelli (eds), *The Politics of Europeanization*, pp. 338–9.

43 C. Radaelli, 'Europeanization of public policy', in Featherstone and Radaelli (eds), *The Politics of Europeanization*, p.41.

44 *loc.cit.*

45 G. Pridham and P. Pridham, *Transnational Party Co-operation and European Integration: The process towards direct elections*, London, Georges Allen & Unwin, 1981; L. Bardi, 'Transnational trends in European parties and the 1994 elections of the European Parliament', *Party Politics*, 1996, vol. 2, no. 1, pp. 99–114; *Simon Hix* 'Parties at the European Level and the Legitimacy of EU Socio-economic Policy', *Journal of Common Market Studies*, Vol. 33, No.4, 1995, pp. 527–54. S. Hix and C. Lord, *Political Parties in the European Union*, London, Macmillan, 1997; P. Delwit and J.-M. De Waele (eds), *La démocratisation en Europe centrale: la coopération paneuropéenne des partis politiques*, Paris, L'Harmattan, 1998; D. S. Bell and C. Lord (eds), *Transnational Parties in the European Union*, Aldershot, Ashgate, 1998; Kenneth Dyson, 'Benign or Malevolent Leviathan? Social Democratic Governments in a Neo-liberal Euro Area', *The Political Quarterly*, Vol. 70, No. 2, 1999, pp. 194–209; R. Ladrech, *Social Democracy and the Challenge of European Union*, London, Lynne Rienner Publishers, 2000; Simon Hix, 'Parties at the European Level', in Paul Webb, David Farrell and Ian Holliday (eds) *Political Parties in Advanced Industrial Democracies*, Oxford and New York, Oxford University Press, 2002; Karl-Magnus Johansson, 'Another Road to Maastricht: The Christian Democrat Coalition and the Quest for European Union', *Journal of Common Market Studies*, Vol. 40, No. 5, 2000, pp. 871–93. E. Külahci, 'European party federations (EPFs) and the EU legitimacy deficit: conceptualising the horizontal pathway', in N. Winn and E. Harris (eds), 'Europeanisation: Regulation and Identity in the New Europe', *Perspectives on European Politics and Society. Journal of Intra-European Dialogue*, 2003, vol. 4, no. 1, pp. 117–45; R. Coman, 'Européanisation et coopération paneu-ropéenne des partis: Une perspective roumaine', *Romanian Political Science Review*, 2003, vol. 3, no. 3, pp. 651–3; P. Delwit, E. Külahci and C. Van de Walle (eds), *The Europarties: organisation and influence*, Brussels, Brussels University, 2004, available at: http://www.sciencespo.site.ulb.ac.be/dos-siers_livres/theeuropartiesorganisation/fichiers/en_bookefpp.pdf; Külahci, *La social-démocratie*; D. Hanley, *Beyond the Nation State: parties in the era of European Integration*, London, Palgrave, 2008; E. Külahci, 'Europarties: agenda-setter or agenda-follower? Social democracy and the disincentives for tax harmonization', *Journal of Common Market Studies*, 2010, vol. 48, no. 5, pp. 1283–306.

46 H. Kriesi, S. Bornschier, E. Grande, R. Lachat, M. Dolezal and T. Frey, 'Glo-balization and the transformation of the national political space: six European countries compared', *European Journal of Political Research*, 2006, vol. 45, no. 6, pp. 921–56.

47 Delwit, *Les partis socialistes...*, pp. 253–84; J. Blondel and M. Cotta, 'Con-clusion', in J. Blondel and M. Cotta (eds), *Party and Government: an inquiry into the relationship between governments and supporting parties in liberal democracies*, London, MacMillan, 1996, pp. 254–60; Carter, Luther and

Poguntke, 'European integration...', pp. 15–16; A. Szczerbiak and P. Taggart, 'Introduction: Opposing Europe? The Politics of Euroscepticism in Europe', in Szczerbiak and Taggart, *Opposing Europe?*, pp. 1–15; N. Conti, 'Domestic parties and European Integration: the problem of party attitudes to the EU and the Europeanisation of parties', *European Political Science*, 2007, 6.

48 Bartolini, *Re-Structuring Europe...*, p. 321.

49 Hooghe and Marks, 'A postfunctionalist theory...', p.20.

50 See, for instance, Delwit, *Les partis socialistes...*, pp. 253–84.

51 Bartolini, *Re-Structuring Europe...*, p. 321.

52 Carter, Luther and Poguntke,'European integration...', p. 16. For a more general analysis of party organisation, see A. Panebianco, *Political Parties: Organization and Power*, Cambridge, Cambridge University Press, 1983; R. Harmel and K. Janda, 'An integrated theory of party goals and party change', *Journal of Theoretical Politics*, 1994, vol. 6, no. 3, pp. 259–87; R. S. Katz and P Mair (eds), *How Parties Organize. Change and Adaptation in Party Organizations in Western Democracies*, Sage, London, 1994; R. S. Katz and P. Mair, 'Changing models of party organization and party democracy: the emergence of the cartel party', *Party Politics*, 1995, vol. 1, no. 1, pp. 5–28; R. Koole, 'Cadre, Catch-All or Cartel? A Comment on the Notion of the Cartel Party', *Party Politics*, 1996, vol. 2, no. 4, pp. 507–23; R. S. Katz and P. Mair, 'Cadre, Catch-All or Cartel? A Rejoinder', *Party Politics*, 1996, vol. 2, no. 4, pp. 525–34; S. E. Scarrow, *Parties and their Members: Organizing for Victory in Britain and Germany*, New York, Oxford University Press, 1995; P. Ignazi and C. Ysmal (eds), *The Organization of Political Parties in Southern Europe*, London, Praeger, 1998.

53 Hooghe, Marks and Wilson, 'Does left/right structure...' pp. 123–4.

54 Blondel and Cotta, *Party and Government...*, pp. 254–60. See also M. Liebman, *Introduction aux doctrines politiques contemporaines: conflits idéologiques et conflits sociaux au XXe siècle*, Brussels, Presses universitaires de Bruxelles, 1984.

55 G. Sartori, *Parties and Party System: a framework for analysis*, Colchester, ECPR Press Classic Series, 2005; P. Mair, *Party System Change:Approaches and Interpretations*, Oxford, Clarendon Press, 1997; S. Bartolini, 'Institutional Constraints and Party Competition in the French Party System', *West European Politics*, 1984, vol. 7, no. 4, pp. 102–27.

56 Mair,'The limited impact...', pp. 47–8.

57 Mair, 'The limited impact...', pp. 31–7.

58 Külahci, 'EU political conditionality...', pp. 394–5 and p. 401; P. Delwit and J.-M. De Waele (eds), *Le mode de scrutin fait-il l'élection?*, Brussels, Editions de l'Université de Bruxelles, 2000.

59 C. Ragin, *The Comparative Method: Moving Beyond Qualitative and Quantitative Strategies*, Berkeley, University of California Press, 1987.

60 R. Hague and M. Harrop, *Comparative Government and Politics: An Introduction*, Hampshire, Palgrave Macmillan, 2004, 6th edn., pp. 82–3; A. Przeworski and H. Teune, *The Logic of Comparative Social Inquiry*, New York, Wiley, 1970.

chapter two | the 'european integration' – cleavage in the party system: the french case

David S. Bell

Introduction

European integration issues are not standard political cleavages – they are matters of 'high politics' that were once (before the first European elections) considered the preserve of the executive and the material for interstate and diplomatic bargaining. However, these issues have become part of the French domestic political arena and have been the vehicle for much wider political action. Governing coalitions have been split by the intrusion of the issues of European integration and opposition parties have been divided by rivalries around the cleavage. It has to be kept in mind, however, that European issues are only one set of divisions amongst many others and not the most important.[1] However, Europe, as an issue, has its effects at the party system level, on party leadership and on factionalism within parties.

A caveat should be entered here: the patterns of influence of European issues on the parties and party systems are difficult to capture in a single description. The issue of Europe enters party competition when it can be exploited by political leaders, but it is not predetermined or predictable. As a result, tracing the impact leads to a marble cake setting rather than a layer cake. In other words, the issue pervades politics and party systems, and forms cleavage lines within parties and between political personalities in search of an audience (or responding to one). European integration may, therefore, lead to a disjunction on certain occasions, but not on others. This is a confusing pattern that will be uncovered in the course of this discussion of the French party system.

From its inception, European integration touched the interests of very significant pressure groups: first coal and steel and then farming, and in recent years it has directly impinged – through market restructuring and the introduction of the Euro – on daily concerns. Moreover, as the main left-right division in French politics has receded (with the end of the socialist 'experiment' from 1981–83) and the importance of this coalition line-up has submerged other factors of division between partners, European integration has emerged with greater significance. This is not very different from developments elsewhere on the Continent with the end of the Cold War, but the size of the pro-Moscow Communist Party and the intensity of debate make for a more fragmented landscape of cross-cutting cleavages than provided by the bipolar left-right conflict. Europe under the Fourth Republic and in the first decades of the Fifth Republic was an additional dimension to the left-right continuum.[2] Europe, however, has not been taken out of party competition; far from it, integration has intermittently moved to the centre stage.

European integration can raise issues of national identity and political decision-making in ways that turn otherwise abstract and technical details into highly-charged issues. Europe meets the conditions whereby there is a case for altering the strength of the parties in that it evokes strongly-held attitudes, has a skewed distribution of opinion and encounters (and enables) strongly-differentiated party views.[3] European integration is, significantly, perceived as a salient issue – and not just by motivated minorities – because a substantial part of the electorate is informed and has an attitude to it. Parties are unable to evade the issue and the adhesion of the French domestic parties to the European groups (in the European Parliament (EP)) bring a European dimension into domestic politics through the need to coordinate action between state and international levels directly.

This issue of Europe is an emotional one and has had high visibility among everyday political issues, not just in election campaigns. But Europe is also a 'position' issue on which parties may appeal to rival bodies of opinion. Thus, the parties can place themselves in a position to appeal to alternative views and exploit these for competitive advantage. 'Position' issues, like prosperity and full employment, are quite unlike 'valence' issues, such as economic growth and the improvement in services, on which people are widely agreed and with which parties try to associate themselves to reinforce their positive image in voters' minds. In addition, the electorate associates different parties with different stances on the European project; party standpoints are strongly differentiated on this issue. There is the further difficulty that Europe as a political issue is an independent variable that is difficult to restrict to pre-defined channels and (similar to the problem of Turkish accession) is liable to force itself on to the agenda.

In the development of a party system, the competition between parties defines the nature of the system itself. Parties look for advantages, taking up and dropping issues that serve the purpose of attracting voters and consolidating their own support.[4] As will be argued, and contrary to one postulate, Europe as an issue does change the party system, with both a negative and positive impact. Hence the integration issue enters through the play of party competition, but elections to the EP introduced a new feature of uncertain consequences into the party system. There has always been an anti-European undertow available and the anti-system parties of the left and the right have exploited this feeling, both of them willing on occasion to put aside their mutual antipathies to campaign against integration.

French public opinion has been traditionally favourable to European integration, but there are opponents and these voters are located predominantly in the popular social classes. They are concentrated on the political extremes, but none of the main parties (with the exception of François Bayrou's small centrist *Modem*) is without its Eurosceptic voters, who endorse the party's general outlook yet remain recalcitrant about integration. Pro-European sentiment is more diffuse, but it has been important in the past (notably in 1965 and 1972) and there have been only a few periods when Europe has not been important. This may be one reason why, in general, the European integration issue is divisive, facilitating splits, schisms and presidential standpoints; it is rarely consolidating.

Party competition has both centripetal and centrifugal effects on individual parties and on the party system. The French party system has gone through three stages of development: one under the Fourth Republic and two in the Fifth Republic. Under the Fourth Republic, the party system was characterised by 'polarized pluralism' (in Sartori's terms) in which the anti-system parties opposed a moderate governing centre.[5] This ended under the Fifth Republic, when a process of bipolarisation was set in motion for the first two decades. This in turn was disrupted after 1984 by a process of fragmentation. What follows is, therefore, an analysis of the cleavages and the cleavage structure in French politics and of how issues can be used for 'heresthetic' manoeuvre in a competitive environment.[6]

The European issue in the evolution of the party system

Integration has changed the environment in which parties have to work and to which political leaders can appeal. New balances have to be found and the interaction between the European issues and the European party system and the domestic party system are intricate. Fifth Republic politics started with a process of bipolarisation as the left-right cleavage supplanted the alignment of the Fourth Republic and as the presidential race intensified that polarisation. This left-right clash, with its wider resonance, seemed to be the dominant trend under the Fifth Republic. In the 1960s, on the conservative right, the coalition quickly consolidated around the figure of de Gaulle and the Gaullist party was the initial beneficiary. Gaullism all but dominated the conservative right in the 1960s as it squeezed the space available for the pro-European Christian democratic sensibility. European integration was a part of this dynamic.

De Gaulle, however, introduced a further twist in the conservative stance hostile to European integration through a series of bruising clashes with the European Commission. De Gaulle's manoeuvre caused difficulties for the opposition parties. He forced the centre, which was more pro-European than the wings, to support the President or the left. In a series of dramatic manoeuvres, de Gaulle differentiated himself from the Fourth Republic's foreign policy and from its elites by promoting a policy hostile to further European integration. But the consequence of these two moves was to divide the left – the extreme left was hostile to integration – and made Gaullism the national ideal that stood against the shadowy menace of 'Europe'. Both these Gaullist positions were appealing options in the context of the party system. Thus, on the right, the conservative parties inherited this Euroscepticism, which has remained a feature of the neo-Gaullist movement although it has diminished in recent years.[7]

On the left, the *Socialist Party* (SFIO), which had defined itself as a 'European' party, found itself in difficulties as a result of President de Gaulle's appropriation of the nationalist high ground on the European issue and divided from its potential alliance partner the *Parti communiste français* (PCF). Communist hostility to European institutions stretched back to the conflict over the European

Coal and Steel Community and the European Defence Community and was, if anything, greater than the Gaullists of that epoch.[8] But the European issue was temporarily defused in the 1970s by the expedient of pushing it into a secondary position, but without the SFIO abandoning its commitment to integration. Thus, with the European issue sidelined, it was possible for the alliance between the communists and socialists to be concluded. President Pompidou's referendum on the enlargement of Europe in 1972 did no more than delay the negotiation of the joint platform of the left, although European policy was explicitly recognised as a point of disagreement. European issues did resurface to divide the left in the mid-1970s, when the alliance underwent internal tensions. In the late 1970s, the Fifth Republic party system achieved a brief symmetry with the 'bipolar quadrille' of the communists and the socialists on the one side and the Gaullists and non-Gaullist conservatives (around President Giscard) on the other.

When elections to the EP took place for the first time by universal suffrage in 1979, the development of a European party system at odds with the French domestic party system started to open up. It is not a minor point that these elections were conducted on a proportional list system and used the country as a 'constituency', unlike the Fifth Republic system (except 1986) of two rounds (if no majority in the first round, the two candidates with the greatest number of votes go to a second round). This technical factor of the electoral system should not be over-stressed, but it played a part in lowering the barrier to entry into the party system. They were, however, 'second order' elections, which have a low turnout, are usually used by voters to warn the government, and are opportunities for minor parties and for single issue parties to enter the party system. As has been noted, they are a popularity test for the government, but the ramifications may extend beyond this immediacy. These parties can be ephemeral, but their effect on the party system can be enduring and the European elections are important for providing momentum to campaigns and to parties. This separation between the domestic system and the European system began in a low-key manner, seeming to confirm integration into Europe, but also providing an opportunity for dissent. In concrete terms, this meant the development of a party system with significant Eurosceptic parties for the European Parliament (significantly, including both right and left wing opponents to integration) and the domestic French party system, better characterised as a divided party system in which the issue emerges more as a cleavage than a primary party system factor.

In 1979, the EP campaign featured two strong anti-European parties, the communists and the neo-Gaullists, but the government was not, on that occasion, the victim of a reprimand handed to the incumbents (as it was in subsequent European elections). This was a high point of the rivalry between President Giscard's centre party and Chirac's neo-Gaullist *Rassemblement pour la République* (RPR) with its anti-European foray known as the 'Cochin appeal', a rallying against the 'party of foreigners', an anti-European statement that thinly disguised an attack on the President. These elections were dominated by the bitter rivalry inside the two coalitions of left and right in which the once dominant parties, RPR and PCF, were being overshadowed by 1970s' newcomers, the *Parti Socialiste* (PS) and the centrist pro-European *Union pour la démocratie française* (UDF). But, that aside, the other feature of European elections as being 'second order' was confirmed, even in 1979.[9]

This facility for small parties became evident in a number of key cases and is one reason for the importance of European elections to the domestic party system – and was a crucial feature in 1984. Significantly, in the 1984 European elections, with the domestic Socialist Party at low ebb and the conservative opposition divided and not fully recovered from losing the presidency in 1981, the conservatives did unite against the Socialist Government; however, Jean-Marie Le Pen's *Front National* (FN) entered the party system with glass-shattering effect, taking 11 per cent of the vote. Le Pen's breakthrough was aided by the merger of the strongly pro-European UDF and the previously sceptical RPR under the centrist leadership of Simone Veil (then EP President) and the consequent opening of a Eurosceptical gap on the right. In 1984, Le Pen's party – in the main, anti-immigrant but also condemning further integration – was at the beginning of an upswing that had started a year earlier (in local elections) and was given increased momentum. At these elections, Le Pen had a platform that enabled the FN to capitalise on its support in the polls and locate itself in the system. The 1984 elections signalled the end of the simple bipolar trend in French politics and contributed to the fissiparous nature of the French party system. A gap was opened up between the domestic French party system and the European party system, which has remained evident since that time. Although a change of government was planned, socialist Prime Minister Mauroy did resign and a new government under Laurent Fabius was installed.

During the 1980s, the integration was less pressing as a party system issue although a number of controversial policies were implemented by the Socialist Governments including the 'southern enlargement', the Single Act and the modernisation of the old 'rust belt industries'. Notwithstanding the developments, 'Europe' became the smoke screen for the Socialist Government's abandonment of a reflationary 'dash for growth' in 1984. In the long term, however, integration was a factor of division within the left. In 1985, President Mitterrand nominated Jacques Delors as Head of the Commission and began a period of dynamic pro-European policy in which Mitterrand supported the Commission to promote faster integration. During the first term of the Mitterrand Presidency (1981–88), and for the Rocard Government (1988–91), this European dynamism was to the benefit of the Socialist Party and gave it a sense of direction in lieu of the abandoned socialist project. However, the manoeuvre linked European integration with an unpopular set of austerity measures and policies that bore down hard on the left's own supporters.

In 1990s politics, the important dividing line was the signing of the Maastricht Treaty and the referendum on it in 1992. Integration was accompanied by a package of highly symbolic measures, by more intrusive policies and strict financial 'convergence criteria', and restrictions on monetary policies. Maastricht became associated with the austere deflationary policies of the Socialist (and Conservative) Governments and with persistent unemployment. A very strong opposition was revealed to the encroachment – as it was depicted – of Europe into the public realm. This opposition had existed before, but it was a potent force and did not subside with the slim 'victory' of the pro-Europeans in the 1992 referendum. For the President, it was the narrowest victory, with 51 per cent of the vote, and it opened a split between the French mainstream parties and their supporters. This was more important on the left than on the right, but not for the extreme parties, which remained in phase with their supporters, but a *'décalage'* was evident for all mainstream political parties. The 1992 referendum had continued the policy of the elite – a 'high politics' imperative to promote European integration – but public opinion had not been fully persuaded. For the Socialist Party, the gap opened up between its supporters in old industrial areas and its European policy, although the communists' radical anti-Europeanism found an echo with its supporters and probably prolonged its influence even as other factors combined to destroy world communism. On the conservative and centrist right, the pro-European vote was mobilised, but a new scepticism ('sovereignty-ist'), more in keeping with traditional Gaullism than with the *Front National*, made progress.

In 1993, there was a conservative landslide at the general election and by the 1994 European elections the party system had shifted substantially, with the decline of the Communist Party and the centrist challenge to the neo-Gaullist RPR. Hence, the referendum on the Maastricht Treaty, far from bringing 'closure' to the European issue, had brought to the fore a substantial opinion opposed to further integration and expressed within both the domestic and European party systems. On the left there was the continuation of the split between the communists and the socialists, but a new fissure developed around the former Minister J.-P. Chevènement, who launched the *Mouvement des citoyens* (MDC), a party strongly opposed to European integration. Within the conservative ranks, the *Mouvement pour la France* (MPF) was founded by the dissident centrist deputy, de Villiers, campaigning against the 'loss of sovereignty' and creating an alternative anti-European party to Le Pen on the right. In the European elections, despite the continuing decline of the Communist Party (which took 7 per cent), the fragmentation of the party system proceeded along with a rejection of the centre governing parties. De Villiers' MPF had big gains, with 13 per cent, Le Pen took 11 per cent and the maverick Radical Party of the Left (pro-European) took 12 per cent – the latter taking votes from Michel Rocard's Socialists, which polled only 14 per cent and ended his presidential hopes even though the conservative centre's candidates took only 25 per cent, hardly an endorsement of Prime Minister Balladur's Government, then in power. This election, projecting new parties into the European Parliament, consummated existing domestic party splits (particularly Chevènement and de Villiers).

European issues could not be ignored. In the run-up to the 1995 presidential elections, Prime Minister Balladur had the support of the centrist pro-Europeans, but Jacques Chirac, trailing in the polls, was tempted by a more radical strategy. Chirac's campaign began to develop a left-leaning 'social' policy (tempting in view of the Socialist Party's near collapse in the 1993 general elections) and at the same time began to water down his commitment to integration, although Chirac never reconciled the differences between his promise to reinvigorate growth through deficit spending and the European Monetary Union (EMU) criteria. However, the intention of making a radical break with Europe to implement a counter-cyclical economic policy could have been imputed to him. This anti-European tack helped to give Chirac the edge over his conservative rival, Balladur, to win the presidential elections of 1995.

Whatever Chirac's real intentions, as the new President he quickly did a U-turn on this 'dash for growth' and other promises, provoking a further distrust of the political elite. In October 1995, President Chirac's Premier Juppé announced a 'plan' to deal with the deficits and to cut costs. Once again the gap between the political class and the public was opened up and strikes across the country caused the essentials of this plan to be abandoned. Economic growth remained sluggish and, despite an austere budget, there were doubts about whether Chirac's Government could meet the EMU criteria without swingeing cuts. Other parties reacted by either, like the socialists, demanding a European response to problems (through an EU 'economic government') or by criticising the President. European integration, far from quarantined at the EP elections, was at the heart of contemporary national assembly cleavages.

It was against this background of ambient dissatisfaction that President Chirac called a snap election for April/May 1997. It is possible that the vigorous disagreements on the left over the Maastricht Treaty may have led Chirac to think that a coalition of the left was impossible but a pre-election compromise was made and it committed the opposition to renegotiating the Euro criteria. As an issue, 'Europe', the Euro and convergence were left hanging; no convincing reason was given for the dissolution and the possibility was left floating that the re-election of the government would provide the authority for a round of deflationary cuts intended to meet the European convergence criteria. In the event, it was the 'plural left' of Verts, 'Chevènementists', communists and radicals led by the socialist Lionel Jospin that won a narrow victory. After the election, President Chirac forced the issue, obliging Jospin, the new premier, to choose between a combined diplomatic constitutional crisis and the European stability pact destined to be ratified that June. With little dissent from the coalition partners (some of them had been anti-Maastricht), Jospin abandoned the idea of changing the Euro criteria, opting instead to work within them.

Despite the hostility of some of the minor parties on the 'plural left' to the Maastricht Treaty, the coalition accepted the timetable; the surprise and satisfaction of coming to power only four years after near obliteration swept their reservations aside and domestic economic growth soon introduced a feeling of well-being. This stance is consistent with the observation that the issue is a function of party position in government or opposition. In order to meet the convergence criteria, taxes were raised (though, critically, on businesses not on individuals) and budget cuts were made (mainly in defence). The government's reduction in unemployment eased in the replacement of the Franc by the Euro in 2002 with minimal controversy. In political terms, Jospin had succeeded in disconnecting Europe from austerity and unemployment so that the Euro was not perceived as the cause of France's economic problems. Moreover, the government also managed to bring about a policy of economic redistribution within the framework set by the European Union.

In events not Europe-driven, it was the rise of the extreme left in 1999 that heralded changes in the French domestic party system. The *Ligue Communiste Révolutionnaire* (LCR) and *Lutte Ouvrière* (LO) allied and polled 5 per cent (to give them five Members of the European Parliament) and the *Verts* returned (10 per cent). In the centre, the Socialist Party revived to poll 22 per cent although its ally, the PCF, took only 7 per cent with an eclectic list, including 'personalities', intended to stave off its decline. Humiliatingly, the RPR polled only 13 per cent and the UDF 9 per cent. Le Pen's FN faltered and its vote fell to 9 per cent, but de Villiers' Eurosceptic MPF combined with dissident Gaullists on a joint list to take 13 per cent, a level connected with the FN's internal disputes. This election also saw the emergence of José Saint-Josse's anti-European *Chasse, Nature, Pêche, Tradition* (CNPT), dedicated to rejecting the EU's laws on game hunting, which they considered to be too stringent. These French European elections in 1999 were the first at which the unambiguously anti-integration parties out-polled the pro-Europeans and the first at which the anti-system parties out-performed the government parties.

At the 2002 presidential elections, the socialist candidate, Lionel Jospin, was eliminated from the first ballot and the run-off took place between the outgoing President Chirac and the extreme right's Le Pen. Europe did not figure in this election, but might have done so if the run-off had been, as anticipated, between President and Premier (Chirac had raised the possibility of an 'avant-garde' Europe, perhaps with the intention of embarrassing Jospin).[10] Chirac was re-elected with 80 per cent of the vote against Le Pen in what was effectively the absence of a serious challenge. President Chirac's easy campaign enabled the creation of a new presidential conservative party – the *Union pour un Mouvement Populaire* (UMP) – federating the conservative, neo-Gaullist and centre right and enabling a sweeping victory in the ensuing general elections. However, this second Chirac presidency was an uncertain one and he faced challenges from within the conservative right – notably from Nicolas Sarkozy. One Eurosceptic faction, *Debout la République*, was formed around Nicolas Dupont-Aignan (and was organisationally ahead of its rivals).

In these circumstances, continuing government unpopularity, the decision to hold a referendum in 2005 on the European Treaty (the 'Constitution') conjured up opposition to integration, both on the right and the left, squeezing the mainstream centre parties.[11] On the conservative and extreme right, the referendum of 2005 on the European Constitution enabled a vigorous defiance of the President's wishes (for a 'yes' vote). Chirac's main competitor, Nicolas Sarkozy, used the occasion to depict the likely impact of Turkey joining the EU in lurid terms.[12] There was also a rearguard action against the Constitution that would 'reduce France to the status of Texas' in the view of the remaining Gaullist faithful.[13] De Villiers denounced the 2005 Constitution, which would, he said, lead to 'France being reduced to one or two votes of 25 or 30 and sometimes to zero, and reduced to 78 then 72 seats in 2009 when Germany has 99' in the Parliament.[14] This campaign, around the defence of France and French values, added credibility in the short term to the 'sovereignty' right although the incompatibility of these demands with government imperatives deprived them of long-term effects.[15] On the right, as on the left, the anti-European positions are at odds with the left-right cleavage that has been central to Fifth Republic party systems.

In the conservative opposition, the campaign enabled the anti-European left to emerge as a major force splitting, once again, the mainstream left from its 'natural' constituency. An effective anti-European campaign was mounted by the extreme left Trotskyite and Communist Parties and split the Socialist Party. Socialist leaders had tried to consolidate the party behind the 'yes' campaign, but tensions with the socialist left (and between presidential candidates) proved impossible to overcome and the campaign fragmented with major figures (former Prime Minister Fabius, for example) going against the party's established line. Competition for the presidential nomination made the exploitation of the European issue a means of differentiation in an otherwise ideologically-weak environment. An unpopular government's referendum, on a badly explained issue, led to the rejection of the Constitution by a substantial margin: 55 per cent voted against the Treaty on a 69 per cent turnout. In the event, this rejection of the Constitution was seen, by the 'left of the left' as their victory. There was satisfaction on the right and extreme right, who also saw it as their victory. This was an overwhelmingly conservative and negative campaign: a rejection of post-industrial society and of European integration as well as of the presumed threats from that process and the intrusion of globalisation into France.[16] This was the 'non' of the insecure, of the middle professions, agriculture, small business and for labour, the threat of deregulation symbolised by the 'Bolkestein' directive.[17] It was not the basis, in other words, for a coalition. On the extreme left, the attempt to create an anti-European and anticapitalist force failed and the Socialist Party maintained its approval of the integration process, although with the internal and external opposition strengthened.

Political parties in the contemporary system

Public opinion in twenty-first century France is divided by the European integration issue – but it is a cleavage that cuts across political alliances and political families.[18] There has been 'a Europeanisation' of the party system and of the parties. Parties contain pro- and anti-integration factions and the issue can divide and unite political actors. In the party system there have been significant pro- and anti-integration parties and these have played important roles in system politics and competition. However, the issue fluctuates in salience and the European integration problem may be pushed down the agenda by other factors. It is not possible to conclude that this one issue defines relationships, but it is possible to say that it is a significant factor. In this it is like other issues, but prudence is required in interpreting its significance at any one point. In 2005, the anti- and/or pro-Constitution vote repeated the old divisions of secular/religious and rich/poor, and repeated the PCF's voting pattern. On the right, the supporters of de Villiers' *Movement pour la France* and Le Pen's *Front National* remain strongly opposed to integration. De Villiers' main role is as a conservative opponent to integration and, by extension, an opponent to Turkey's entry into Europe. In party competition terms, this enabled a pro-integration space to be exploited.

At the beginning of 2002, the centrist politician, François Bayrou, increasingly dissident within the conservative right, struggled to make his voice heard, but after the European election of 2004 he emerged as a component player in the French party system. Bayrou's UDF used its support for European integration to carve a niche for itself in the much more reserved, if not Eurosceptic, centre-right (joining, for example, the *Verts'* Cohn-Bendit in an appeal for a federal Europe).[19] In the 2004 European elections, the UDF was resolutely pro-European and was rewarded with 12 per cent of the vote (eleven seats) and believed that its independent position on the centre-right had been reinforced. Bayrou then sought to create a federalist ginger group, *le Pôle démocratique*, in the European Parliament with the Italian Marguerite list and some of the more Europeanist European People's Party MEPs. It is a measure of the change of opinion that only Bayrou's centre has been aggressively pro-European; all the other parties posed, in one way or another, as the defenders of the public against Europe. Bayrou criticised the *'franchouillardise'* of other conservatives, notably Nicolas Sarkozy.[20] Bayrou's main success came in the presidential elections of 2007 and, at that point, he transformed the UDF into a new party, the Democratic Movement, which became widely known as the 'MoDem', but had little or no success at the subsequent general and local elections. The MoDem party is directly descended from Giscard's UDF coalition of centre parties, but shorn of its anti-European sections.[21]

Since the European elections of June 1984, Jean-Marie Le Pen's *Front National* has been the main anti-system party. However, Le Pen's party did not rise on the issue of European integration, but on its standard triptych of unemployment, crime and immigration combined with a general anti-establishment rhetoric that found a ready audience. Le Pen describes the party as the 'national right' and it is the nation and nationalism that keeps this set of issues together in a plausible manner. Le Pen is on the alert for threats to the French nation and to what the *Front National* regards as a lack of vigilance of the political class (accused of selling out) to this menace. Europe, of course, figures in the 'bestiary', although not with consistency. In the early twenty-first century, Le Pen's position had become appreciably more Eurosceptic. Moreover Le Pen, once favourable to the Euro, decided following the Maastricht Treaty to harden the FN's anti-integration position. European integration, providing a populist theme (political class against the people) gave Le Pen a plank for his platform and this was, for a party organised around a national personality (rather than local notables) highly important in the success of the FN. However, it should be kept in mind that the FN's success at European elections has not automatically fed in to the domestic French political system; in fact, it has struggled to achieve representation in the National Assembly.

Thus, in the early twenty-first century, Le Pen's position had become appreciably more Eurosceptic. By 2000, Le Pen was proposing the renegotiation of all the European treaties, if not the complete withdrawal of France from Europe and, since the mid-1990s, the emphasis was on protection of French industry and small business. In 2002, Le Pen was denouncing the Maastricht Treaty, the Amsterdam Treaty, the Schengen Agreement and calling for the re-establishment of frontiers and customs posts.[22] On the Constitution, the FN's *National hebdo* remarked that 'Giscard has, typically, sold out France once again' by creating a super-state and relegating France to 'the status of a provincial government'.[23] Although FN supporters see themselves as less European and more French than the voters of other parties, Europe – relative to issues such as crime, immigration, pensions and poverty – does not rank top amongst the preoccupations of the FN's voters.

Throughout the Fourth Republic and for most of the Fifth Republic, the Communist Party made the opposition to Europe its own, although it soon came to be rivalled by the Gaullists. Europe was an issue where its anti-Europeanism conformed to the interests of the world communist movement in Moscow. Anti-Europeanism enabled the PCF to seize the nationalist, not to say xenophobic, high ground and mobilise its activists also on a note of strident patriotism. But within the party system, the Communist Party is allied to the pro-European Socialist Party and it survives as a political force thanks to its local implantation. However, this local representation depends on its continuing alliance with the Socialist Party and that, in turn, means that the PCF's hostility to Europe has to be muted to avoid clashes with its coalition partner. Hence, communist anti-Europeanism is emphasised and downplayed as a function of its relations with the socialists, sometimes within the space of a parliamentary term (as it was from 1997–2002).

But Europe, in one way, has become a test of the Communist Party's commitment to a governmental coalition. On the one hand, there is the temptation to appeal to the anti-European instincts prevalent on the left, and especially amongst its supporters while, on the other hand, there is its continuation as a credible political party in close coalition with the socialists. Grumbling approval became the Communist Party's position when it supported the Jospin government in 1997, but that stance opened up the anti-European space on the left. One way leads ultimately to joining the Trotskyite anti-system opposition and the other to support for the much larger Socialist Party – Europe as an issue is a marker of these stances within the party system. Communists have run vigorous campaigns against the Maastricht Treaty and in 2005 they promoted a left-wing opposition to the Constitution. There is abundant evidence of discontent on the left waiting to be expressed through unions and political parties and, given the PCF's decline, a switch to the anti-European part of the spectrum cannot be ruled out. However, the PCF polled worse in 2007 than in 1999 or 2002 and with only 5.25 per cent of the vote its number of MEPs was reduced from six to two.

One reason for this failure was the pressure from the left of the left in the form of the Trotskyite parties that have flourished and now form a significant part of the political party system (10 per cent or more in some elections). There are three main Trotskyite parties. Electorally, the least significant is the *Mouvement pour un parti des travailleurs*, which ran Gérard Schivardi as a candidate in 2007, but was not prepared to abandon the anti-European terrain to its rivals and it wanted a break from the EU and the Maastricht Treaty annulled. Although it polled insignificantly, it is important as an entryist force in the *Force ouvrière* unions and, politically, may be a more consistent pressure than the 'bigger' parties.

Lutte ouvrière (LO), the second Trotskyite party, also devoted most of its energies to trade union and social movements. It began running with Arlette Laguiller as a presidential candidate in 1974 and has presented her at every presidential election since then. For many years this was a token candidacy, but in 1995 Laguiller polled 5.3 per cent. The LO has emerged as a small but significant force in the party system. Its breakthrough came at the European elections in 1978 when it polled 3.3 per cent. The LO also ran a successful European campaign in 1999. Its proclaimed objective is to create a great revolutionary party, one that would take the place of the Communist Party, and opposition to European integration is a standard part of its rhetoric. The LO is secretive and sectarian and is a difficult partner on the rare occasions it consents to work with others.

However, 2002 saw the emergence of the *Ligue Communiste Révolutionaire* (LCR), around its candidate Olivier Besancenot, representing a third electoral force on the left of the left. The LO ran the 2004 European elections in tandem with the LCR (one of the rare occasions on which they managed to collaborate) and with 5.3 per cent of the vote they took five seats in Strasbourg, calling for a 'left-wing rejection' of the EU Constitution.[24] For the extreme left, the issue of the European Constitution was a way of reinvigorating their position and reinforcing the division between itself and the 'governmental' left, while at the same time undermining the Socialist Party's social support. LCR's view was the EU could not possibly be reformed and it wanted new institutions.[25] With the emergence of the LCR as a real rival for the leftist vote, the LO has faded and the tribune role has been taken over by the more flexible party. The LCR is more in tune with the 'post–modern' issues now motivating the extreme left than is the LO and is correspondingly anti-European.

As a political party, the ecologists made a first hesitant appearance in the 1970s and then at the European elections of 1979, when they polled 4.39 per cent. By 1989, the party was able to poll 10.39 per cent in the European elections (to take nine seats) and in 1992, when the Socialist Party was in meltdown, it polled 13.9 per cent in regional elections, followed by 11 per cent in the 1993 general elections (but won no seats). This inability to capitalise on favourable circumstances left the main left-wing party in the movement – *les Verts* – dominant, but convinced that its best hope of progress was to ally with the socialist left. Thus, although its vote was not as high as the early 1990s, it was rewarded with influence as it became an essential part of the coalition. It is another component of the left that is pro-European.

Les Verts are generally pro-European and their most vigorous populist, Daniel Cohn-Bendit, was the leader of their 1999 European list. In 2004, they were the only party to run a truly Europe-wide campaign with common slogans and posters and demanded a 'united Europe' as a counterweight to the United States. *Les Verts* have looked to Europe to solve problems and have supported initiatives with an environmental thrust. Daniel Cohn-Bendit and the ecological theorist and activist Alain Lipietz argued that the Constitution had to be accepted as a package.

Lipietz praised the possibility of 'write-in' campaigns, noting also that the EU's aims included ecological and social objectives as well as public services.[26] But even minorities in *Les Verts* express reservations about the inadequacies of what they call the 'neo-liberal Treaty'.

One of the original Europeanist Parties, the Socialist Party has long taken pride in its pro-European credentials.[27] There were reservations about some aspects of integration – notably the European Defence Community (EDC) over which the party split – in the 1950s, but its support for the process and attacks on those, like de Gaulle, who impeded it were a standard feature of the party's policy.[28] In the 1980s and 1990s, when the party attained real power, it promoted European integration in significant ways and the developments from the Single Act that removed trade from the state regulators onwards, including Eureka, the Euro and the Schengen Agreement, can be traced back to the socialists in office. Although the 1980s produced many initiatives, they were largely at an elite level and there was a low level of public anxiety about Europe at this time.

Yet there has always been a debate inside the Socialist Party, often provoked by a minority of Eurosceptics, and that scepticism has increased since the mid-1990s as the party has been nudged by the extreme left into a more nuanced position. Coalition difficulties kept the socialist leadership on the fence on issues such as the EU Constitution for a long time and the rise of scepticism in the party itself made this fence-sitting the best option for a weak leadership. Partially, this hesitation by the PS is a consequence of the near defeat in the 1992 referendum on the Maastricht Treaty, but also of coalition politics in which the socialists have to deal with Eurosceptic partners such as the communists. There has also been the rise of an anti-European left factions – the *Nouveau Monde* and *Nouveau Parti Socialiste* – within the Party, who deplored the stability and growth pact and who saw an increasingly neo-liberal union being developed (some were strongly in favour of federalism).[29] However, some critics did not see the Constitution as sufficiently federal because it reinforced the Council of the EU, made the Council an uncontrolled legislator, failed to provide for an economic government and did not greatly enhance the European Parliament's position.[30]

These socialist factions are a bridge to the extreme left and in the factional struggle for dominance inside the socialist 'presidentiables' the appeal to Eurosceptics might get a vital margin of support. The PS had laid down six conditions that would make the Constitution acceptable but, as in 1997, there was a muted European response to this demand.[31] There were similar splits over the desirability of Turkey's entry into the EU.[32] It was in order to prevent the party tearing itself apart that First Secretary François Hollande's leadership delayed affirming its position on the Constitution and then organised an internal consultation of party members to decide its line. This internal consultation overwhelmingly supported the 'yes' campaign, but the left and former Prime Minister Fabius broke ranks to campaign against the Constitution. Fabius, was the only 'presidentiable' who opposed the Constitution while Ségolène Royal and Dominique Strauss-Kahn both supported the 'yes' campaign. Opposition to the Constitution did not give Fabius the upper hand and it was not a factor in Ségolène Royal's sweeping victory in the PS 2006 presidential 'primaries'.

Conclusion

European integration has been developed by its founders as a way of overcoming the deficiencies of the European state system. In the 1950s or 1960s, these deficiencies hardly needed to be underscored as the memory of two World Wars was still vivid, but as the generations move on, the need for integration, which seemed evident at one time, has become less clear. This has allowed the primary national reflex, which, as the wars remind us, is the bias for the European state to re-emerge, but focused on integration and contesting the process. This should not be a surprise to students of European history, but it does leave the parties of European integration vulnerable to ambush, as it did during the Fourth Republic.[33]

European elections are rarely decisive and seldom involve the abstruse and technical issues with which the European Union deals (still less with those within the European Parliament's remit). European elections are characterised, however, by new entrants into the party system and these have given impetus to rising movements.[34] This does not mean that all the small parties that have emerged at European elections have all become significant participants in the national party system. Many small parties (such as the MDC) have subsequently dwindled or failed to stay the course. However, European elections do provide mobilising potential and a chance for the small parties to move out of the shadows of the larger organisations. In this way, the European platform is usually (though not invariably) a national one and the issues promoted by the small parties (corruption, crime, foreign policy) are not necessarily those of European integration.[35]

European integration, starting with the narrow endorsement of the Maastricht Treaty in 1992, exposed the gap between the political elites and their party supporters.[36] Europe has thus given impetus to existing splits in the system and is one of the issues where these are most clearly expressed. However, European integration under the Fifth Republic party system is the wedge for the exploitation of other cleavages, even though it has not been the cause of the remaking of the national party system. There is a continuing left-right split in French politics, but there have been instances when this has been overcome and it could happen again, and Europe could be the issue that creates a fundamental divide (by carving out a new centre, for example).

European elections and referendums enable voters to express dissatisfaction with the role of the governing party. This can be shrugged off – as it was when the UMP was rebuffed in June 2004 – but it can represent a further weakening of the government majority in a fragile coalition. It is not, however, necessarily the opposition that gains from the government's setback in elections that do not redistribute national power. European elections are more of a 'protest' (in the sense that voters' primary loyalties remain unchanged) than a deliberate choice.

Competition is the dynamo of Western party systems[37] and is both external, between parties (sometimes within coalitions) and internal, resulting in factionalism (that may result in splits and new party formation). These elements are fully evident in the French party system of the Fourth and Fifth Republics and 'Europe', as an issue, is liable to present unpredictable opportunities to competing politicians. In the first phase of the Fifth Republic until Mitterrand's election in 1981, dominated as it was by the left-right division, the competition was manifest mainly in factionalism and in competition for position within the coalitions of the right and left. After 1981, the left-right division began to weaken and the problem of European integration emerged again from its socialist eclipse.

Mair's postulate about 'depoliticisation' is pertinent here[38]. The working of the institutions constructed by European integration is dependent on detailed and technical bargaining. This is not amenable to quick and simple description, nor do these compromises fit easily into many of the party belief systems. Politics in Europe retains the characteristic of what Weber calls the 'slow boring of hard boards'. It was once thought that, because the business of the institutions was arcane, there would be a momentum of Europeanisation that would proceed inexorably without interference. This has turned out to be wrong and 'Europe' as an all-purpose issue has intruded into the agenda of other matters and proved as amenable to exploitation in party competition as other issues not of 'high politics'.

It must be concluded, from an admittedly small-scale study, that the development of the party system and the pattern of party politics is bound up with European integration through the European parliamentary system and the elections. Europe is not insulated from domestic politics and party system competition has many dimensions, not the least of which is the integration issue itself. Whether this was, as might be inferred, something that the initiators of the integration project would lament or whether it should be lamented is not the concern here; however, the 'depoliticisation' of the process has ramifications that go beyond the 'high politics' of European nation states.

In France, European integration has to be embraced by any presidential contender. No serious mainstream candidate can be a Eurosceptic and to evince such a position would be to undermine France's position on the European stage, disqualifying them in the eyes of the majority of the electorate. This makes integration much more difficult to deal with than in the first four decades of the Fifth Republic, when submerging it in other problems or representing it as a part of grand strategy was possible. It remains the case, however, that European issues can emerge or be pushed on to the agenda as a means of destabilising presidential coalitions and that, in this competition, the opponents of further integration or enlargement have a purchase on the political system that can be potentially destructive.

European integration has, from its outset as the European Coal and Steel Community, been a source of division or cleavage in the French party system. Europe has largely been an elite issue in post-war politics. European integration is generally supported in France, but there are reservations. Moreover, in terms of party politics, Europe has not always received overwhelming endorsement, perhaps because the benefits – not always recognised – have been widely distributed. Unlike other cleavages, the European integration issue can cut across parties and the left-right cleavage dividing them – occasionally making for new coalitions or line-ups – and has pitted sections of partisan support against each other. The notion of integration alone can cause these realignments, but it is usually in combination with, or in addition to, other issues that it is particularly potent. Thus the problem of finding support for the European Defence Community was to be instrumental in the defeat of the Mendès France government in February 1955. Usually, dissatisfaction with other policies and/or the comportment of the leadership are expressed in dissidence on the issue of European integration. If the paths of European integration and European elections are to be followed through, then it has to be noted that the institutions that have evolved since the first elections provide opportunity structures of uncertain implications, some of which are available for European integration. European integration is the chosen battleground for anti-system parties and it enables them to invoke a sense of patriotism, 'them and us', defence of the 'menu peuple' and reaffirmation of the nation.

Notes

1 P. Mair, 'The limited impact of Europe on national party systems', *West European Politics*, 2000, vol. 23, pp. 27–51 and R. Andersen and J. Evans 'Values, Cleavages and Party Choice in France, 1988–1995', *French Politics*, 2003 (March), vol. 1 (1), pp. 83–114.

2 A. Alexandre and X. Jardin, 'From the Europe of the nations to the European Union?', *British Elections and Parties Review*, 1997, vol. 7, pp. 185–206.

3 D. Butler and D. Stokes, *Political Change in Britain*, Harmondsworth, Penguin, 1970, p. 233.

4 P. Mair, *Party System Change*, Oxford, OUP, 1997.

5 G. Sartori, *Parties and Party Systems*, Cambridge, CUP, 1976.

6 A. Guyomarch, 'The European dynamics of evolving party competition in France', *Parliamentary Affairs*, 1995, vol. 48 (1), 'Heresthetic' is Riker's term.

7 J. Evans, 'Contrasting attitudinal bases to Euroscepticism amongst the French electorate', *Electoral Studies*, 2000, vol. 19 (4), pp. 539–61.

8 F.D. Willis, *France, Germany and the New Europe*, Stanford, Stanford University Press, 1968, Ch.7.

9 K.H. Reif and H. Schmitt, 'Nine Second Order National Elections', *European Journal of Political Research*, 1980, vol. 8, pp. 3–44.

10 *Le Monde,* 10.1.4

11 In the European elections of 2004, 60 per cent of voters were animated by discontent with the government, *Le Monde* (Sofres), 7.5.2004.

12 *Le Monde*, 11.5.4.

13 *Le Figaro*, 7.11.2.

14 *Le Figaro,* 13–14.12.3.

15 A. Mergier *et al.*, *Le jour où la France a dit non,* Paris, Plon, 2005.

16 *Les Echos*, 30.5.5.

17 *Le Monde*, 31.5.5.

18 S. Abrial *et al.*, 'Stabilité et recomposition du système de partis français', *Revue politique et parlementaire*, 2002 (Sept–Dec.), no. 1020–1021, pp. 228–43.

19 *La Croix,* 14.6.0.

20 *Libération,* 13.9.3.

21 B. Dolez, 'La liste Bayrou ou la résurgence du cournat démocrate-chrétien?', *Revue française de science politique*, 1999, vol. 49 (4–5), pp. 663–74.

22 *Le Figaro*, 26.4.2.

23 *Le Monde,* 3.7.3.

24 A. Krivine, *Le Monde,* 23.10.3.

25 *La Croix,* 6.2004.

26 *Politis,* 2.10.3.

27 G. Lemaire-Prosche, *Le P.S. et l'Europe*, Paris, Edns Universitaires, 1990.

28 Willis, *France, Germany...*, pp. 262–4.

29 *Le Monde*, 26.9.3.

30 *Le Monde,* 3.7.3.

31 *Libération,* 1.9.3.

32 *Le Monde,* 27.11.2.

33 Sartori, *Parties and Party Systems,* Ch. 7.

34 S. Bartolini, 'La structure des clivages nationaux et la question de l'intégration européenne', *Politique européenne,* 2001, no. 4, pp. 15–45.

35 C. Anderson, 'When in doubt use proxies', *Comparative Political Studies,* 1998, vol. 18, pp. 125–38.

36 P. Taggart, 'A touchstone of dissent', *European Journal of Political Research,* 1998, vol. 33, pp. 363–88.

37 R. Ladrech, 'Europeanization of political parties', *Party Politics,* 2002, vol. 8, pp. 389–404.

38 Mair, 'The limited impact...'.

chapter | the europeanisation of the
three | german party system

Isabelle Hertner and James Sloam

Introduction

The main political actors of the Federal Republic of Germany (Parliament, the media, public opinion and interest groups) have for a long time supported the idea of European integration. The process of European integration seemed to provide West Germany (1949–90) with both peace and prosperity after the catastrophe of the Second World War. Initial concerns that Chancellor Konrad Adenauer's (1949–63) policy of *Western integration* (*Westintegration*) would cement divisions between the two Germanys during the Cold War (raised by the opposition Social Democratic Party) had completely subsided by the 1960s. For over three decades, the positive conception of the European Community (EC)/European Union (EU) went unchallenged within the German system, and European policy remains dominated by a 'basic consensus' (*grundkonsens*) in favour of the integration process. European policy experts from the two main 'catch-all parties' (*volksparteien*), the Social Democrats (*Sozialdemokratische Partei Deutschlands* (SPD)) and the Christian Democrats (*Christlich Demokratische Union/Christlich-Soziale Union* (CDU/CSU)) continue to co-operate and formulate common policies. This is not to say that the great advances in European integration since the 1980s have not had an impact on German politics, but to make the point that inter-party conflict on European issues is rare.

European integration is one of several key dynamics that has impacted on German political parties and their approach to the EC/EU. Advances in the quantity and quality of integration across a range of policy areas have led to the *domestication* of EU politics (something that has concerned the German states – *Länder*) and demanded more effective coordination across policy areas. Equally, German reunification forced the country to undergo a painful period of restructuring (e.g. effective wage devaluation) and cuts to public spending, which placed the model of *co-operative federalism* – defining relations between sub-national (state), national (federal) and supranational (EU) governance – under stress.[1] The direct and indirect impact of reunification – from the resource crunch in German public finances to increased voter volatility (particularly in the new *Länder* of Eastern Germany) also resulted in a less stable political climate. German politics ultimately evolved from an impressively stable two-and-a-half party system – the CDU-CSU, the SPD and the centre-right *Free Democratic Party* (FDP) – in the fifty years after the formation of the Federal Republic to a five-party system at the beginning of the twenty-first century. On one level, these changes increased the *conditionality* of German support for EU policies. On another level, much remains the same, as the new political parties that emerged in the 1980s and 1990s – the *Bündnis 90/Greens* (the Greens) – and the *Party of Democratic Socialism* (PDS)/ *Left Party* (LP) have largely been absorbed into the pro-European consensus. The Europeanisation of German political parties has therefore unfolded within a complex matrix of internal and external dynamics. As a consequence, European policy is caught up in an intense interplay between the 'uploading' process of seeking to integrate Europe around Germany's own institutional models, policy preferences and ways of doing things, and a 'downloading' process of domestic adaptation to EU integration by the doctrines of primacy and direct effect enshrined in Community law.[2] Since the direct impact of the EU on overall party competition in Germany is very low (given the *basic consensus* and typically low public interest in EU affairs), this chapter will concentrate on the Europeanisation effect in terms of party programmes (EU policy).

The German party system and European integration

From the outside looking in

The inclusion of Germany in the system context of the EU could potentially influence all structural properties of the party system.[3] In this context, national parties from different member states may even 'Europeanise' each other through bilateral or EU-level contacts.

We agree with Mair that Europeanisation has had important *indirect* effects on national party systems.[4] Given that many important decisions now take place at the EU level, parties are less able to influence policy in key areas due to the lack of a European party system and the lack of transparency of intergovernmental negotiations. In particular, the European Stability and Growth Pact (supported by the stability-oriented interest rate policy of the European Central Bank) have severely reduced the room for manoeuvre with regard to increases in public borrowing and spending, limiting the possibilities for expansionist monetary policy. A further area where national policy has been constrained is in the area of the Internal Market. Also known as the Single Market, its completion has placed pressure on the member states to reduce public subsidies and deregulate key sectors of the economy. European Union Competition Policy, for example, has led to a number of controversies in Germany, where the state has been forced to withdraw support from certain industries (as in the case of state guarantees for regional banks – *Landesbanks*). The pressures to adapt have also been strong in the banking, energy and telecommunication sectors, where the European Commission has pushed for further liberalisation.

Not only has the policy space that is available for competing parties been limited as a result of EU decision-making, but also the range of policy instruments available to national governments has been reduced. It can, therefore, be argued that the indirect effects of Europeanisation put considerable constraints on national party systems, and – given the lack of opportunities for contestation of parties at the EU level[5] – parties thus have little opportunity to act authoritatively within the developing system of European governance.[6] Obviously, the impact of a market-oriented integration process in these areas has been most marked on centre-left and left parties. While parties can set out policies that contradict these realities in a populist manner – as the PDS/LP in Germany have certainly done in the past – the predicament has been more serious for the SPD. Adapting to EU norms added to the pressure to introduce welfare reforms (to reduce public spending) and to reduce and withdraw state benefits and subsidies. The political consequences for the SPD of Gerhard Schröder's *Agenda 2010* reform programme – that introduced controversial 'welfare-to-work' style policies to the labour market/benefits system – were dire, as core supporters left in droves to enable the lift-off of the new Left Party.

However, Mair perhaps paints too bleak a picture of this Europeanisation effect (focusing on the downloading side of the equation). In fact, as Bartolini argues, the EU can also provide opportunities for political parties.[7] A very good example of this is the Greens in Germany (and across Europe in general). On the one hand, EU governmental engagement helped to de-radicalise the Greens in Germany[8] while, on the other hand, it has provided the opportunity to pursue environmental issues (that cross national boundaries), e.g. the championing of organic farming provisions by Renate Künast, Green Minister for Consumer Protection, Food and Agriculture (2001–5). The opportunities for shaping the EU are far better for political parties in Germany than in other countries (e.g. the United Kingdom) given the lack of party competition in this area. They have the freedom to play a more patient, 'long game', which pays greater dividends in the EU polity. The opportunity structures provided by the EU therefore depend heavily upon the institutional (party) and national structures explored below.

Finally, it has become apparent that the EU constraints placed upon parties are open to change. In the face of extreme pressure from the global financial crisis, government and party actors at the national level have, for example, been able to effectively challenge (and even openly 'flout') EU provisions on government intervention in the Internal Market and on levels of public spending (i.e. with regard to the deficit criteria). In Germany, as elsewhere, the credit crunch has led to huge increases in public spending (and public debt) alongside large-scale government intervention in the private sector (in particular, the financial, real estate, and automotive industries). For this reason, it is important to remember that the impact of Europeanisation is transient in its nature.

From the inside looking out – internal dynamics in the German party system

In the national context, it is important to emphasise once more the fact that there is in Germany a strong inter-party consensus on the general goal of EU integration. Since the late 1950s, this elite consensus and the permissive consensus that characterised mass/elite relations in this area was a major political resource for successive German governments.[9] Thus, even when the elite took decisions opposed by public opinion as a whole – such as the maintenance of Germany's role as *paymaster* of the EU, and the giving up of the Deutschmark in favour of the

Euro – they were passed almost unanimously in Parliament. The continued commitment of German elites to multilateralism, Europeanised national identity and the integration project has been facilitated by these wider circumstances, giving them the confidence to promote initiatives for deeper integration.[10]

The sharp downturn in the German economy and greater tensions in the German federal system,[11] which came about partly as a consequence of German reunification in 1990, increased the importance of material concerns. This gradually had an impact on Germany's relations with the EU. Elite support for the EU and the integration process has somewhat hardened within the last decade and important differences of emphasis have emerged between the federal and the *Länder* level. Moreover, public support for European integration is not as stable as it used to be. German parties need to be more careful than in the past and take mass opinion into consideration. While it is hard for them to gain any political advantage from opposition to the EU and/or its policies, they now stress the specific benefits for Germany in a way they did not in the past. In this regard, the 'exaggerated multilateralism' of Helmut Kohl's tenure as Chancellor (1982–98) was replaced by the 'pragmatic multilateralism' of the Schröder Chancellorship (1998–2005).[12] Schröder was less afraid to assert German interests over issues ranging from the EU budget, to the weighting of votes in the Council, and to the imposition of transition periods for the free movement of workers from the accession countries of East Central Europe. Chancellor Merkel's 2005–9 Grand Coalition (CDU/CSU and SPD) adopted a more diplomatic tone than Schröder – described by Foreign Minister Steinmeier (SPD) as 'self-assured modesty' – but was prepared to assert German interests more forcefully than under Kohl. Following the September 2009 elections, it may be expected that the 'self-assured modesty' of Angela Merkel will continue with its new coalition partner, the FDP.

To analyse the direct impact of European integration on national party systems, Mair suggests two variables: the *format* and *mechanics* of the party system.[13] It is argued here that the German party system has changed significantly since the 1980s. Yet these changes cannot be attributed *directly* to the process of European integration, when Mair's two variables of Europeanisation are taken into account.

Let us begin with the format of the German party system, i.e. the number of relevant parties in contention in the national arena. (West) Germany's relatively stable 'two-and-a-half party system' of the 1960s and 1970s[14] – dominated by the two 'catch-all parties'[15] and with the liberal FDP, acting as the 'kingmaker' – has developed into a fluid five-party system on the federal level.[16] However, this triangular dynamic of party competition was undermined by the arrival of two new parties. First, in 1983, the post-materialist Greens entered the Bundestag, and secondly, in 1990, after German reunification, the socialist PDS. Given their genesis in the protest movements of the 1960s and 1970s, the Greens first presented themselves as an 'outrider', anti-establishment party. Yet alongside increasing electoral success came the intensification of divisions between 'realos' (pragmatists) and 'fundis' (fundamentalists). By the 1990s, however, the pragmatists had clearly gained the upper hand, and the Greens entered the federal government in 1998 as junior partner to the SPD. In the East German system, party competition was in effect banned. The PDS was the legal successor to the Socialist Unity Party (SED), which governed the one-party system and one-party state of the GDR. Initially at least, the party was supported by the 'losers' of reunification and those (mostly former functionaries) who remained loyal to the regime, and evolved into a 'regional protest party'.[17] In 2005, the PDS co-operated with the Electoral Alternative for Labour and Social Justice (WASG), and in 2007 the two groupings merged to form the Left Party (*Die Linke*).[18] Both the LP and the Greens are positioned to the left ('traditional' and 'post-materialist', respectively),[19] but the emergence of the LP has clearly narrowed the strategic alternatives for the Social Democrats, who have thus far ruled out an electoral coalition with the LP at the federal level.

The CDU/CSU, currently, has only one major competitor at the federal level: the SPD. The FDP is generally viewed as an ally and the preferred coalition partner of the Christian Democrats. The September 2009 elections confirmed this preference. The three far-right/extreme-right parties in Germany – the National Democratic Party (NPD), the German People's Union (DVU) and the Republicans (*Republikaner*) – together polled less than 3 per cent in the 2005 federal elections.[20] While they have scored some successes in second-order elections,[21] their impact upon the party system is small given their failure at the national level, their dwindling membership, and the costs of abiding by a *basic law* that forbids the existence of anti-constitutional parties.[22]

In the period between 1965 and 1998, three new political parties, explicitly referring to the EU integration process, have taken part in national elections,[23] but none of these parties gained seats in the Bundestag or European Parliament (EP) and disappeared quickly.

To summarise, the number of relevant parties at national level has increased, leading to a fragmentation of the German party system. However, the arrival of the two relevant parties (the Greens and the LP) cannot be directly linked to European integration. The Greens emerged out of the peace/ecological movement of the 1960s and 1970s (and through the emergence of the post-material cleavage in German politics), and the PDS was born out of reunification as the communist successor party in East Germany. Given the fact that European integration has not created significant divisions with and between political parties in Germany, we agree with Mair that 'to the simple question of whether Europe has had a direct impact on the format of national party systems, the equally simple answer must be an unequivocal "no"'.[24]

This raises the question: have the mechanics of the German party system, i.e. the modes of interaction between the relevant parties, been 'Europeanised'? Despite the emergence of some fault lines between the parties – as with, for example, the prospective EU enlargement to Turkey[25] – in Germany there is no discernible conflict within the party system over European integration.[26] Even the LP, a strong critic of the current market-oriented EU and an equally strong proponent of a *social Europe*, is generally supportive of the European integration process. If anything, lines of conflict over European policy exist most conspicuously between the parties at the federal level, and the parties at the regional level. The German

Länder have a more particularistic view of European integration and have on occasion – as in the case of Bavaria under Edmund Stoiber (CSU Minister-President
from 1993–2007) – become vocal critics of the loss of powers to Brussels.

Nevertheless, in no other large EU member state has the elite consensus around
the European project been as stable as in Germany, where hard Euroscepticism
remains a 'dark matter' for all relevant parties.[27] Euroscepticism is geographi-
cally and ideologically confined to the margins of the German political system.
According to Lees, the PDS was the only one of the five parties that lay outside the
European policy consensus and could be classified even as a 'soft Eurosceptic'[28]
and this mild Euroscepticism has 'softened' further since the PDS merger with the
WASG. This does not mean that there is no difference between the parties in their
European positions.[29] On certain issues, such as EU enlargement, their policies
differ considerably. However, the strong role of *co-operative federalism* with its
pressures to achieve compromise between the two legislative chambers, and the
fact that Germany is usually governed by a coalition of at least two parties, creates
a powerful constitutional logic for consensual politics. These factors have acted
as important constraints against temptations to mobilise Eurosceptic sentiments in
the German party system.[30] Furthermore, in terms of party competition in domestic elections, 'almost nothing points to the pro- versus anti-European conflict line
becoming a relevant cleavage dimension'.[31] This is not to deny the importance of
the Europeanisation effect on political parties, but merely to emphasise the more
indirect effects discussed above.

The Europeanisation of German political parties

The process of Europeanisation has had little impact upon the political strategies
of German parties. The EU is not a controversial issue among German political
elites and the public does not generally view European-level issues as having a
major bearing on their day-to-day lives (as in most member states this reflects a
'knowledge gap' rather than a 'legitimacy gap'). We agree with David Hanley, a
political researcher, that programmatic change is the most visible party response to
European integration,[32] followed by organisational change. This section will therefore concentrate on the impact of Europeanisation on party programmes (in terms
of EU policy) and decision-making in this area with regard to *European policy
networks* (both at the domestic and the EU level). Seeing Europeanisation as a
multidirectional process, this study will analyse how integration shapes German
parties' programmes and organisational structures, and also the parties' efforts to
shape the outcomes of EU integration in ways that suit their own interests.

Party programmes (EU policy)

The first point to make is that European policy has grown markedly in its importance in recent years. As discussed above, European integration has long been supported by a cross-party consensus, but European issues are gradually coming to the
fore in the political arena as German parties have sought to integrate the EU into

their policy programmes. Therefore, parallel to the advances in European integration that took place in the 1980s and 1990s, EC/EU politics became an increasing feature of party manifestos over this period. Figure 3.1, based on Manifestos
Research Group (MRG) data,[33] shows that references to the EC/EU have increased
by over 60 per cent amongst the long-established parties (SPD, CDU/CSU and
FDP) and almost tripled amongst the parties overall since the 1980s. We would
therefore suggest that the incorporation of EU policy into all other policy areas is
indispensable for a party with governing aspirations. Even the LP, the nearest to
an 'outsider' of the five relevant parties, cannot ignore the EU. In fact, Figure 3.1
shows that the PDS, in its efforts to establish credibility (as a viable party of the
'hard left')[34] and pursue its preference for more EU-level regulation, had the most
positive references to the EU of all German parties in its 2002 manifesto. The data
clearly shows that the EU has become more prominent in election manifestos, so
we must delve more deeply to fully understand the development of EU policy in
the individual parties.

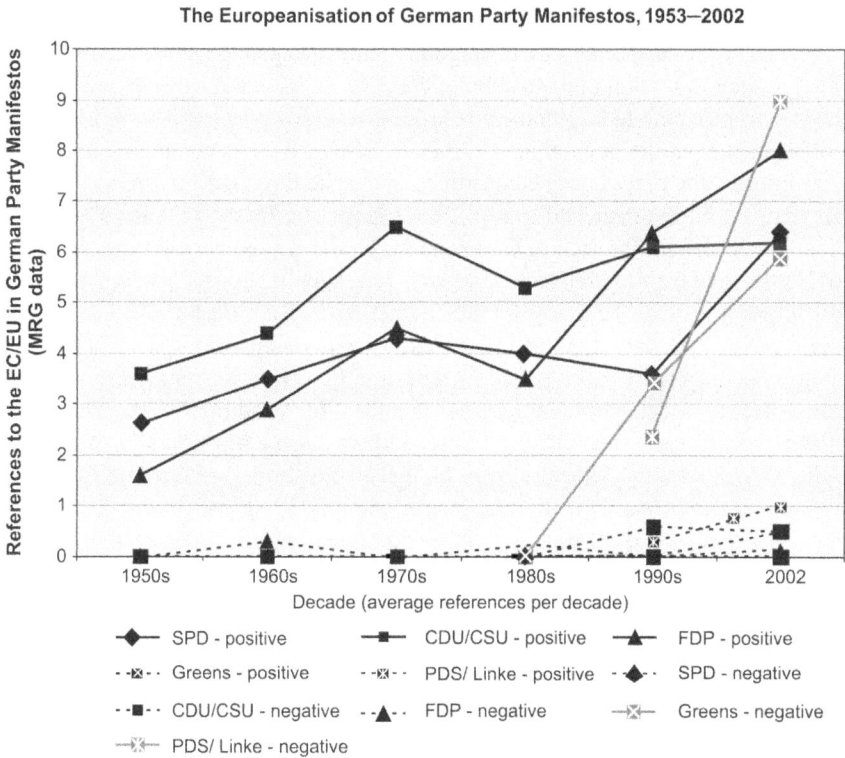

Figure 3.1: The Europeanisation of German Party Manifestos 1953–2002

The catch-all parties

SPD European policy was dominated by a basic consensus in favour of European integration from the 1960s onwards. Although the consensus was somewhat disrupted in the 1990s, and after the party came into power under Gerhard Schröder in 1998, underlying support for European integration has remained strong.[35] This might seem surprising considering that integration placed a number of traditional social democratic policy areas under considerable strain (as mentioned above in relation to the Internal Market and the Single Currency). Since regulation (and ownership) of public services is and has been constrained by European integration, some degree of confrontation (both directly and indirectly) with 'cherished notions regarding the role of the national state' was inevitable.[36] However, for German Social Democrat politicians, it has been difficult to oppose EU policy directly, taking into account the institutionalised nature of German support for European integration. Thus, EU-level constraints remain largely ignored in federal electoral campaigns, even if they severely limit the room for manoeuvre of competing political parties.[37]

SPD European policy has undergone significant change since reunification. First, policy formation in opposition in the early 1990s was characterised by strategic and programmatic pluralism. European politics was not very high on the SPD's agenda at the beginning of the 1990s. But, given its commitment to a social Europe, the party became concerned about the direction Europe was taking. At first, the SPD threatened to reject the Maastricht Treaty, criticising the EC's democratic deficit, the lack of European parliamentary power, and the transition of Europe to a market (that lacked a social dimension). However, a large majority of the party ratified the Treaty in the Bundestag in December 1992. The second period of change started in the mid-1990s, when divisions within the SPD leadership were mirrored by a confused European policy. This was partly the result of the existence of competing ideological streams – old (traditional) left, new (postmaterialist) left and modernising centre, and was also a consequence of the plurality of actors at the federal level. The leadership 'troika' of Gerhard Schröder, Oskar Lafontaine and Rudolf Scharping in the mid-1990s was erratic and inconsistent with regard to EU policy, and their rhetoric often contradicted official party policy. From their regional power-bases, this new generation of SPD leaders was prepared to take a more critical stance on European integration – Schröder, for example, as Minister-President of Lower Saxony, suggested that the postponement of the Euro might not be a bad thing. The cross-party consensus on the EC/EU made it nevertheless impossible for the mainstream parties to campaign effectively against Europe – the failure of Dieter Spöri, SPD candidate in the 1992 Baden-Württemberg state election, seemed to prove this point.[38] From 1996 to 1998, the party concentrated on domestic policy issues, in a last push to dethrone Chancellor Kohl, and were pragmatic and consistent about their (albeit more conditional) support for European integration. This approach was characterised by Schröder's insistence that Germans *should be Europeans because they want to be, not because they feel they have to be.* The emergence of a new generation of SPD leaders socialised with European integration as a given fact allowed a more self-confident EU (and foreign) policy focused more strongly on national interests.[39] For example, Chancellor Schröder's insistence on a new distribution of votes in the European institutions[40] represented his wish for a 'normalised' discourse (liberated from the constraints of Germany's past) in Europe. Yet as the SPD prepared for government in the late 1990s and entered power in 1998, a more coherent and nuanced European vision gradually evolved. This was also successfully integrated into the party's overall policy platform, so that references to European issues increased by over 60 per cent between the 1980s and 2002 (see Figure 3.1).

Like most Christian democratic parties in Europe, the CDU is integrationist. The party characterises itself as 'Germany's European party' (*Europapartei Deutschlands*), stressing its commitment to the process of European integration since its beginnings in the 1950s.[41] Once again, this can be broadly verified by MRG data (see Figure 3.1), which shows that the CDU/CSU has consistently put European issues to the fore since the early years of the European Community. Helmut Kohl, Chancellor from 1982 until 1998 (and CDU party chairman from 1973 until 1998), has certainly been the key figure in the Europeanisation of the CDU. Kohl had a strong personal interest in the pursuit of European integration, especially in the aftermath of German reunification, viewing German unity and the unification of Europe as 'two sides of the same coin'. Moreover, his incumbency during a period when the integration process gained renewed momentum (starting in 1986 with the commitment to a Single European Market) provided an opportunity to pursue goals that simply were not available in the previous and following years.[42] Ever deeper integration was the *leitmotiv* of Kohl's European policy, and the EMU was the centrepiece of this policy.[43] In fact, any reservations over the (uneven) development of the EC/EU reflected a desire for more not less political union. One of the few examples of CDU national politicians rocking the boat over European integration was the 1994 Schäuble-Lamers paper, which called for a 'core Europe' (with respect to Economic and Monetary Union). This reflected a concern that the integration process should progress more systematically and pragmatically without diluting or destabilising the EU. However, the implicit suggestion in the paper that some states should be excluded from the forthcoming single currency was quickly dismissed by Kohl. Between 1998 and 2005, the CDU was in opposition. The removal of the party from power, added to the resignation of Kohl as party chairman, led to a greater focus on domestic policy. Just as any criticism of the European policy consensus emanated from SPD regional politics, the internal criticism of the pro-integration approach came from Christian Democrat state premiers. The most strident critic was CSU Minister-President Stoiber, who disapproved of the level of German payments to the EU budget as well as the nature of EMU and the general extension of Brussels' powers without a clear delimitation of competences. In Lees's terms, the CSU under Stoiber was characterised by 'soft Euroscepticism'.[44] A more subtle difference of opinion over European policy within the CDU/CSU exists between the foreign policy experts and European policy experts. Foreign policy experts are prominent in the parties and advocate US relations/Atlanticism (sometimes at the expense of EU affairs) – they are also more impressed by globalisation than Europeanisation.

When, in 2005, the Grand Coalition came to power, the 'coalition contract' (*Koalitionsvertrag*) dedicated a long section to European politics.[45] Though Social Democrat-Green foreign and European policy (1998–2005) had been fiercely criticised by the Christian Democrat and Liberal opposition, common European policy positions were agreed rather smoothly. Key points were support for the Constitutional Treaty (to be interpreted as strong commitment to EU integration in general), further de-bureaucratisation and deregulation at EU level, a reformed Lisbon Agenda as well as closer co-operation in security matters.[46] The one real area of dispute – the issue of EU enlargement to Turkey – was also easily overcome as the decision for accession negotiations to begin had already been taken. After 2005, the SPD governed as the junior partner in a Grand Coalition with the Christian Democrats and therefore retained a strong influence on Germany's EU policy. Nevertheless, it is difficult to measure social democratic influence on EU policy under the Grand Coalition, since everyday EU policy coordination is a somewhat 'shared domain' between the two coalition partners. Chancellor Merkel is a CDU politician; the Foreign Minister Steinmeier belongs to the SPD; and the responsibility for the coordination of EU policy is held by the Economic Ministry under successive CSU minister.[47] As a consequence, German EU policy under the Grand Coalition needs to be understood as a compromise between the two *Volksparteien*, even if they do not always agree on every issue.

The minor parties

The FDP, as a liberal party and the strongest supporter of free markets and free competition in the German system, has been a clear advocate of European integration over recent decades. As the junior coalition partner in the Kohl governments (1982–98), the FDP held the foreign office and so was itself deeply involved in the European integration process during that period. In fact, Hans-Dietrich Genscher (Foreign Minister from 1974–82 under SPD-FDP coalitions and 1982–92 under CDU/CSU-FDP coalitions) was one of the key actors in German European policy during this period. His efforts to 'upload' liberal policy on to the European level can clearly be seen through his active role in the agreement of the Single European Act in 1986, and he was widely credited with helping to convince Kohl to go along with French plans for EMU without a parallel *European Political Union*.[48] In terms of the party's election manifestos, Figure 3.1 shows that the Europeanisation of FDP policy since the 1980s has been very significant (with positive references to the EC/EU more than doubling during this period). This is indicative of both the party's hold on the foreign office and the emergence of an EC/EU that is broadly favourable from a liberal, market-oriented perspective. This is not to say that the FDP takes a totally uncritical line on integration. The party has advocated reforms to improve efficiency (decision-making, regulatory and democratic) with an emphasis on the completion of the Single Market in an enlarged EU.[49]

The Greens are in many ways the most Europeanised of Germany's political parties ('We Greens see ourselves as a European party')[50]: a core interest in European issues allied to constitutionally embedded activism at the EU level (explained below). The programmatic commitment to European affairs is quite obviously a reflection of the need to pursue environmental policy on a supranational level, and – as with the other German parties – the party's manifestos have increasingly turned to European issues in recent decades (see Figure 3.1). While the FDP wishes to see the EU become more efficient in market terms, for the Greens the priority is regulation and common standards to protect the environment. The Greens are also fervent advocates of a democratisation of the EU through the European Parliament.[51] Efforts to 'upload' policy on to the EU level nevertheless faced a reality check when the Greens entered government in 1998. Joschka Fischer, Germany's first Green Foreign Minister (1998–2005), had a particular responsibility for European affairs in view of Chancellor Schröder's clear preference for domestic politics. For Fischer and Environment Minister, Jürgen Trittin, this involved a large amount of pragmatism in highly complex inter-governmental negotiations and relations with their senior coalition partner, the SPD. Trittin, for example, was put in the invidious position of withdrawing German support for a car recycling directive (under direct orders from Schröder) in 1999 due to concerns about its impact upon the German car industry. However, involvement in intergovernmental politics at the European level has also provided opportunities, and the Green Party has been proactive in pursuing its agenda. Fischer's famous speech at the Humboldt University in 2000 was an important contribution to the debate about democratic reform of the EU and was backed up by the German Government's insistence on the establishment of an Intergovernmental Conference on institutional reform.[52] Remembering also the influence of Künast in consumer affairs (see above), it appears that a well networked party can make a difference in specific policy areas. Today, fervent Green support for European integration is tempered by concern over the nature of the EU – environmental standards, democratic accountability and over-centralisation – but the party is deeply committed to and engaged in shaping EU politics, policy and polity.

The Left Party has the most ambivalent relationship towards the European Union of all the electorally relevant German parties. Though the LP supports the principle of European integration, it intends to 'fight against its present neo-liberal constellation'.[53] Given the tight constraints (perhaps even 'straightjacket') within the EU for parties of the left (see above), it is perhaps unsurprising that PDS/LP has become increasingly interested in European issues (even if its radical programme has little chance of implementation). In fact, Figure 3.1 shows that the PDS in 2002 made the most (positive and negative) references to the EU of all the parties in its election manifesto. The EU not only provides an opportunity for the promotion of socialist principles on a national level, it provides a platform for the party to support policies to *fix the ills* of globalisation and establish a more democratic and 'people-oriented' EU. Among its shopping list of priorities, the LP calls for the introduction of a European minimum wage, harmonisation of taxes (to end 'social dumping'), greater regulation of arms exports and more direct democracy.[54] The Left Party's commitment to European issues is likely to remain. Oskar Lafontaine, the party's most high-profile leader, has long believed in the centrality of the EU for the attainment of socialist goals.[55]

The Fringe parties – the Far Right

The far right in Germany has distinct views on the EU and European integration. Though the degree of focus on European politics is variable, it is a common (almost integral) theme given these nationalist parties' strong opposition to the ceding of national sovereignty to a 'foreign' body (linked to an 'increasing lack of freedom and totalitarianism'), immigration in general (disturbingly related to the 'cultural and biological destruction of the peoples of Europe'), and the enlargement of the European Union (with particular reference to Turkey).[56] They support a 'Germany for the Germans ... a stop to increasing immigration'.[57] All three parties argue for a 'federation of fatherlands' and 'of Christian and Western values' as opposed to the current EU.[58] In recent years, social questions (in the face of increasing unemployment and economic hardship) have led to the development of anti-capitalism and anti-globalisation as major themes.[59] In this context, the EU is seen as a neo-liberal tool for Anglo-Saxon or US hegemonic interests. Though the influence of these parties overall is very small, one point worth mentioning is that they are the only true anti-European parties in Germany, and have tried to use this fact to their advantage: 'No-one wanted the inflationary Euro-money. Without asking the people it was forced upon us.'[60]

Party organisation

While the ideologies of parties and programmes have been affected by Europeanisation, the internal adaptation of party organisational structures to European integration has gained increasing attention.[61] With regard to European policy making, recent studies have pointed to the shift of power within national political parties in favour of national party elites and/or EU specialists.[62] We consider EU specialists to be a heterogeneous group of actors consisting of Members of the European Parliament (MEPs), national politicians with an EU brief (such as MPs active on European committees, party spokespersons for EU affairs, and ministers of European affairs), and staff with an EU brief (people employed by parties concerned with the management and organisation of EU-related activities).[63]

Though each of the German parties is embedded in a different network, it is important to draw out a few common features. First, European policy takes places almost exclusively on the national plane. The further from the centre of European policy making in Berlin, the less Europeanised the parties become. However, the only areas where the *Länder* have managed to unite (in the *Bundesrat*, the upper chamber) were over the need for greater insight into intergovernmental negotiations, plus a clearer division of powers between Brussels, Berlin and the German regions. Secondly, we must make the obvious but fundamental point that parties have far fewer resources to devote to the less salient area of EU politics in opposition than in government. However, in Germany this is much less the case than in other countries. Not only do German parliamentary committees have an important and largely non-partisan role in European policy, but German parties may also tap into the vast resources of their political foundations. The SPD-aligned Friedrich Ebert Foundation (FES), for example, with an annual budget of €111 million in 2007 (over half of which is spent on international activities) and offices in 26 European states,[64] plays a pivotal role in maintaining good contacts between the SPD and its centre-left sister parties in other member states. The political consensus enables European policy groups to concentrate on the detail of policy rather than the domestic consequences of their positions (as is the case for the major parties in the UK). Conversely, there is the fact that European policy – which is less partisan – allows a large degree of continuity in government ministries (and autonomy for officials in the relevant ministries).

In the case of the German catch-all parties, a number of findings are worth mentioning. Deeper European integration has not resulted in a noticeable increase in the number of EU specialists working on EU issues within the party organisations or national and sub-national parliaments.[65] However, the number of those whose remit is affected by European politics has clearly grown. EU specialists are involved in the drafting of programmes, but the role of individuals seems to depend on their overall influence within their party. German MEPs enjoy a very high degree of independence and autonomy that is rooted in the importance of their regional base for re-selection. National party leaderships of the SPD and CDU have very little influence on candidate selection and can therefore hardly ensure discipline or hold MEPs accountable.[66] An indicator of an MEP's status within the party is whether they are present on the party executive committee (*Vorstand*). On the whole and in cross-national comparison, both the SPD's and the CDU's EU specialists (especially MEPs) are only 'moderately' integrated into the party, and party-family affiliation does not appear to affect the degree of integration.[67] As with other member state representatives, MEPs from the German catch-all parties are quite likely to vote in a national rather than a party political bloc in the EP when key national interests are at stake. The European policy consensus thus gives German parties quite an advantage when working for common interests, e.g. on behalf of the powerful car industry.

Raunio argues that European integration consolidates the centralisation of power and top-down decision-making by providing party leadership within an arena (the EU) where the party organisation exercises little if any control over its representatives.[68] When a party is in government and thus involved in the European-level decision-making process, particularly in the Council of Ministers and the European Council, the autonomy of the party leadership in driving policy is increased. The reason behind this is the difficulty that parties have in mandating ministers ex ante and holding them to account ex post when they engage in EU decision-making.[69] Neither the SPD nor the CDU subject their ministers to significant ex-ante or ex-post controls.[70] It can therefore be concluded that European integration has caused a shift of power within the two German *Volksparteien* in favour of national party elites.

Conclusion

This chapter has argued that – despite many common features – the German party system provides a unique context for Europeanisation. While clear differences between the German parties still exist, the basic consensus over the positive nature of European integration has encouraged German parties to pursue a 'long game', and discouraged them from using the European Union as a 'political football'.

Key changes in the German party system have resulted from a number of (essentially domestic) factors including the cost of regenerating the East German economy, the rigidity of the German labour market, and the difficulty of achieving reform within an interlocked federal system. A downturn in the German economy placed further pressure on public spending, further exacerbating tensions within a country that had become more diverse in economic, political and social terms.

According to Mair, Europeanisation can have direct and indirect effects on national parties and party system. In a direct sense, Europeanisation has only played a marginal role in party system change in Germany given the lack of real conflict over European policy, and the strong support of the political, media and business elites for the European project. The German party system has changed significantly since the 1980s with the number of relevant parties increasing from two-and-a-half to five relevant parties at the federal level. These changes, however, cannot be attributed directly to European integration. The impact of Europeanisation might also be indirect: by removing certain policy areas from the exclusive authority of the national political arena, Europeanisation exerts an important, but nevertheless indirect influence on the way in which parties compete with one another. In the case of Germany, there is no doubt that European integration placed limits on the policy options that could be pursued by the two former main governing parties (SPD and CDU/CSU). This may continue with the new governmental coalition between liberals and Christian democrats. The EMU and the Internal Market established a centripetal force for the main governing parties that has increased the space for smaller parties on the left and the right (though not the far right) of the political spectrum. The impact of integration was more restrictive for the SPD as it appeared to forestall a major demand-side spending programme, placing further pressure on the welfare state and encouraging reformist policies that split the SPD and allowed the emergence of the new Left Party on the national stage. Therefore, even though the policy space, repertoire and instruments available to German parties have been limited due to the process of European integration, political competition has not become depoliticised.

To summarise, although one can find little direct impact of Europeanisation on the German party system, there is significant evidence of indirect Europeanisation. This very much confirms the Mair/Ladrech paradox set out in the introduction to this book – that we are witnessing 'the Europeanisation of individual parties and the non-Europeanisation of party systems'. One of the main areas where Europeanisation has taken place is at the programmatic level, where European policy has become increasingly important for politically relevant German political parties (irrespective of their ideological position). In other words, the 'downloading' of policy from the EU level has precipitated greater efforts to 'upload' policy from the national level. Whilst German support for European integration has become more 'conditional', this has actually lead to intensified engagement in the EU policy-making process rather than opposition to or disengagement from EU affairs. The lack of party competition over Europe has allowed German parties to focus on uploading policies to shape the EU (and promote national policy agendas) without the fear of appearing too integrationist. In this context, the German parties – with varying degrees of enthusiasm and success – have sought to operationalise EU-level contacts to promote their policy goals. To this end, they have sought to engage with a wide range of domestic and European-level actors, resulting in a genuine multidirectional Europeanisation effect.

Notes

1   C. Jeffery, *Recasting German Federalism: The Legacies of Unification*, London, Continuum, 1999.

2   K. Dyson, 'The Europeanization of German governance', in S. Padgett, W. E. Paterson and G. Smith (eds), *Developments in German Politics 3*, Basingstoke, Palgrave, 2003, pp. 161–83.

3   O. Niedermayer, 'The Party System: Structure, Policy, and Europeanization' in K. Dyson and K. Goetz (eds), *Germany, Europe and the Politics of Constraint*, Oxford, Oxford University Press, 2003, pp. 129–46.

4   P. Mair, 'Political parties and party systems', in P. Graziano and M. Vink (eds), *Europeanization: New Research Agendas*, Basingstoke, Palgrave, 2007, pp. 154–66.

5   S. Hix, *What's Wrong with the European Union and How to Fix it*, Cambridge, Polity, 2008.

6   Mair, 'Political parties...'.

7   S. Bartolini, *Restructuring Europe: Centre Formation, System Building, and Political Structuring between the Nation State and the European Union*, Oxford, Oxford University Press, 2005.

8   E. Bomberg and N. Carter 'Greens in Brussels: shapers or shaped?', *European Journal of Political Research, 2006*, 45, pp. 99–125.

9   W. E. Paterson, 'Germany and Europe' in Padgett, Paterson and Smith (eds), *Developments*, pp. 206–26. Although West European integration was initially opposed by the SPD (which at the time saw it as an obstacle to an early German re-unification), given the success of the European integration process in 1950s (particularly for the export-oriented West German economy) and the consolidation of the German Democratic Republic (GDR) the Social Democrats had become convinced *Euroenthusiasts* by the time of their watershed Bad Godesberg conference in 1959.

10 S. Bulmer, C. Jeffery and W. E. Paterson, *Germany's European Diplomacy: Shaping the Regional Milieu*, Manchester, Manchester University Press, 2000.

11 H. Kitschelt and W. Streeck (eds), *Germany: Beyond the Stable State*, London, Frank Cass, 2004.

12 J. Sloam, *The European Policy of the German Social Democrats: Interpreting a Changing World*, Basingstoke, Palgrave, 2005.

13 P. Mair 'The limited impact of Europe on national party systems', *West European Politics*, 2000, vol. 23 (4), pp. 27–51.

14 J. Blondel, 'Party systems and patterns of government in western democracies', *Canadian Journal of Political Science*, 1968, vol. 1 (2), pp. 180–203.

15 O. Kirchheimer, 'The catch-all party', in P. Mair (ed.), *The West European Party System*, Oxford, Oxford University Press, 1990, pp. 50–60.

16 Niedermayer, 'The Party System...', and J. Sloam, 'Catch-all parties catching less: the 2005 election and the decline of the German Volkspartei', in A. Miskimmon, W. E. Paterson and J. Sloam (eds), *Germany's Gathering Crisis: The 2005 Federal Election and the Grand Coalition*, Basingstoke, Palgrave, 2008.

17 D. Hough, *The Rise and Fall of the PDS in Eastern Germany*, Birmingham,

Birmingham University Press, 2002.

18 D. Hough, 'Smaller parties and the "normalization" of the German party system', in Miskimmon, Paterson and Sloam, *Germany's Gathering Crisis.*

19 C. Lees, '"Dark matter": institutional constraints and the failure of party-based Euroscepticism in Germany', *Political Studies*, 2002, vol. 50, pp. 244–67, p. 260.

20 Germany's far-right parties have recently avoided electoral competition with each other. The two largest parties, the NPD and DVU, in particular, established the *Deutschlandpakt* to avoid splitting the vote.

21 Far right parties in Germany passed the 5 per cent threshold in five West German states in the late 1960s (NPD), in the 1989 European elections (Republicans), and in four eastern German states and two western German states (DVU and NPD) since the early 1990s.

22 U. Backes, 'The electoral victory of the NPD in Saxony and the prospects for future extreme right success in German elections', *Patterns of Prejudice*, 2006, vol. 40 (2), pp. 129–41. Backes shows that overall party membership of the Republicans, NPD and DVU fell by about half between 1990 and 2005.

23 The decidedly pro-European *Europäische Föderalistische Partei* in the 1960s, and the Eurosceptical *Bund freier Bürger – Offensive für Deutschland* (BfB) and the Initiative Pro D-Mark- Neue Liberale Partei (Pro-DM) in the 1990s.

24 Mair, 'The limited impact...', p. 31.

25 On the theme, Turkish integration to the EU, the SPD has taken the position of supporting entry (if the accession criteria are met) whilst the Christian Democratic Parties have only supported a 'privileged partnership'. The issue of Turkish enlargement can also be related to domestic issues. The SPD has been supportive of the naturalisation amongst the large immigrant Turkish community in Germany whilst the CDU/CSU has placed more focus on the need for the Turkish community to 'integrate' into German society.

26 T. Poguntke, 'Europeanization in a consensual environment? German political parties and the European Union', in T. Poguntke, N. Aylott, E. Carter and R. Ladrech (eds), *The Europeanization of National Political Parties: Power and Organizational Adaptation*, London, Routledge, 2007, pp. 108–33.

27 Lees, '"Dark matter"...', pp. 244–67.

28 Lees, '"Dark matter"....', pp. 244–67, see also A. Szczerbiak and P. Taggart (eds), *Opposing Europe?: The Comparative Party Politics of Euroscepticism – Volume 1: Case Studies and Country Surveys*, Oxford, Oxford University Press, 2008.

29 R. Sturm and H. Pehle, *Das neue deutsche Regierungssystem*, Opladen, Leske & Budrich, 2001, p. 148.

30 Poguntke,'Europeanization...', pp. 108–33

31 Niedermayer, 'The Party System...', p. 129.

32 D. Hanley, 'Christian Democracy and the paradoxes of Europeanization', *Party Politics*, 2002, vol. 8 (4), pp. 463–81.

33 I. Budge, H.-D. Klingemann, A. Volkens and J. Bara, *Mapping Policy Preferences: Estimates for Parties, Electors, and Governments 1945–1998*, Oxford, Oxford University Press, 2001; H.-D. Klingemann, A. Volkens, J. Bara and I. Budge, *Mapping Policy Preferences II: Estimates for Parties, Electors and*

Governments in Central and Eastern Europe, European Union and OECD 1990–2003, Oxford, Oxford University Press, 2007.

34 Given its association with the former East German state party (the SED), the PDS was never more than a fringe part in the more populous states of Western Germany (with approximately three times as many people as in the new states of Eastern Germany) until its merger with the WASG in 2007.

35 Sloam, *The European Policy...*

36 R. Ladrech, 'The Left and the European Union', *Parliamentary Affairs*, 2003, vol. 56, pp. 112–24, p. 121.

37 Dyson, 'The Europeanization...'. EU- level constraints have, in fact, been instrumentalised by the SPD leadership to help justify unpopular measures (e.g. privatisations) amongst its members and the left wing.

38 N. Reinhardt, 'A turning point in the German EMU debate: The Baden-Württemberg regional election of March 1996', 1996, *German Politics*, vol. 6 (1), pp. 77–99.

39 Sloam, *The European Policy...*

40 H. Haftendorn, *Coming of Age: German Foreign Policy since 1945*, Lanham, Rowman & Littlefield, 2006.

41 Christian Democratic Union (CDU) *Die CDU hat sich seit den Anfängen der europäischen Integration unter Bundeskanzler Konrad Adenauer immer als die Europapartei verstanden*, http://www.cdu.de/politikaz/europa.php (accessed 1 July 2008).

42 Bulmer *et al*, *Germany's European...*

43 Paterson, 'Germany and Europe...', pp. 209–26.

44 In policy terms, this manifested itself as support for a Judeo-Christian Europe, flanked by a social market economy, and a power structure based on subsidiarity. Christian Social Union (CSU), *Unsere Politik: Europa*, www.csu. de/partei/unsere_politik/aussenpolitik_europa/europa/index.htm (accessed 1 June 2008).

45 German Federal Government *Gemeinsam für Deutschland. Mit Mut und Menschlichkeit. Koalitionsvertrag von CDU, CSU und SPD*, http://www. bundesregierung.de/Content/DE/__Anlagen/koalitionsvertrag,property=publi cationFile.pdf (accessed 1 June 2008).

46 Ibid.

47 Merkel can make use of the Chancellor's 'guideline competency' (*Richtlinienkompetenz*), supported by the Chancellor's Office. However, the Chancellor's office is poorly staffed; the EU affairs division consists of no more than 15–20 members and is not actually able to steer EU policy except for issues with special relevance to the chancellor. Therefore, the role of the Foreign Office and the Economics ministry in defining everyday EU policy should not be underestimated. See T. Beichelt, 'Over-efficiency in German EU Policy Coordination', *German Politics*, 2007, vol. 16, (4), pp. 421–33.

48 K. Dyson and K. Featherstone, *Road To Maastricht: Negotiating Economic and Monetary Union*, Oxford, Oxford University Press, 2000.

49 Free Democratic Party (FDP), *Forderungskatalog der FDP im EP an die Deutsche Ratspräsidentschaft*, http://europa.fdp.de/sitefiles/downloads/931/ Forderungskatalog_FDP..pdf (accessed 1 June 2008).

50 Bündnis90/The Greens *Themen: Europa*, www.gruene.de/cms/themen/rubrik/13/13329.europa.htm (accessed 1 June 2008).
51 Bomberg argues, 'the German Greens have come a long way since the mid-1980s when their fundamentalist members of the European Parliament (MEPs) called for an end to collaboration with "a scandalously, pre-constitutional undemocratic condition"', E. Bomberg, 'The Europeanisation of Green Parties: exploring the EU's impact', *West European Politics*, 2002, vol. 25 (3), pp. 29–50, p. 36.
52 Equally, the intergovernmental platform provided by the EU allowed Trittin to make a positive contribution to saving the Kyoto protocol at the Bonn Climate Change Conference in 2001.
53 The Left Party (LP) *Politik: Europa*, http://die-linke.de/politik/themen/positionen_a_z/europa/ (accessed 1 June 2008).
54 Ibid.
55 O. Lafontaine and C. Müller, *Keine Angst vor der Globalisierung. Wohlstand und Arbeit für alle*, Bonn, Dietz, 1998.
56 NPD 'Europaprogramm der NPD', http://partei.npd.de/medien/pdf/Europa-programm_Netz.pdf (accessed 10 January 2009), pp. 3–4.
57 DVU 'Partei-Programm', http://www.dvu.de/pdf/Parteiprogr.pdf (accessed 10 January 2009), p. 1.
58 NPD, 'Europaprogramm der NPD', p. 3. Republikaner 'Bundesparteiprogramm', http://www.rep.de/upload/CMS/Die_Republikaner/pdf/programm_pdf_neu.pdf (accessed 10 January 2009), p. 10.
59 B. Sommer, 'Anti-Capitalism in the name of ethno-nationalism: ideological shifts on the German extreme right', *Patterns of Prejudice*, 2008, vol. 42 (3), pp. 305–16.
60 NPD, 2009, p. 3.
61 Poguntke,'Europeanization...', pp. 108–33, and R. Ladrech, 'National Political Parties and European Governance: The Consequences of "Missing in Action"', *West European Politics*, 2007, vol. 30 (5), pp. 945–60.
62 E. Carter, 'European integration and internal party dynamics' in Poguntke *et al.*, *The Europeanization of...*, pp. 1–27.
63 Ibid.
64 Friedrich Ebert Foundation (FES) *International Co-operation*, http://www.fes.de/inhalt/Dokumente_2008/fesenglish.pdf (accessed 1 June 2008)
65 Poguntke, 'Europeanization...', pp.108–33.
66 Ibid.
67 N. Aylott, L. Morales and L. Ramiro. 'Some things change, a lot stays the same: comparing the country studies' in Poguntke *et al.*, *The Europeanization of...*, pp. 190–210.
68 T. Raunio, 'Why European integration increases leadership autonomy within political parties', *Party Politics*, 2002, vol. 8 (4), pp. 405–22.
69 S. Hix and K Goetz, 'Introduction: European integration and national political systems', *West European Politics,* 2000, vol.23, no. 4, pp. 1–26.
70 Aylott *et al.*, 'Some things change...', pp. 190–210.

chapter four | europeanisation and partisan structure in italy

Nicolò Conti and Luca Verzichelli

Introduction

The period of the *First Italian Republic* (1948–1992) was characterised by a very stable political elite, while the following years – the *Second Italian Republic* – were met with a sudden and intense change in the party system that determined a significant renewal of the political elite and, as a consequence, a transformation of the political discourse.[1] We will measure continuity and discontinuity of the European party discourse, first within each of these two phases and then later discuss the changes that occurred between the two phases. To begin, we should make some general reference to the interaction between European and domestic party politics and, more specifically, to the connection between European integration and the evolution of *coalition governance* in Italy. At least two historical turning points deserve a closer look, since they seem to harmonise change at the domestic and at the supranational level. During the 1970s, a Grand Coalition at the domestic level, including the Communist Party, came together with the deepening of the European Economic Community that led to the creation of the European Monetary System. Then, at the beginning of the 1990s, the end of the First Republic coincided with the development of the crucial *vincolo esterno*,[2] which was created by the negotiation of the European Monetary Union. During the 1970s, developments in party attitudes towards issues of foreign policy, as well as of European integration, marked the shift of the Italian system from polarised pluralism to a more moderate multiparty system. In addition, the European Union (EU) external constraint has been a crucial factor in determining the collapse of the First Republic and the establishment of a bipolar (with some elements of a majoritarian) democracy.[3] As we will document in the chapter, these critical junctures in the EU process are also turning points in the domestic scene marked by shifts in the attitudes toward the EU of the Italian parties.

Europeanisation and Italian party system

In this section, we introduce the problem of the impact of the European issue on the Italian party system. For this purpose, the study has been based on the analysis of a broad range of documents produced by the party central office and party leaders such as party manifestos, parliamentary debates on cabinet crises or inaugurations, ad hoc party conferences on Europe and party congress acts (see list in the

Appendix). The analysis of this rather diverse body of documents shows that for a long period of time the integration process has been viewed in Italy as a matter of geo-political choice. For this reason, it has been at the centre of confrontations between principled positions in favour and against European integration. In this respect, it is necessary to recall that after World War II (WWII), for almost fifty years, Italy had the Christian Democrats (DC) as the major partner of every governing coalition. At the same time, Italy had the largest Communist Party (PCI) of the West as the main opposition party, whose electoral support reached as much as one third of the total vote and equalled the one vote of the DC. Before the crisis in the electoral support for these two parties in the 1980s, they alone represented as much as two-thirds of the electorate. Hence, no other party was able to challenge such figures, the other relevant parties relying on levels of support at below 10 per cent or, in the case of the socialists at the time of their maximum electoral strength, just above 10 per cent. It is clear that in Italy for almost fifty years after WWII, party attitudes toward European integration have been mainly a matter of confrontation between the two main actors of the party system, who brought their principled views into the politicisation of this issue, with the other minor actors approximating their positions relative to the DC or the PCI, depending on the party with which they were aligned.

Considering the large distance between their broad ideological positions, the attitudes of these two parties towards the European Economic Community (EEC) reflected the pattern of ideological polarisation of the party system. Precisely, the DC had been the main vehicle of a vision that brought together pro-Europeanism and Atlanticism. This vision had been at the centre of government foreign policy that was led for about fifty years by the Christian Democrats. All parties taking part in the coalition government have been urged by the DC to advance this principle. Furthermore, full acceptance of the international commitments of the country, established for the most part by the initiative of the DC and represented in particular by membership of NATO and the EEC, had been a precondition imposed on any party that wanted to join the government coalition. In particular, it had been the precondition for the parties of the left – the socialists in the 1960s and the communists a decade later – in order to become part of a majority supporting the government.

Nevertheless, the benevolent attitude towards European integration of the Italian Government was challenged by the communists, who first opposed the EEC when their ideological distance from government was greater. Then, when the party shifted to a more moderate position in the mid-1970s and joined, for a few years, the majority supporting a DC single-party government, the Italian Communist Party evolved into broad acceptance of the EEC. However, the PCI continued to promote a model of integration that was alternative to the one pursued by the DC and on a different EEC trajectory. The party was opposed to the ongoing situation. It proposed a programmatic platform including a larger involvement of the working class in the European decision-making process, the parliamentarisation of the EEC through the European Parliament (EP) – diminishing the relevance of the Commission and the Council, but also through a larger control of domestic parliaments on the EEC allowing, for example, the rejection of any decision taken by national parliaments that conflicted with domestic interests.

The third actor of the Italian party system, the Socialist Party (PSI), shifted between the two positions represented by the PCI on the one side and the DC on the other. The PSI changed its main political strategy, moving from an alliance with the communists to a thirty-year lasting alliance with the Christian Democrats, and also moved from a reserved – occasionally even hostile – attitude towards the EEC, to a more sympathetic and even supportive one. To this picture, we can add the case of minor actors, such as the lay parties (liberals, republicans, and social democrats), small forces around the centrist positions of the political spectrum, whose relevance was increased, despite their small electoral size, by their participation in government on a regular base. Their underlying attitudes towards the process of European integration were supportive but, apart from the distinctive role of some more prominent figures,[4] their influence was quite limited and their contribution to the Italian foreign/European policy quite irrelevant – these remained a privileged domain of the Christian Democratic Party.

Finally, the attitude towards European integration of the extreme right party, *Movimento Sociale Italiano* (MSI), should also be mentioned. With nationalism at the centre of its ideology and opposing any attempt that could reduce the scope of national sovereignty, this neo-fascist party was always hostile to the EEC. The MSI was a small party permanently excluded from any alliance with mainstream parties and left at the margin of the political scene. Therefore, its role in the politicisation of the European issue in the Italian party system has been very limited.

As a consequence of the shifts in the positions of individual parties, the model of competition characterising the Italian party system varied over time. It originally featured a pattern of deep polarisation, but this decreases over time. However, the question of European integration proved a competitive issue until the final phase of the First Republic. At the beginning of the 1980s, the gap between the two main political actors of the Italian party system, the DC and the PCI, was very wide, with the former adopting a discourse of fervent support and even celebration of the EEC and the latter adopting a soft Eurosceptic discourse. From the end of the 1980s, the two parties came to unprecedented convergence on the issue of European integration, finally making it a rather consensual issue. As for the PSI, until the beginning of the 1960s, this party represented to some extent an alternative choice to DC and PCI. In fact, the socialists developed an attitude that was in between that of the two main forces of the time. On the one hand, this consisted of broad acceptance of the process of European integration while, on the other hand, it consisted of dissatisfaction and criticisms towards the Common Market, its outcomes and future developments. As we have seen, this is a similar strategy to that adopted by the communists during the second half of the 1960s and, even more convincingly, in the 1970s. Until it was politically feasible, the PSI was very careful in marking a distance from both the DC and the PCI. However, as the distance between the two parties lessened, the space for movement by the socialists was in turn lessened and their position ultimately overlapped with that of Christian democrats.[5] In any case, the ability of the socialists to develop an alternative European discourse from the one of the Christian democrats and of the communists should not be exaggerated. In fact, their attitude of delegation to the real holder (the DC) of the foreign and European policy of the country[6] overall prevailed.

The patterns of party competition over the European issue, in the forty years after the early steps in the integration process, have been characterised by a change from *polarised* to *moderate* competition. The political stance on the European issue has become simpler over time, moving from a multiplicity of alternative positions on the EEC (rejection, reserved support, unconditional support) to a simplified one presenting closer positions (reserved and unconditional support, and finally diffuse unconditional support at the beginning of the 1990s). Radicalism of the positions on EEC was gradually banned from the political discourse of the three main political actors, with their reciprocal distance reduced. The situation evolved from one of three distinctive views on European integration, to one in which the stance of the DC and the PSI were practically indistinguishable. The shift of the PCI to more benign attitude to integration and, since the early 1990s, to openly pro-European attitudes when it was renamed the Democratic Party of the Left (*Partito dei Democratici di Sinistra* (PDS)), drove the DC and the PSI to adopt even more supportive positions. Clearly, these two parties attempted to mark a distance from the communists. Hence, as long as the PCI evolved into a more supportive position on Europe, the internal divisions or reservations in these two parties were undermined. Somehow paradoxically, the shift in the position of the communists (whose determinants stemmed from both external and domestic factors, i.e. the failure of communism in central and Eastern Europe and the alliance with the Christian democrats in the 1970s) was ultimately responsible for the restructuring of the largely enthusiastic European rhetoric of the Italian parties. When the PDS came to a position of principled support for European integration, this prompted the end of the DC's role as guarantor of the international commitments of the country and it brought about an unprecedented and diffuse Europhilia within the system.

It is possible to draw from the pre-1994 period some implications that explain party attitudes towards the EEC/EU. In the case of Italy, three factors have been particularly influential: broad ideology, distance from the centre of the political spectrum and government/opposition status. The ideological dimension of party response showed that the divide was mainly characterised as confrontation between a Eurosceptic left and a pro-European centre. The degree of support or opposition to the EEC has changed deeply over time. Change has been much stronger within the left: for the communists the shift was one from 'hard' to 'soft' Euroscepticism, and then later to pro-Europeanism; for the socialists – and much earlier – the shift was from 'soft' Euroscepticism to pro-Europeanism. However, in the centre (the DC), there was less movement and any change basically concerned an increment in the level of intra-party unity in supporting the process of European integration.[7] Surely, we can contrast the attitudes of the left with those of the centre as this represents the main pattern of party competition of the First Republic. However, it would not be meaningful to contrast the left to the right because (apart from one minor right-of-centre party[8]) until the 1990s the Italian right was mainly characterised by the extremism and political isolation of a minor fringe party, the MSI.

Hence, the main discontinuity we have observed is the U-turn of the left on European issues. As argued elsewhere,[9] a change in the position of the left is a common trend throughout Europe. In other countries, the realignment has not been as dramatic as in Italy; here, the left has long been characterised by an exceptional radicalism. In the end, hard Euroscepticism in Italy has been the typical attitude of radical parties, either of the left (PCI until the end of the 1960s) or of the right (MSI until the beginning of the 1990s). Their varying distance from the centre of the political spectrum, which is occupied by moderate parties, seems therefore another determinant of their attitudes.

The other relevant factor to explain party attitudes in the pre-1994 period is the one of the government/opposition status of parties. The magnitude of such impact is extremely important: under the First Republic, support for the process of European integration was always a precondition to enter government. This precondition has been largely managed by the DC, which has imposed on the various coalition partners a favourable stance towards the main international commitments of the country. In fact, we have seen that left-wing parties develop more supportive positions on European integration as they moved closer to the government arena. This was the case of the PSI in the 1960s, and similarly of the PCI in the 1970s. Finally, in Italy no party in government ever took an openly Eurosceptic stance until 1994; at the same time, the act of joining the government or a majority supporting the government has been a relevant function of accepting the principles of pro-Europeanism.

Since 1994, however, the situation has changed to a large extent. As shown by other analyses,[10] after the ratification of the Maastricht Treaty, European integration was discussed by parties in a more attentive way than in the past and a growing plurality of positions seemed to emerge. This led to a more articulate party discourse and has forced (even if with some relevant exceptions) party elites to take more explicit positions, avoiding for example the traditional 'good willing' or the 'don't complain/don't explain' mode of the DC. In fact, Eurosceptic stances gained new relevance after 1992. First, we should consider that before the regionalist Northern League turned towards Euroscepticism in the mid-1990s,[11] two extreme parties (the MSI and the small reconstructed Communist Party) presented a set of clear arguments against the Europe of Maastricht.[12] For the very first time after the PCI conversion to a more moderate stance, the ratification of the Maastricht Treaty witnessed the firm opposition of the two extremes (although less so than in the past) of the political spectrum. In a few years, these two parties would be transformed from 'excluded extremes' to relevant coalition parties,[13] without first totally rejecting their negative vision of the EU.

Overall, the pattern of party competition over the EU seems more complicated in the period from the mid-1990s onwards. There are real differences in the attitudes of centre-left and centre-right parties.[14] Furthermore, there are internal variations among the parties included in the same coalition, and for some cases there are also differences within the same party over time. This makes the picture for the *Second Republic* quite diverse, marked by huge discontinuities when compared to the pre-1992 period, and characterised by dynamism suggestive of another realignment of Italian party positions on the EU after the convergence that occurred at the end of the 1980s. Ideology and the distance from the political spectrum seem again the main determinants of party attitudes.

Ultimately, this case seems to confirm the cross-national tendency to have a more pro-European centre-left than the centre-right and broad support for the EU from mainstream parties as opposed to a rejection from peripheral parties.[15] By contrast, the expectation to take a moderate stance in the European discourse of the government parties[16] cannot be confirmed in the Italian case. Interestingly, in this country the government/opposition status of parties no longer holds a strong influence. This is certainly due to the interplay with another institutional factor: the level of inclusiveness of the Italian Government. Italy is a country where an extremely large number of parties are represented in the electoral institutions and governments need to rely on the confidence vote of small parties to have a majority. This, together with the high level of alternation in government experienced in the last decade, creates a situation where virtually no party is permanently excluded from the governmental arena – even extreme parties have been involved in sharing government responsibilities. This factor could represent an incentive for parties to differentiate their positions, specifically on European integration, without fear of paying the cost of exclusion from the competition to govern. In particular, this can explain why extreme parties have had no strong incentive to moderate their attitudes towards the EU in the race to take part in a government coalition. This situation distinguishes Italy's Second Republic from its predecessor – and from other countries – in which peripheral parties are systematically excluded from government and their fierce Eurosceptic rhetoric is, consequently, isolated from government.

All in all, the competition over the EU issue has overlapped with – and even strengthened – the dominant pattern of competition of the party system. Indeed, conflict over the European issue produced *divergence* when the polarisation of the party system was higher until the mid-1970s. Then, from this period until the beginning of the 1990s, it produced *convergence* as polarisation was lower, following the shift of the Italian left into more moderate positions and the inclusion of the communists in a grand coalition. Finally, it produced *divergence* again from the mid-1990s onwards, when party competition abandoned consensus to embrace a tendency towards bipolarity. In this respect, we propose for the Italian party system the argument of the *internalisation* of the European issue along the established lines of party division: a process largely characterised by a *fit* between the conflict over EEC/EU and the domestic patterns of party competition. The European issue has neither disrupted the Italian party system, nor has it created a new cleavage. On the contrary, competition over the EU has been internalised by the established patterns of competition characterising the party system, and it might also have contributed to their reinforcement.

Europeanisation and individual parties

Ideology and policy stance

From polarisation to convergence in the Cold War period

Moving to a more in-depth analysis of individual parties and their attitudes toward the EEC/EU, we start with the Christian Democrats (DC) – the main party of the Italian party system at the time of the First Republic. The main coalition partner of every government for almost fifty years, from post-World War II to the early 1990s, the DC's party leaders strongly supported all key decisions in the integration process. A solid pro-Europeanism was rooted in the party ideology, and it seems that since the very beginning of the period starting from the end of WWII, the party had an approach of principled pro-Europeanism. In spite of this, some evolution in specific aspects of the party vision of Europe can be found over time, as well as some intra-party tensions.[17] This does not affect the overall picture of a party characterised by long-established Europhilia. Nevertheless, a lack of salience of the European issue in the political discourse of the DC is often visible in the documents.[18] Moreover, shifts in the preferences on some specific aspects can be registered. Overall, in spite of an undoubtedly high level of commitment to European integration, the party did not always produce programmatic statements covering specific aspects of the integration process, such as the ones of the institutional enforcement of the EC or of its international role.

This phenomenon can be explained only by looking at the peculiar nature of the DC's politics: many observers agree that activism in the European field depended less on the party than on the initiative of various individuals such as prime ministers or ministers of foreign affairs. This resulted in a 'polycentric presence' of the DC in matters of foreign policy in general, and of European affairs in particular,[19] which revealed a lack of strategy and discontinuity in the party's European activism. Ultimately, this led to a low-profile and an underdeveloped foreign policy, secondary to the party's main concern for domestic problems. The DC's European policy was essentially reactive and, as Bull argued,[20] it was characterised more by *flawed* than by *genuine* Europeanism. This image matches the evidence that we have produced on the party preferences on European integration – always supportive, but at several points lacking proactive programmatic commitment. From the mid-1980s on, we have experienced an increase in the speed of supranational integration, yet the party political discourse often proved silent in this field.

As mentioned above, the Communist Party (PCI) was the Italian party providing the longest-lasting opposition to European integration. From its very beginning, the integration process was seen by the PCI as one face of Atlanticism, driven by the United States and seeking to establish US hegemony in Western Europe. In the communist ideology, the persistence of a strong and non-externally constrained nation state was essential for the improvement of workers' conditions. Its threat would entail a challenge to workers' aspirations, since they would be pushed to shift the focus of their mission from working class improvement and struggle for power to the defence of national sovereignty against foreign imperialism. Only the Soviet state was considered the most sophisticated instrument in the hands of the working class and this justified its leading role in the world communist movement, at least until the 1960s. In fact, from the analysis of the party's documents, the attitudes of the Italian communists towards European integration seem very negative until the end of the 1960s. Then, the party started to develop a more pragmatic orientation, even if attitudes remained very negative, as it shifted from attempts to stop the integration process and annul its outcomes to demanding significant reforms. From our analysis, it seems that the beginning of the 1970s can be taken as a watershed: the PCI ceased to present the EEC as a by-product of US imperialism, and there was a move to support some kind of integration, thus shifting the overall attitude to European integration from hard to soft Euroscepticism.

The PCI opposed European integration longer than any other party. The analysis of party documents shows that opposition was voiced through explicit critical statements. Shifts in the party preferences were often preceded by a period of silence on the relevant aspects. Once the party shifted to a pro-European position, the documents become more articulate as they developed an alternative model of integration. A difference also emerged between the 'internal' discourse, mainly devoted to defend an *alternative vision* of Europe, and the electoral appeal, centred on the need to affirm the pro-European change of the party, and to capture the Europhilia of Italian public opinion.[21]

The third party selected for our analysis of the First Republic scenario, the Socialist Party (PSI), was traditionally characterised by the difficult relationship with the two giants of the party system.[22] In fact, all the positions expressed by this party on the issue of European integration were to some extent influenced by its peculiar character as *third actor* on the political spectrum. Immediately after WWII, the subordination of the socialist leaders to the Communist Party prevented its leadership from promoting the federalist ideas that characterised some of its sectors during the years of the anti-Fascist resistance. The analysis of official documents reveals a relative silence on the European issue in the internal debate, at least until the mid-1950s. The electoral manifestos for the 1948 and 1953 elections did not present any reference to the project of the integration of Europe. Even the opening speech of an important party congress (1957), which marked the start of a pathway of 'autonomy' from the Communist Party as well as the subsequent electoral platform, neglected to debate the future of European integration. Nevertheless, already during the second half of the 1950s, the party could mark its autonomous position from the PCI on European integration, voting in favour of the European Atomic Energy Community and abstaining on the parliamentary ratification of the European Coal and Steel Community. When the time was ripe to open the government arena to the PSI, one sensitive issue to be discussed within the party was the official position on the EEC. As a sign of this, some of the most eminent yet isolated pro-European figures of the left were recruited by the party (e.g. Antonio Giolitti).

Nonetheless, the PSI remained reluctant to accept the traditional 'market-oriented' idea of the EEC, and there was no real active participation of the socialist elite in the debate on a more integrated Europe. The European policy (as well as most of the whole package of international policy) was delegated to the DC following the fundamental 'agreement' that the centre-left government would not make any changes to the international commitments of Italy.[23] Since the 1970s, we can find a clear preference of the socialists for more integration, mainly voiced by a claim for supranational institutional enforcement (support for the monetary system, celebration of the EP direct elections, and creation of a genuine single market). The overall attitude of the party during the 1970s can be estimated as a form of Europhilia even if, overall, the party still proved silent on many important issues, showing its nature as a minor party, more ready to react to the moves of the other party competitors, than to develop its own agenda.

In the 1980s, when the party was led by Bettino Craxi and by a new core of leaders in their forties, the PSI started to make increased reference to the European scene in its discourse. This strategy was oriented to reach a double goal:

- to show the legitimacy of the PSI to play a role, vis-à-vis the 'exceptional' power of the largest Communist Party of Western Europe; and
- to assess the closeness between a European model of efficiency largely managed by socialist parties in government, and a greater role of the Italian socialists.

From this perspective, we can affirm that during the 1980s the pro-Europeanism of the PSI was primarily an attempt to strengthen a specific message (and a socialist leadership) at the domestic level.[24]

Moving to the last part of the First Republic period, we note that after 1985, the political debate was, instead, almost totally dominated by domestic questions, such as the problem of the alternation between a socialist and a Christian democratic executive chief, and the hard conflicts between the leaders of the two parties of the left, the PCI and the PSI. As a consequence, the issue of European integration was almost totally neglected in political debate. For example, it disappeared from the party congress debates, as well as from the manifestos for the last two elections in the First Republic (1987 and 1992). There are various reasons for this decline in interest. In general, parties supporting the cabinet were displaying a greater lack of policy inspiration, which in a few years would lead to a crisis for the whole political system. This is particularly true for the two most important government actors, the PSI and the DC, whose elites were at this point totally unable to manage the new demands. In fact, while the increasing voices about the 'costs of the integration' probably had an important role in the escalation of the protest party Northern League, the government leaders could not consider themselves as the sole 'pro-European defenders'. The opposition on the left was now clearly divided between a small anti-European extreme (the new Communist Party, the RC) and a fully pro-European party, the PDS (then renamed DS, the main successor of the PCI), plus a number of new actors with pro-European attitudes, like the radicals and the greens. Therefore, government parties, including the PSI, limited themselves to appeal to the necessity to 'remain in Europe', meeting the challenges of the *vincolo esterno* and following the stimuli coming from the supranational arena.[25] In comparison, the party discourse of the late PCI/early PDS was mainly oriented towards a repositioning of its general guidelines and followed the more sympathetic attitudes toward the EEC of most European social-democratic parties.

The post-1992 period – the rise of new patterns of competition over the European issue

We have seen that, since the 1980s, Italy has become one of the most pro-European member states, with the broad support of all the main parties and enthusiastic public opinion. At the same time, Italy arrived at this position after a process of realignment over several decades, when fierce opposition to the Common Market from parties on the left gradually evolved into more supportive and pragmatic attitudes. This issue that had polarised left-wing parties declined and they shifted from the extreme to the core of the party system. Alberta Sbragia described the phenomenon as follows: '… once the PCI changed its position and supported Italian participation in the European Community, it became difficult to find anyone who questioned the appropriateness of the Italian participation in the process …'[26]

Nevertheless, since 1994, all positions from hard Euroscepticism to fervent pro-Europeanism are again represented in the Italian party system. Before 1994, there was very little between the two positions of principled support and principled rejection of the Common Market, since any moderate/pragmatic approach to the issue of European integration was hardly represented in the Italian party system. In particular, the first discontinuity to note is that the two major parties of the centre-right, *Forza Italia* and the National Alliance (*Alleanza Nazionale* – formerly the MSI), show hints of Euroscepticism at different points in time. Their political discourse moves back and forth from soft Euroscepticism to vagueness, to broad unspecific pro-Europeanism, where the latter is mainly comprised of supportive rhetoric largely used to gain legitimacy in the domestic, as well as the international, arena. In fact, support for European integration from these two parties is never issue-specific (apart from the project of a common foreign and security policy that is strongly supported by the National Alliance). Instead, it is mainly framed through support for the broad idea of integration. *Forza Italia* and the National Alliance alternate between hints of support for the general idea of integration to issue-specific stances of Euroscepticism, an underlying attitude that, at some point, has been qualified as one of 'soft Euroscepticism'.[27] In particular, the record of *Forza Italia,* the largest Italian party and the main partner of every centre-right government, was striking and it goes very much against the supposed pro-Europeanism that this party argued elsewhere.[28] In fact, as shown by the electoral manifestos, *Forza Italia* had the lowest level of programmatic commitment to EU issues in the entire party system. While the National Alliance's rhetoric refers more favourably to the EU, it alternates between pro-European and Eurosceptic stances.[29]

More specifically, *Forza Italia* and the National Alliance converge on the broad principle of the defence of national interests in the EU. The other area of convergence is that concerning the institutional setting, where their preference is for an option that can secure the national sovereignty through intergovernmentalism. Otherwise, on other issues the distance between these two parties is remarkable. For instance, the National Alliance is very interested in the outcomes of the EU in terms of international politics, but it does not consider Italy strong enough to play an autonomous role. Conversely, the EU is seen as capable of establishing a European presence in the international arena, something that in the end would also enhance the international role of Italy. The party also shows an interest in the capacity of the EU to protect the European economies from the challenges emerging from globalisation. The focus is to protect those goods made in the EU from the low-cost production of goods in Third World countries. In particular, the EU is seen as the environment where a defence strategy can be more successfully achieved. In their view, the effects would be balanced by the solidarity and inter-dependence among the economies of the member states. In comparison, the priority of *Forza Italia* is to create an ever-larger free-market area, more than a federal and politically-integrated entity. With respect to this priority, the question of the international role of the EU is underdeveloped, while a strong preference is expressed in favour of a prominent international role for NATO, enhanced by contributions from the EU and its member states.

In 2008, *Forza Italia* and the National Alliance merged to create a new party, People of Freedom (PDL),[30] but the merger was not successful and a large section of the former National Alliance split from PDL in 2010 to pursue a different policy agenda. Meanwhile, the stance taken by the PDL on the EU proved hesitant and confused, probably as a result of the different orientations of its party factions.

On the other side of the political spectrum, many analyses show that the Italian left has Europe at the centre of its programmes, more so than the parties on the right.[31] The Italian People's Party (*Margherita*– a party then merging into the Democratic Party)[32] developed the traditional commitment of the Christian democrats towards the idea of a united Europe, while the social democrats (PDS/DS[33]) reflect the positive commitment of this party family that has marked the distance from a cautious past, at least in the last two decades. These two parties are strongly committed to the principle of an *ever-closer union*. Both support the idea of a federal Europe and, therefore, of an intense political integration. They are in favour of a supranational mode of integration and are much more critical of intergovernmentalism. This translates into having a preference for the enhancement of the powers of the European Parliament and the Commission to the detriment of those of the Council. They also aim to promote a European identity through common citizenship. In the international arena, they are in favour of a strong role for the EU and the creation of a European military force. These parties have also proposed a permanent seat for the EU on the Security Council, while in their view NATO should be transformed into an instrument of the United Nations.

It has been argued that, following a cross-national pattern, parties have eventually swapped their positions on the EU.[34] In line with this trend, Italy's left has become more pro-European than the centre-right. On the whole, the picture of contemporary Italian parties can be seen in the light of two points of view proposed by the comparative analyses of party attitudes.[35] The first one concerns the European vocation of the centre-left[36] that was particularly visible when it was led by former EC President, Romano Prodi. Alternatively, at the extremes of the political spectrum, hard Euroscepticism seems a solid feature. Throughout the period, the small Communist Party (*Rifondazione Comunista*) showed strong opposition to European integration and the radical right-wing party, the Northern League,[37] was also fiercely opposed to the EU. This creates a serious problem of division within the two main coalitions, where moderate parties have to face the challenge of the European protest of the extreme parties they align with, in order to have a majority in the country. In particular, *Rifondazione Comunista* defined the EU as an instrument of Americanisation, and also as an international technocratic power often associated with the IMF and WTO. The party voted against the ratification of the Maastricht Treaty and it was also against monetary union and the creation of a Central European Bank. Interestingly, and contrary to the centre-left, this party mainly represents the negative outcomes of the integration process, particularly in terms of the domestic impact of the EU. European politics is defined as a cause of the diminishing quality of life of the lower classes and of the disadvantaged social groups, and also the cause of a period of stagnation in consumer demand. At the other extreme of the political spectrum, the Northern League strongly criticises the consequences of European integration. EU institutions are accused of participating in a process of state-building that aims to replace nation states with a new super-state aimed at preventing local identities from developing any further. Moreover, this regionalist party expresses a pessimistic evaluation of the impact of the EU on the main goal promoted by the party, i.e. the self-determination of the northern regions of Italy, as well as on its targeted social groups, such as northern farmers, milk producers and small firms.

All in all, the main tendencies that emerged in Italy after the abrupt party system change between 1992 and 1994 could be summarised as follows:

- *A constellation of preferences* has emerged as party attitudes can be ordered between two poles ranging from fervent support to strong opposition to the EU.
- Support for the EU has ceased to be an issue of consensus.
- *Euroscepticism has become significant*: at some point in time the number of parties with a degree of Euroscepticism and their respective ability to attract votes has become majoritarian in the country.
- *Right-of-centre parties are more Eurosceptic* than left-of-centre parties, with the far left (*Rifondazione Comunista*) being the only Eurosceptic party of the left wing. The centre-left is more committed to the EU theme than the centre-right and the two extremes are also rather committed. The sign of this commitment varies; it is positive for the centre-left, negative for the two extremes (more so for the Northern League), whereas the centre-right is less committed and more cautious in terms of attitudes.[38]

Europe proves to be a divisive issue for party competition and, interestingly, follows a pattern that is not very different from what happens with other issues.

Organisation

This section addresses the representative structure of the Italian delegation in the European Parliament (EP). Two general problems that are also common to the other member states – namely the national nature of the selectors and the lack of a full harmonisation of electoral rules – certainly contribute to the creation of such a structure. However, the subordination of the Members of the European Parliament (MEPs) to their domestic party selectors has always been particularly strong in the Italian case. For example, comparative research on national delegations within the EP shows that Italian and French MEPs are much more involved compared with British and German MEPs, as noted by the high degrees of substitutions.[39] This phenomenon can be explained by the fact that the careers of the Italian MEPs are often inserted into patterns of national political careers. In other words, access to the EP is not reserved for 'EU specialists' who are experts in European policies and issues. Conversely, relatively older politicians recruited from the national political *filières* are usually selected for EP seats and, nearly always, they clearly show a preference for national political engagement.

A first reason for the low level of Europeanisation of the Italian representatives in the EP is the nature of the selection procedures: the electoral system used so far (a PR system with five large constituencies and one to three preference votes according to the size of the constituency) does not help in structuring a clear competition between candidates with different appeals and competencies. Additionally, the internal rules implemented by the domestic parties of the First Republic[40] and later by the new political actors of the Second Republic do not encourage any involvement of party activists in the selection procedures of MEPs. As a result, the composition of electoral lists is left entirely to the national party executives. The chances of election for outsiders, even if genuine EU experts, are very limited.

Data presented by Pasquinucci and Verzichelli covering the characteristics of the EP personnel elected in the first six legislative terms confirm that the Italian MEPs tend to be mainly 'stepping stone' politicians, very much constrained by the patterns of a domestic political career.[41] Between 1979 and 1999, an average of 45.4 per cent of Italian MEPs had a regional/local electoral background and an average of 40.8 per cent had experience as national MPs. Customarily, they plan a return to domestic politics. This explains why the Italian electoral cycle, particularly in general elections but also regional elections, results in the withdrawal of rather a high percentage of Italian MEPs who prefer to run for domestic electoral offices.

Conclusion

As the present book illustrates, the Europeanisation of political parties is a multi-dimensional phenomenon. We found that European integration is an issue that has been internalised by the Italian parties following the established lines of conflict that operate in the domestic system. In the Italian case, the European issue has helped shape the patterns of party competition and we believe it has even reinforced them. We also found that, in some cases, the party discourse adapted to the change in the environment marked by the growing penetration of Europe into domestic arenas, either in terms of more supportive attitudes or of more Euroscepticism. It seems that the European issue is meaningful for the mechanics of the party system (namely the patterns of competition), while it has not impacted on its format (the units of the party system). In fact, in Italy we do not find splits in party or parties whose creation/dissolution can be re-conducted predominantly to European integration. As for the mechanics, it is true that the degree of attention paid by party elites to the specific problems of the debate on a *closer relationship with the EU* has been low sometimes, especially when we consider that we are dealing with one of the six founding members of the EEC. This could certainly reinforce Mair's argument concerning the growing depoliticisation of European issues.[42] In this chapter, we did not investigate problems of disconnection of the party in public office, in government or in parliament, from the direct control of EU issues. Certainly, the lack of a dedicated discourse and programmatic stance may suggest a disconnection in the party management of such issues. At the same time, the role of experts and technocrats in guaranteeing the compliance of Italy with the EU challenges in the most crucial steps of the EU process, as well as their capacity to fill the gap of an unstable political scene, have also been documented.[43] However, this work shows that the patterns of competition over the European issue are also quite clearly defined and they have helped produce different positions on Europe on the political scene. Several trends developed at different times: programmatic divergence in the form of polarisation until the 1970s, convergence from the 1970s until the early 1990s, and again divergence from the 1990s onwards. Overall, we did not find evidence of 'misfit' between the cleavages at work in Italy and the party competition on Europe but, instead, an overlap between the party system mechanics and competition over the EU integration issue. Additionally, the patterns of recruitment of Italian MEPs have not produced any substantial change, as they have been secured in the national career patterns under the firm control of the party central office.

We would like to conclude this work observing that in the Italian case, the EU has been politicised by parties largely by means of internalisation. We have seen that the European theme has been managed by domestic parties through absorption and without paradigmatic change, i.e. the change in format and mechanics searched for by Mair in his analysis.[44] However, since the 1960s, the European issue has proved relevant and it has even contributed to shape the ideology, the programmatic supply and the coalition politics of the individual parties, a case confirming the Mair/Ladrech paradox.

Appendix

List of analysed documents

Parties of the First Republic

Party	Title	Year	Type of document
1	*L'ordine internazionale*	1943a	6
1	*Idee ricostruttive della Democrazia Cristiana*	1943b	6
1	*Il programma della Democrazia Cristiana I*	1944a	6
1	*Il programma della Democrazia Cristiana II*	1944b	6
1	*Pensando al dopo: la politica del buonsenso*	1944c	6
1	*Atti del Consiglio Nazionale della DC*	1945	5
1	*Atti del I Congresso Nazionale della DC*	1946	4
1	*Atti Congresso Nouvelles Equipes Internationales*	1950	5
1	*Atti del IV Congresso Nazionale della DC*	1952	4
1	*Programma governativo*	1954a	3
1	*Tre ordini del giorno della Direzione Centrale della DC*	1954b	5
1	*Atti del V Congresso Nazionale della DC*	1954c	4
1	*Atti della Direzione Centrale della DC*	1955	5
1	*Atti del VI Congresso Nazionale della DC*	1956	4
1	*Mozione conclusiva del Consiglio Nazionale della DC*	1957a	5
1	*Risoluzione della Direzione Centrale della DC*	1957b	5
1	*Accordo programmatico tra la DC e il PSDI*	1958	3
1	*Atti del VII Congresso Nazionale della DC*	1959	4
1	*Atti dell'VIII Congresso Nazionale della DC*	1962a	4
1	*Programma elettorale DC per la IV legislatura*	1962b	2
1	*Accordo politico-programmatico per il governo*	1963a	3
1	*Mozione partiti democratici-cristiani paesi CEE*	1963b	5
1	*Accordo politico-programmatico tra DC, PSI, PSDI e PRI*	1964a	3
1	*Atti del IX Congresso Nazionale della DC*	1964b	4
1	*Atti del X Congresso Nazionale della DC*	1967	4
1	*Idee, struttura e iniziativa della DC*	1969	4
1	*Un impegno unitario e di solidarietà democratica*	1973	4
1	*Un rinnovato impegno della DC*	1976a	4
1	*Il programma della DC*	1976b	1

(contd)

Party	Title	Year	Type of document
1	*Il programma elettorale della DC*	1979a	1
1	*La Democrazia Cristiana per l'Europa*	1979b	2
1	*Atti del XIV Congresso della DC*	1980	4
1	*La Dichiarazione d'intenti di De Mita*	1982	4
1	*Un programma per garantire lo sviluppo*	1983	1
1	*Sintesi della relazione di De Mita*	1984a	4
1	*Un futuro sicuro per l'Italia con una DC forte in Europa*	1984b	6
1	*Sintesi della relazione di De Mita*	1986	4
1	*Un programma per l'Italia*	1987	1
1	*Atti del XVIII Congresso Nazionale della DC*	1989a	4
1	*Con la Democrazia Cristiana nella prospettiva del 1992*	1989b	2
1	*La Linea strategica della DC*	1992	1
2	*Preparazione dell'VIII Congresso del Pci*	1956	5
2	*Cosa vuole il Pci per il MEC*	1958a	6
2	*Per una maggioranza di sinistra*	1958b	6
2	*Gli artigiani e il MEC*	1958c	6
2	*Il programma elettorale del Pci*	1963	1
2	*E' ora di cambiare*	1968	6
2	*Il programma dei comunisti per un governo di svolta democratica*	1972	1
2	*Atti del XIV Congresso*	1975a	4
2	*I PC dell'Europa occidentale sui problemi dell'agricoltura*	1975b	5
2	*Le proposte dei comunisti per la politica economica*	1976a	6
2	*Il programma del PCI*	1976b	1
2	*Il programma dei comunisti per l'VIII legislatura*	1979a	1
2	*10 Giugno. Il voto al Pci è importante, è necessario*	1979b	6
2	*Vota comunista*	1979c	6
2	*Un programma per cambiare*	1983	1
2	*Agricoltura. Consumatori. Inflazione. Tre facce della disfatta dei governi italiani*	1984	6
2	*Il Pci per la X legislatura*	1987	1
2	*Relazione introduttiva al Congresso di Rimini*	1991	4

(*contd*)

Party	Title	Year	Type of document
2	*Pds. L'opposizione che costruisce*	1992	1
3	*Relazione di Nenni al Congresso*	1957	4
3	*Per una politica di alternativa democratica*	1958	1
3	*Il programma del Psi*	1963a	1
3	*Relazione di Nenni al Congresso*	1963b	4
3	*Il programma socialista*	1968	1
3	*Le proposte politiche dei socialisti*	1972	6
3	*Il programma del PSI*	1976	3
3	*Idee per un programma*	1979	3
3	*Governare il cambiamento. Conferenza di Rimini*	1982	5
3	*Programma Psi per la nona legislatura*	1983	1
3	*Tesi del Psi per il 43 Congresso*	1984a	4
3	*Discorso di Craxi a Milano campagna europee*	1984b	6
3	*Programma Psi per la decima legislatura*	1987	1
3	*PSI. Un governo per la ripresa*	1992	1

Parties of the Second Republic

Party	Title	Year	Type of document
4	Un programma per gli Italiani	1994a	1
4	Il partito popolare è il cuore dell'Europa	1994b	2
4	*Tesi per la definizione della piattaforma programmatica dell'Ulivo*	1996	1
4	*Europa, un impegno popolare*	1999	2
4	*Rinnoviamo l'Italia, insieme*	2001	1
5	Relazione introduttiva al Congresso di Rimini	1991	4
5	Pds. L'opposizione che costruisce	1992	1
5	*Per ricostruire un'Italia più giusta, più unita, più moderna*	1994a	1
5	*Il programma del Pds per le elezioni europee*	1994b	2
5	*Tesi per la definizione della piattaforma programmatica dell'Ulivo*	1996	1
5	*Piattaforma dei Democratici di Sinistra per le elezioni europee*	1999	2

(contd)

Party	Title	Year	Type of document
5	Rinnoviamo l'Italia, insieme	2001a	1
5	*Per una Unione Europea protagonista del governo del mondo*	2001b	5
6	*Dall'opposizione per l'alternativa*	1992	1
6	*Europee '94. A sinistra c'è un'altra Europa*	1994	2
6	*Ricominciare da sinistra per l'alternativa*	1996	1
6	Un'alternativa per l'Europa. Pace, lavoro e democrazia	1999	2
6	*Programma politico*	2001	1
7	No title	1994a	1
7	*Programma per l'Europa*	1994b	2
7	*100 Impegni per cambiare l'Italia*	1996	1
7	Relazione di Berlusconi congresso di Assago	1998	4
7	*Il Manifesto per l'Europa di Forza Italia*	1999	2
7	*Piano di governo per una intera legislatura*	2001	1
7	*Nessuno può mettere l'Italia sotto tutela 14/01/02*	2002	7
8	*Discorso di Bossi al II Congresso Federale della Lega Nord*	1994a	4
8	*Programma elettorale esteri della Lega Nord per le elezioni politiche*	1994b	1
8	*L'Europa della Lega Nord*	1994c	2
8	*Discorso di Umberto Bossi all'Assemblea Federale della Lega Nord di Torino*	1995	5
8	*Programma elettorale per la Padania*	1996a	1
8	*Discorso di Umberto Bossi alla Camera dei Deputati*	1996b	7
8	*Intervento di Bossi al Congresso Federale Straordinario della Lega Nord*	1998a	4
8	Intervento di Bossi alla Camera su fiducia al Governo Prodi	1998b	7
8	*Elezioni Europee 1999. Per una Padania libera in un'Europa libera*	1999	2
8	*Intervento di Bossi a Pontida*	2000a	5
8	*Discorso di Bossi a Venezia*	2000b	4
8	*Piano di governo per una intera legislatura*	2001a	1
8	*Discorso di Bossi a Pontida*	2001b	5

(contd)

Party	Title	Year	Type of document
8	*Intervento di Bossi al Congresso Ordinario della Lega Nord*	2002	4
9	*Il programma della destra di governo*	1994a	1
9	*12 giugno. La nuova Europa*	1994b	2
9	*Le tesi del congresso di Fiuggi*	1995	4
9	*100 Impegni per cambiare l'Italia*	1996	1
9	Conferenza programmatica	1998	5
9	*Programma di AN per le elezioni europee*	1999	2
9	*Libero, forte e giusto. Il governo che vogliamo*	2001a	1
9	*Piano di governo per una intera legislatura*	2001b	1
9	*Piattaforma politico-programmatica del II congresso nazionale*	2002	4

Notes:

Party: 1. Christian Democrats **2.** Italian Communist Party **3.** Italian Socialist Party **4.** Italian People's Party/*Margherita* **5.** Left Democrats **6.** *Rifondazione Comunista* **7.** *Forza Italia* **8.** Northern League **9.** National Alliance.

Type of document: **1.** General election platform **2.** European election platform **3.** Cabinet inauguration **4.** Party congress platform **5.** Intra-party debate **6.** Other party programmatic document **7.** Party leader's parliamentary speech.

Notes

1 Although the chapter presents the results of a joint work, Conti is particularly responsible for the section on 'Europeanisation and Italian individual parties' and Verzichelli for the section on 'Europeanisation and Italian party system', while the introduction and the conclusion have been written jointly.

2 K. Dyson and K. Featherstone, 'Italy and EMU as a "Vincolo Esterno": empowering the technocrats, transforming the state', *South European Society and Politics*, 1996, vol. 2, pp. 272–99.

3 M. Cotta and P. Isernia, *Il gigante dai piedi di argilla*, Bologna, Il Mulino, 1996.

4 For example, the liberal Gaetano Martino, Minister of Foreign Affairs in the EEC founding years of 1954–57.

5 In particular, the argument of the *vincolo esterno* (external constraint), which was so strong in the Christian Democrats' defence of European integration, also became a strong element of the socialist pro-Europeanism. As stated by prominent socialist De Michelis, corrective adjustments with a Community label would be the only way to 'overcome our own lack of discipline' (G. De Michelis, 'A nation's game of leapfrog', *The Independent*, 7 August 1990, p. 15, quoted in V. Bufacchi and S. Burgess, *Italy after 1989: Events and Interpretations*, London, Palgrave, 2001, p. 36.

6 However, it should be underlined that the socialists were quite active when De Michelis was Minister of Foreign Affairs. In particular, at the time of the Italian presidency in 1990 he contributed to push forward closer economic and monetary union in the EEC.

7 N. Conti and L. Verzichelli, 'La Dimensione Europea del Discorso Politico: Un Analisi Diacronica del Caso Italiano (1950–2001)', in M. Cotta, P. Isernia and Luca Verzichelli (eds), *L'Europa in Italia,* Bologna, Il Mulino, 2005, pp. 61–116.

8 We refer here to the Liberals (PLI).

9 M. J. Gabel and S. Hix, 'Defining the EU political space', *Comparative Political Studies*, 2002 , 35 (8), pp. 934–64.

10 N. Conti, 'Party conflict over European Integration in Italy: a new dimension of party competition?', *Journal of Southern Europe and the Balkans*, 2006, vol. 8 (2): 217–233; N. Conti and V. Memoli, 'Italian parties and Europe: problems of identity, representation and scope of governance in the Euromanifestos (1989–2004)', *Perspectives on European Politics and Society*, 2010, vol. 11 (2), pp.166–81.

11 There has been in this party a sense of dissatisfaction with the outcomes of European integration, since the process itself changed the preconditions to attain the main party goal, the self-determination of the more developed northern regions of Italy. At an earlier stage, support for European integration and for the Euro was seen by the Northern League as a tool for the more competitive North to exit the nation state. In reality, after the accession of the country in the Euro area since first stage, the integration process changed the process by which the exit-orientation of the North might grow. This step was represented as a success of national unity, and so the process itself turned somehow against the party.

12 P. A. Daniels, 'Italy and the Maastricht Treaty', in S. Hellman and G. Pasquino (eds), *Italian Politics*, vol. 8, Bologna, Il Mulino, 1993, pp. 178–191.

13 More specifically, the MSI, then renamed National Alliance (Fiuggi, January 1995), had already become a government party in 1994, while the communists became part of a centre-left majority between 1996 and 1999 and took part in the government in 2006–2008.

14 See on this Conti, 'Party conflict ...'; Conti and Memoli, 'Italian parties...'.

15 L. Hooghe, G. Marks and C. Wilson, 'Does left/right structure party positions on European Integration?', in G. Marks and M. Steenbergen (eds), *European Integration and Political Conflict*, Cambridge, Cambridge University Press, 2004, pp.120–140.

16 N. Sitter, 'The Politics of opposition and European Integration in Scandinavia: is Euro-Scepticism a government-opposition dynamic?', *West European Politics*, 2001, vol. 4. N. Sitter, 'Opposing Europe: Euro-scepticism, Opposition and Party Competition', *SEI Working papers* 56 and *OERN Working papers* 9, University of Sussex, 2002.

17 For example, see in the 1950s the intra-party struggle opposing the Euro-sceptical left-wing faction to the party leadership; and in the early 1970s, the criticisms of the system of European constraints coming from the US loyal right-wing faction.

18 Conti and Verzichelli, 'La Dimensione...'.

19 A. Pilati, 'Obiettivi e vincoli dei partiti sulla scena internazionale', *Politica Internazionale*, 1982, vol. 2.

20 M. Bull, 'The European Community and 'Regime Parties': A Case Study of Italian Christian democracy', *EUI working papers*, 1994; M. Bull, 'The Italian Christian Democrats'*, in *Political Parties and the European Union*, London, Routledge, 1996, pp.139–154.

21 T. Ammendola and P. Isernia, 'L'Europa vista dagli italiani: i primi vent'anni', in M. Cotta, P. Isernia and L. Verzichelli (eds), *L'Europa in Italia: Elite, opinione pubblica e decisioni*, Bologna: Il Mulino, 2005, pp. 117–170.

22 W. Merkel, *Prima e dopo Craxi*, Padova, Liviana, 1986.

23 N. Kogan, *Storia politica dell'Italia repubblicana*, Roma, Editori Riuniti, 1977.

24 W. Merkel, *Prima e dopo Craxi*.

25 Dyson and Featherstone, 'Italy and EMU...' pp. 272–99; C. Radaelli, 'The Italian state and the Euro: institution, discourse and policy regimes', in K. Dyson (ed.) *European States and the Euro*, Oxford, Oxford University Press, 2002, pp. 212–237.

26 A. Sbragia, 'Italy pays for Europe: political leaders, political choice and institutional adaptation', in M. G. Cowles, J. Caporaso and T. Risse (eds), *Transforming Europe: Europeanisation and Domestic Change*, Ithaca, Cornell University Press, 2000, p. 93.

27 Conti, 'Party conflict...'.

28 F. Cavatorta, S. Kritzinger and R. Chari, 'Continuities and change in party positions towards Europe: an examination of Italian parties' Euro-Manifestos', *Journal of European Public Policy*, 2004, vol. 6, pp.954–974.

29 N. Conti, 'Tied hands? Italian political parties and Europe', *Modern Italy*, 2009, vol. 14 (2), pp. 203–216; Conti and Memoli, 'Italian parties...'.

30 A few months after its creation, the party gained over 37 per cent of votes in the general elections.

31 Conti, 'Party conflict...'and 'Tied hands?...'; Conti and Memoli, 'Italian parties...'.

32 The Democratic Party was created in 2007 when the Left democrats merged with *Margherita*. Today, it is the main party of the centre-left, having gained 33 per cent of the national vote in the 2008 general elections.

33 This party represents the largest heir of the Italian Communist Party (PCI) that dissolved in the early 1990s. It has moved from a post-communist legacy to a more moderate social democrat platform. Dissident members from the old PCI created a separate and more extreme party, *Rifondazione Comunista*.

34 Gabel and Hix, 'Defining the EU...'; R. Ladrech, *Social Democracy and the Challenge of European Union*, London, Lynne Rienner Publisher, 2000.

35 The picture of a divided party system on the issue of European integration is confirmed in the aftermath of the last European elections of 2004. After the vote, the members of the centre left with a Christian democratic background who traditionally belonged to the EPP decided to move to the Group of the Alliance of Liberals and Democrats for Europe, in order distance themselves from *Forza Italia* and from the EPP that hosts them and that has recently shifted to a more Eurosceptic position.

36 Ladrech, *Social Democracy...*; L. Hooghe, G. Marks and C. Wilson, 'Does Left/Right Structure Party Positions on European Integration?', in *Comparative Political Studies*, vol. 35 (8), 2002; L. Ray, 'Measuring party orientations towards European Integration: results from an expert survey', *European Journal of Political Research*, 1999, vol. 36, pp. 283–306.

37 We define Northern League as a radical right-wing party, in line with the definition given in the most recent literature, see for example T. Gold, *The Lega Nord and Contemporary Politics in Italy*, New York, Palgrave, 2003.

38 An evident case of unease with the EU of the Italian centre-right is that of the (non-party affiliated) pro-European minister of Foreign affairs Ruggero – a former General Director of WTO in 1995–9 – who was forced to resign from the Berlusconi government (January 2002) because of a serious conflict over European affairs with other more Eurosceptic ministers (especially the ones from the Northern League).

39 S. Scarrow, 'Political career paths and the European Parliament', *Legislative Studies Quarterly*, 1997, vol. 2, pp. 253–63; L. Verzichelli and M. Edinger, 'A critical juncture? The 2004 European elections and the making of a supranational elite', *The Journal of Legislative Studies*, 2005, vol. 11 (2), pp. 254–74.

40 L. Bardi and L. Morlino, 'Italy: Tracing the Roots of the Great Transformation', in R. Katz and P. Mair (eds), *How Parties Organize: Change and Adaptation in Western Democracies*, London, Sage, 1992, pp. 242–277.

41 D. Pasquinucci and L. Verzichelli, *Elezioni europee e classe politica sovranazionale 1979–2004*, Bologna, Il Mulino, 2004.

42 P. Mair, 'Political parties and party systems', in P. Graziano and M. Vink (eds), *Europeanization: New Research Agendas*, Basingstoke, Palgrave Macmillan, 2006, pp. 154–166.

43 Dyson and Featherstone, 'Italy and EMU...', pp. 272–99.

44 P. Mair, 'The limited impact of Europe on National party system', *West European Politics*, 2000, vol. 4, pp. 27–51.

chapter five | a differential europeanisation? the political parties of the united kingdom[1]

David Hanley and John Loughlin

Introduction

The Europeanisation[2] of the United Kingdom's political parties, both individually and taken together as a party system, is a highly uneven process. We introduce, however, a refinement, in that we distinguish between two distinct party systems within the United Kingdom (UK). First is the system of state-wide parties, operating across all the territories of the UK, with the exception of Northern Ireland, the latter being always politically *sui generis*. These parties include the Labour, Conservative, Liberal-Democrat and Green parties, who seek representation in the Westminster Parliament. Secondly, there are the devolved territorial institutions of the UK in Wales, Scotland and Northern Ireland, which are the seats of a different party competition. We might even speak of distinct decentralised party systems, where cleavages, ideological issues and party configurations differ from the UK-wide system.[3] The UK system increasingly resembles that of Spain or the federal states such as in Germany and Belgium, where state-wide parties contest regional elections, regionally-based parties contest state-wide elections and some parties only contest the regional elections. Furthermore, the regional branches of state-wide parties are developing varying degrees of autonomy from their London 'parents' in what remains a dynamic process of territorialisation. These processes have intensified in the UK following the 1998 devolution programme. Even without 'Europeanising' pressures, therefore, it would be logical to treat the peripheral parties separately; but, in fact, the effects of Europeanisation may have been greater here than on the state-wide parties.

Europeanisation and British party system

The main section of this chapter, then, will be divided into two parts: analysis of the state-wide parties, and then of the territorial systems. Before embarking on this micro-analysis, however, it is necessary to return to the macro-level and consider the questions of cleavage and party competition.

It is commonplace to remark that the political cleavages within the United Kingdom produced a bipolar system – a 'two-class, two-party' system.[4] The Conservative Party represented the interests of big landowners and industrial capitalists as well as the Church of England. The lower classes were first represented in the nineteenth century by the Liberal Party, then by the Labour Party from the first quarter of the twentieth century. The potential for a church/state cleavage was never allowed to develop, thanks to the adroitness of the governing classes in incorporating Catholics into the political process early in the nineteenth century. Guaranteed political rights and the control of their schools, Catholics were free to vote along class lines like anyone else. Furthermore, Great Britain was quite a complex society from a religious point of view with two established churches and a variety of others. No clear-cut church-state cleavage could emerge as happened in Catholic countries. It was long believed that the centre/periphery cleavage had been similarly subsumed into the dominant class cleavage, at least so far as the creation of political parties was concerned. Rich Scots and Welshmen could vote Tory, the poor voted overwhelmingly Labour; there seemed no space for parties based on identity or culture, alongside the state-wide behemoths. But rapid socio-economic change after World War II, culminating in the divisive and voluntaristic policies of the Thatcher era, opened up new space for territorial politics.[5] By the 1970s, nationalist parties in Scotland and Wales challenged Labour hegemony in those two countries, one consequence of which was the ill-fated referendums of 1979. During this period, however, 'Europe' was largely absent from the political debate except in the form of a strong dose of Euroscepticism, both within Labour and the nationalist parties. In Northern Ireland, the 'Troubles' were at their height and, although the moderate nationalist Social Democratic and Labour Party was strongly pro-European, Sinn Féin, the hard-line political wing of the IRA, was resolutely anti-EC. Like Thatcher, it saw the EC as a threat to national sovereignty.

In systemic terms, therefore, Europeanisation latches on to a system strongly predicated on social class cleavage, into which territorial cleavages have increasingly forced their way. Clearly at the macro level, it is possible to speak of a whole new cleavage generated by Europeanisation, namely that between integrationists and, for want of a better term, 'sovereignists' (from the French 'souverainistes'). Some evidence for this claim will be seen shortly in the way in which individual parties have had to position themselves on the issue of integration, but we can already see the effects at macro level. The most spectacular is the creation of new sovereignist parties. First, the Referendum Party, which is closely associated with the late millionaire James Goldsmith, that served as a launch pad for the United Kingdom Independence Party (UKIP). This party has demonstrated its appeal in two European Parliamentary elections.[6] It has also begun to stand in national contests, clearly aiming to function as more than a single-issue party (unlike its Danish equivalent, which only contests European elections). One can obviously argue about its future prospects (could it, for instance, be sidelined if the Conservatives moved to a totally Eurosceptic line?). The point is, however, that it has already made an impact on the UK party system, clearly expressing the presence of a new cleavage. But, as in other countries, such as France, this cleavage runs *within* parties as well as *between* them. Both Labour and the Conservatives have their Euro-enthusiasts and their Eurosceptics. It is therefore a matter of the balance of forces between these groups and how they affect the overall orientation of the party.

Inseparable from questions of cleavage are those about the nature of party competition. Europeanisation has had subtle but limited effects here; we would agree with Mair's findings about most of the party systems of the EU, namely that the parties have managed to control the effects of Europeanisation to a high degree.[7] Because EP elections have to include some degree of proportionality, the UK has used a regional list system, which gives forces such as nationalist parties and Greens a realistic chance of representation in the European Parliament (EP). To that extent, Europeanisation can be said to have modified the nature of party competition. Yet this applies only to the EP arena, which the British political class regards as a mere 'second-order' election[8]; even here, proportionality has been severely limited compared with, say, the Netherlands or Finland, both of which use a nationwide system. In the crucial elections to Westminster, the first-past-the-post system remains intact because both main parties, Labour and Conservative, believe that it works to their advantage over time; it may allow their rivals periods in office, but the pendulum always swings back to them, seeming to exclude smaller parties like the Liberal Democrats (until the Coalition Government of the 2010 May election). This shows the limits of Europeanisation on parties; they can, under European influence, allow a more generous form of suffrage for an institution they regard as less important, but no European pressures will be allowed to modify elections seen as vital.[9]

In systemic terms, then, Europeanisation would seem to have had some noticeable effect on the cleavage structure and a much more limited one on the rules of competition. But we now need to look beneath this framework at how individual parties have been affected.

Europeanisation and individual parties

State-wide parties

Ideology and policy stance

The Conservative Party (also called the Tory Party) has trodden a varying itinerary on European issues. Its most decisive move came in the 1960s when Harold MacMillan, and particularly Edward Heath, pushed the then governing party to apply for UK membership of the EEC, a move which, after two rebuffs, eventually succeeded under Heath's premiership in 1973. Economic considerations were presented as paramount (hence the continuing popularity of the term 'Common Market' to refer to the European Economic Community) and the notion of the EEC as a guarantor of peace was also important for this generation of politicians who had fought in World War II. The consequences of UK membership were played down so far as possible, particularly in what amounted to a wholesale reordering of UK foreign policy priorities (the 'retreat from Empire') and the likelihood of further political integration. The next generation of Conservative politicians had a more critical attitude to the (now) European Union (EU), however. If Margaret Thatcher signed up to the Single European Act, it was in the belief that the EU could be kept purely as an internal market without any necessary implications for further common policies or political unity. During the long Tory reign from 1979 to 1997, the party increasingly polarised between the militantly neo-liberal Thatcherites (Europe as purely a free-trade zone) and pro-Europeans, ready to accept increasing amounts of economic and political integration. The latter camp included party heavyweight politicians such as Kenneth Clarke, Michael Heseltine and Douglas Hurd.[10]

John Major's premiership attempted to straddle the gap between these pro-Europeans and the mass of the party in the country with increasing difficulty as various 'little Englander' MPs rebelled. Major sought symbolic gestures from his EU partners (the famous opt-outs, of which the single currency was the most important), but these were not enough to stem the growing 'fissiparousness' within the party, which was an important factor in its defeat in 1997.

The question of integration has produced a clear decantation within the Tory party, most notably within its EP delegation. Pro-integration Members of European Parliament (MEPs) have been deselected or marginalised or have simply quit,[11] and the parliamentary group of the European People's Party (EPP) has felt itself forced to offer the Tories and some of their Eurosceptic allies, such as the Czech ODS, what amounts to a separate status within the EPP parliamentary group (see next section).

Such concessions by the EPP did not seem, however, to have achieved their ostensible objective of reducing the challenge posed by the out-and-out rejection-ists of the UKIP, whose progress in the 2004 EP elections came mainly at Tory expense.[12] Under Michael Howard, the Tory response to UKIP was to move further in the direction of the Eurosceptics, with outright refusal of the Euro and draft European Constitution, while making demands for repatriation of some common policies such as fisheries. Tory intakes in the EP and House of Commons appears increasingly to be Eurosceptic, with the Europhile 'big beasts', like Clarke, seemingly further isolated. This was recently confirmed by the Europscepetics' contribution to the creation in 2009 of the new EP conservative group, namely the European Conservatives and Reformists (ECR).

Historically, the Labour Party's resistance to the Common Market was based on aspirations to a sort of 'socialism in one country'. It began to change under the leadership of Harold Wilson, who accepted the case for EEC entry on economic grounds. This economic realism prevailed when Labour was returned to office in 1974. To quell any dispute within his party, Wilson put the question of membership to a referendum, in which the 'yes vote' triumphed by two to one in 1975.[13] Divisions within his cabinet (whose members were given freedom to campaign for a 'no vote', if they wished) ran roughly parallel to those within the nation at large, and it seemed that the question of British membership was resolved within the ranks of Labour. But the problems of governing through the turbulence of the 1970s and the trauma of the 1979 defeat unleashed a period of sectarian infighting and scission within the party. Initially, the socialist left took the ascendancy, and the famous 1983 manifesto, dubbed 'the longest suicide note in history' by Gerald Kaufman MP,[14] promised withdrawal from the EEC, as well as unilateral nuclear disarmament and a package of statist economic policies. It took a good decade to put Labour back on a pro-European trajectory, and the main influence in this process was probably awareness among union leaders and politicians alike that Europe offered a more promising field for the promotion of a progressive social agenda than was possible in Thatcherite Britain. Euro-friendly rhetoric aside, however, the so-called 'New Labour' of Blair and Brown accepted, whether by conviction or in the name of electoral realism, most of the shibboleths of Thatcherism: reduction of the state's economic role, including privatisation (of services as well as industry) wherever possible; marginalisation of organised labour in the policy process; and a liberal trade policy.

The Labour Party's record in office suggests that its European objectives are little different from those of Thatcherism; from Brown's constant hectoring of governments that he sees as overprotective of their economies, to the appointment of Peter Mandelson as EU Trade Commissioner, to the seeking of working alliances with governments of neo-liberal views (Aznar, Berlusconi, and new EU entrants), there is a consistent neo-liberal approach to European policy. Against this background, accompanied by an unstinting 'Atlanticism' on wider questions of foreign policy, the periodic declarations of enthusiasm for further integration by Blair (cf. his episodic support for joining the Euro or for the draft Constitution) ring particularly hollow. What New Labour really stands for is an 'Atlanticist Europe', deregulated and opened up to competition, in which the 'European social model', as developed by social democrats and Christian democrats over the years, is regarded as an expensive luxury and where any common foreign or security policy can only be dovetailed to NATO (i.e. the United States) specifications. Its main allies have, logically, been the Spanish and Italian right, plus various supporters among the new entrants. Most of Labour's leadership elites, and their younger acolytes who increasingly fill the backbenches via careers as parliamentary assistants, share this utilitarian orientation, while those in favour of greater integration or a more social Europe are pushed to the side. Whether this minimalist, neo-liberal model of Europe is a direct effect of British involvement in the EU or, more likely, a reflection of wider global pressures on the UK economy and society, remains, however, a moot point. But certainly the Labour Party's position on Europe has shifted considerably.

The Liberal Party and its successor the Liberal Democrats (frequently shortened to 'Lib Dems') have long been the most enthusiastic advocates within the UK of European integration, even if their commitment falls some way short of federalism.[15] The Lib Dems favour joining the Euro and passing the draft Constitution. As a party with a free-market tradition they are keen supporters of the Single Market, but would go further than their rivals in supporting measures such as an integrated European financial sector, firmer fiscal incentives to make polluters pay and encouragement for the use of energy-conserving materials. Even the Common Foreign and Security Policy should be run by Qualified Majority Voting, though the party believes in retaining a national veto on purely defence questions. The libertarian heritage of the party surfaces in its support for the Schengen Agreement and a common asylum policy. British liberalism has always favoured decentralising policies, so it is no surprise to see the Lib Dems advocating the representation of regions, on appropriate issues, in the European Council. Generally, the party is keen on subsidiarity and concerned to involve national parliaments more in EU decision-making so as to reduce the 'democratic deficit'.

Permanently excluded from national office, the Lib Dems have found the EP, where they have usually been a key element of the European Liberal Democrats (ELDR) group, a useful place in which to argue their case. Europeanisation has probably not changed the party fundamentally; rather it has increased the strength of previously held convictions.

The Green Party has relied heavily on the EP to achieve any public prominence; the Westminster electoral system is a handicap to its hope of achieving representation there. The Green Party is also weak in local government, though the 2003 elections to the Scottish Parliament brought it seven MSPs. British Greens, like many of their colleagues, harbour deeply ambivalent attitudes to Europe, though the Scottish Green Party was more upbeat about the draft Constitution than the Green Party of England and Wales.[16] The European Green Party deliberately draws its remit to cover all Europe beyond the EU, as far as Georgia. This is a way of saying that the free-market, capitalist, EU, with its indifference to the real needs of the environment, may not be a cause worth investing in. It is possible also that some British Greens who are strongly individualist, yet also quite traditionalist in their way, are quite resistant to continental political culture, with its strong bargaining ethos and reliance on compromise, preferring what they see as a more principled way of conducting politics. The party certainly attracts those of libertarian and individualistic temperament, who often seem to have difficulty with the compromise and shared discipline required by successful mass structures. Green British MEPs can be relied upon to criticise the EU on any number of policy fronts, from the (in their eyes) environmentally-destructive Common Agricultural Policy, to EU backsliding on human rights and lack of institutional transparency to the inadequacies of foreign aid policy. By any judgment, the party would have to be placed nearer the Eurosceptic end of the spectrum.

Organisation

The main implications of Europe for Conservative Party organisation have been felt both at the party's centre and at its periphery. It is commonplace to remark on the increasingly Eurosceptic profile of candidates at both national and European elections, but it has not been necessary for the party's Central Office to set up new structures (unlike Labour – see below) to achieve this aim. The ageing, white, overwhelmingly middle-class membership of the party is arguably even more hostile to Europe than parts of the leadership.[17] These 'true blues' are unlikely to choose candidates with integrationist sympathies. Nevertheless, there have still been sufficient pro-European Tory parliamentarians for them to organise in a loose faction, while the Europhobes have also created their own ginger groups, such as the virulent Bruges Group. Europeanisation has thus affected the internal structures of the party.

Another direct result of European pressures could be seen in the disastrous choice of Iain Duncan Smith as party leader, in which the membership was, very foolishly, allowed a decisive say. The victory of 'IDS' owed everything to his fervent Atlanticism and dislike of Europe and nothing to his totally inadequate political skills; the membership was simply choosing an image of itself writ large.

Smith's leadership did bring one key change in Tory external relations, however, and this was in relation to the European People's Party (EPP). John Major and Chris Patten, the most European of recent Tory elites, had secured membership of the EPP parliamentary group for Tory MEPs in 1991, but the party as such never joined the EPP because of the latter's explicit federalism. Even group membership brought increasing tension, however, as Eurosceptic MEPs found themselves being asked to vote (and refusing to do so) for motions that had a visible integrationist content. Relations had become execrable, and it is an open secret[18] that the Tories were about to leave the EPP group and recreate a sort of autonomous conservative group like that shared with Danish conservatives in the past. Duncan Smith had made a number of conditions for staying, and when he was replaced by Michael Howard in a 'velvet coup', the EPP group chairman, Pöttering, caved in and accepted these conditions, in order to keep the Tories within the fold and guarantee the EPP's status as the largest group.[19] This did not persist to the 2009 European elections, which witnessed the creation of the conservative ECR group (European Conservatives and Reformists).

The Labour Party has on the face of it undergone considerable change in the context of Europeanisation. No separate structures have been created for European elections, where the seats are simply amalgamations of Westminster seats. However, important changes have occurred with regard to the selection of MEPs and their role in party decision-making. William Messmer showed how the use of the National Executive Committee (NEC) panels enabled the leadership to gain control of candidate selection, an operation made much easier by the adoption of multi-candidate constituencies, where the NEC can determine the order of the list. Much of Labour's enthusiasm for the semi-proportional system now in use can be ascribed to the possibility that it affords the national leadership the opportunity of removing control of candidate selection from local activists.[20] Certainly, according to Wring, Baker and Seawright, this move enabled the centre to empty the EP group (known as the EPLP – European Parliamentary Labour Party) almost overnight of most of its 'awkward squad'. By their count, barely a third of retiring MEPs identified as 'old Labour' (believers in state socialism) were given winnable positions on regional lists in 1999[21] – those remaining were loyal Blairites.

A reward for MEPs' loyalty came in the form of what Messmer calls 'the link system', whereby EPLP spokespeople are attached to the appropriate office in Whitehall as part of the ministerial team in that policy area. This possibility of influence on policy certainly gives MEPs incentives to toe the party line (though few MEPs seem to detect any real influence on policy on their part), and this arrangement also gives Labour's central leadership an early input into EP decision-making, what Messmer calls[22] an 'early warning system'. Thus by a system of sticks and carrots (tighter candidate control plus positions of apparent influence), the Labour leadership tightened up control over its MEPs.

How far this is due to EP-specific factors alone is, however, unclear. The Labour leadership has been attempting to regain control over elected officials at all levels since the early 1980s, when infiltration of the party by *trotskisants* of the Militant tendency was perceived as a real threat, especially in Liverpool, where the Militant-run city council oscillated between farce and tragedy.[23] The modernisers around Blair needed central control of candidates wherever possible, so as to determine the type of person elected, namely market-friendly, mildly pro-European Atlanticists, and not the 'old Labour' state socialists often picked by constituency activists. All kind of devices have been used by the Labour centre to wrest control of candidate selection from local activists, including bribing retiring MPs and cynical use of parity legislation.

European integration has only at best been a secondary factor in changing Labour organisation to a more centralist direction. The struggle to gain central control over candidates goes back beyond Blair to the Kinnock leadership, as the 'modernisation' of the party began after the crushing defeat of 1983.

Peripheral parties

In this section, Scotland and Wales are analysed together while Northern Ireland is treated separately. Scotland and Wales are both part of the party system of Great Britain, in that they have both state-wide parties as well as regional national-ist parties. Northern Ireland should be regarded as a separate party system from that in Great Britain. Before analysing in detail the peripheral parties' positions on Europe, it is worth noting that up to the 1980s, all nationalist and regionalist parties across Europe were divided with regard to European integration. Some were broadly in favour of European federalism, but the more separatist nationalist parties opposed European integration. As nationalists, they rightly perceived the European project as a threat to the nation state and therefore to their own politi-cal projects of achieving statehood for their own 'stateless' nations. Additionally, as they moved towards the political left, and even Marxism, they saw European integration as a capitalist programme and a 'rich man's club', in which their own 'nations' would be marginalised or excluded.

Yet, by the 1990s, this hostility had changed and the nationalist as well as the re-gionalist parties (with the exception of Sinn Féin) had shifted their opinion. Again, this is a pan-European phenomenon. Whereas the nationalists had seen 'Europe' as a threat to their ideological positions, they now saw it as an opportunity to by-pass their national governments in a new 'Europe of the Regions'. They recognised that European integration was weakening the traditional nation state and that this was an opportunity for them. Although the extent of nation-state weakness was prob-ably exaggerated by scholars in the 1990s, the perception, nevertheless, encour-aged the nationalist parties to revise their ideological positions. This is quite clear in the Scottish and Welsh cases, where the Scottish Nationalist Party (SNP) and Plaid Cymru (PC) adopted strongly pro-European positions. Indeed, the Labour Party itself encouraged this positive approach to European integration during the devolution referendum campaigns in 1997. Compare the 1979 referendums, when Europe was barely mentioned, with 1997, when it was central to the arguments put forward by those in favour of devolution from the London-based government to the SNP and PC. Those opposed to devolution, the Conservatives and the 'vote no' campaigns, were also sceptical about Europe.

Scotland and Wales[24]

Both the Scottish Nationalist Party (SNP) and Plaid Cymru (PC) support European integration and most EU policies. The SNP, however, has not completely abandoned its traditional nationalism and is opposed to a European federation in which nation states would disappear. Each member state must retain its own sovereignty in respect of constitutional, fiscal and other matters of vital national importance. Plaid Cymru has not pronounced on this, but has stated that it wishes 'to place Wales at the heart of government in Europe'.

During the period of their Euroscepticism, both parties were in favour of simple independence – the Scottish and Welsh nations had a right to their own states. Now this has been modified to 'independence in Europe'. The SNP argues that this is necessary in order for Scotland to have a full voice in Europe and not simply that of a region, which is its present status. Although PC has been coyer about coming out explicitly in favour of independence, it advances a similar argument. Wales needs to be independent in order to promote Welsh values and interests, e.g. agricultural and economic interests. This applies particularly to protecting the rights and welfare of the Welsh language. Both parties believe that Scotland and Wales, as independent nations in the new Europe, would take place alongside other small nations such as Ireland, Denmark, Finland, Latvia, etc. and be fully represented in the Council of Ministers and other EU institutions. On the other hand, although they have retained a dose of nationalism, they are also in favour of a common foreign policy and a common defence and security policy, both of which would seriously diminish their autonomy as sovereign member states.

On a number of more specific policy issues, the two parties are largely in agreement. Both welcomed the draft Constitutional Treaty, but the SNP favoured holding a referendum on the issue. Both favoured the enlargement process, but the PC is worried because Wales lost an MEP under the new arrangements, while half of the new member states, with smaller populations than Wales, now have full member status. The two parties are in favour of the Euro and believe it will bring economic benefits to their countries (although it is less certain that the Scottish and Welsh populations support this view). Again, the SNP favours a referendum on the issue, while PC supports a timely introduction 'under conditions of democratic control' and the guarantee of protection for the smaller economies of Europe. On economic policy, the SNP argues that Scottish independence is crucial for economic development in Scotland, as the country is tied to an economic policy designed for the overheated south east England. This means that Scottish exports are priced out of the market. It is in favour of the Single Market, but taxation and social security should remain under member state control. In its literature, PC says little about economic policy except to support local regeneration and greater access to EU structural funds.

On social policy issues, the two parties adopt a more social democratic position compared to the more neo-liberal stance of UK governments, whether Conservative or Labour, which have consistently opposed any strengthening of this at EU level. The same is true of issues such as environmental policy and sustainable development, and agricultural policy (although both support the recent reforms of the Common Agricultural Policy). The SNP is opposed to the EU Common Fisheries Policy, arguing that fishing is of vital national importance for Scotland. It wishes to see the management of Scotland's fishing returned from Brussels and London to Edinburgh. However, it would like to see Scotland qualify as an Objective One status region, as achieved by parts of Wales, and argues that the failure to do so was due to a miscalculation by the UK Office of National Statistics.

This analysis shows that both parties have significantly modified their separatist nationalism of the 1970s to reformulate their political project along the lines of 'independence in Europe'. They are ranged alongside the Euro-enthusiast parties, and there is a clear distance between them and the UK Independence Party (UKIP) and even the Conservatives and, in important respects, the New Labour Party. At the same time, how to realise the dream of 'independence in Europe' is not very clear. If Scotland became independent (at least a possibility), it is not clear whether this would be accepted by the rest of the UK nor, indeed, by the other member states of the EU. Furthermore, independence within Europe is a goal with a contradiction at its heart, as was illustrated by the inconsistency of both parties in seeking independence while wanting common foreign, defence and security policies.

We have dealt mainly with the nationalist parties in Scotland and Wales. The main state-wide parties, however, are also present in both countries. The Labour Party is the biggest of these, followed by the Liberal Democrats, with the Conservatives reduced to a rump. The UK Independence Party has no greater following than it does in England. There is the added complexity that electors send MPs to Westminster, SMPs to the Scottish Parliament, AMs to the National Assembly for Wales, as well as MEPs to the EP. Generally speaking, Welsh and Scottish MPs are more pro-European than their English counterparts, although there are important exceptions to this. MEPs tend to be more pro-European for obvious reasons (although we should not forget that UKIP has several MEPs) and sceptics tend to be socialised into the European system once they become active in the EP, though very often it is pro-integration candidates who tend to get themselves selected in the first place.[25] What is interesting is that the Scottish and Welsh sections of both the Labour and Conservative parties are also more pro-European than the nationwide parties as a whole, and this is also reflected in the SMPs and AMs. We need to qualify this by pointing out a difference between the Scottish Parliament and the National Assembly of Wales (NAW). The former has developed a more vigorous European policy than the latter, despite the pro-European rhetoric that was used to justify the 'yes' vote, particularly in Wales.[26]

Northern Ireland

Although Northern Ireland is part of the United Kingdom, it has a quite separate political history and culture. The traditional Labour and Conservative parties have not contested the Northern Ireland elections. These differences make its political cleavages distinct from those in Great Britain. Basically, the fundamental cleavage concerns what is known as the 'constitutional question', that is whether Northern Ireland should remain part of the UK or whether it should leave and join with the Irish Republic. This cleavage has divided the two governments of the UK and Ireland and has fed the violent conflict between nationalists and unionists. Each side has generated its own parties, movements, organisations and paramilitary groups. Until the 1980s, the European Community was marginal to the conflict and, from 1979, EP elections were mainly another expression of the internal conflict. Nevertheless, political parties from within the two communities took distinctive positions with regard to European integration. Unionist parties tended towards Euroscepticism, with the Ulster Unionist Party (UUP) aligning with the British Conservatives and the more extreme Democratic Unionist Party (DUP) under the leadership of the Reverend Ian Paisley denouncing Europe as a 'Roman Catholic plot'. On the nationalist side, there was greater polarisation with the Social Democratic and Labour Party (SDLP), led by John Hume, whose politics were close to European federalism and Christian democracy, being strongly in favour and Sinn Féin being strongly opposed.

What is interesting about the Northern Ireland case, however, is that although the EC had little direct impact on the 'Troubles', except in providing various kinds of funding, it did alter the parameters within which the conflict was fought out. Basically, as continuing European integration began to treat as relative the centrality of the nation state and national sovereignty, the problem could be formulated differently. Rather than being an irreconcilable clash between two competing claims of sovereignty over the same piece of territory by two sovereign governments, it was now reformulated in such a way as to allow for a more flexible and subtle interpretation. Sovereignty was now conceived as capable of being divided and flexible rather than indivisible and rigid. This led to the signing of the 1998 Good Friday Agreement and the complex sets of institutions that emanated from that, including the power-sharing Assembly. Although the institutions took some time to function properly, nevertheless, this has completely changed the parameters of Northern Ireland politics and there reigns now a kind of peace. 'Europe' is the wider context and background that made this possible.

The positions of the parties towards Europe have also slightly changed. The DUP continues to be suspicious of the 'Roman' aspects of the integration, but the Unionist Party now has a number of members much more favourable towards the EU, thanks to their experience of working in the European institutions. The SDLP continues to have a strongly pro-European attitude even if the party lost to Sinn Féin the seat that they always had won since the elections began in 1979. Sinn Féin, for its part, although it has not fully endorsed the EU, now sees it as a 'significant terrain for struggle' and occupies its two seats in the Parliament (the second from the Irish Republic); it still does not occupy its seats at Westminster. It is interesting to see that the division now is between the two unionist parties and Sinn Féin on the one side and the SDLP on the other. For example, the UUP, DUP and Sinn Féin all oppose a European Constitution as an infringement of the rights of nation states (although they are thinking of different nation states), while the SDLP fully endorses it. Sinn Féin is also concerned that common foreign, defence and security policies will infringe Irish neutrality. On the other hand, Sinn Féin and the SDLP both strongly endorse the Euro as it will bring north and south of Ireland closer (the Republic has already adopted it), while the two unionist parties, expressing British nationalist Euroscepticism, oppose it. Furthermore, as parties of the left, both Sinn Féin and the SDLP endorse the social policy and social rights agenda of the EU, while the UUP and DUP are critical of them.

Conclusion

It might be helpful in the conclusion to subject our analysis of the British case to the series of general, comparative questions raised by Robert Ladrech and Peter Mair about the possible effects of Europeanisation on domestic party politics.[27] Ladrech raised the likelihood of opportunistic strategy by parties seeking to exploit the European Union as an issue; in some cases, this might even lead to the creation of entirely new parties, but it was certainly likely to inspire strategic changes by existing parties and possibly alter the internal balance of the latter. He also felt that EU issues would figure more in party programmes but, more importantly, would be linked to policies previously regarded as part of the domestic field; some of these linkages might be subtle. Peter Mair, for his part[28] considered the possible effects of Europeanisation on the format and mechanics of party systems, and asked whether Europeanisation helped or hindered what is widely perceived as an increasing 'depoliticisation' of national politics. The evidence presented here would suggest that 'Europe' has probably encouraged depoliticisation more than the opposite, as the majority of British voters see it as making politics even less attractive than national issues. In any case, European elections, which already have very low turnouts, tend to be about national and even local issues for those who do bother to vote. Politics is thus increasingly an elite-driven activity that alienates the mass of people.

Taking first the exploitation of Europe as an issue, this has obviously been going on for some forty years, probably most spectacularly within the internal politics of Labour. Two points are worth making here. First, the mainstream parties have mostly managed to keep the issue within their control. The UK Independence Party and the Referendum Party are recent arrivals on the political scene, and it remains to be seen how much they can affect the behaviour of the potential parties of government. Given the salience of the European issue, it says much for the hegemonic capacity of the two major parties that they have kept new forces off the electoral radar screen for so long, and it would be unwise for the newcomers to expect huge progress, especially given the rigours of the Westminster electoral system.

Secondly, Europe is more important in decanting internal *rapports de force* within the two big parties than it is as a real issue between them. Put crudely, both are pragmatic Europeans and intergovernmentalists; this is why they are so careful to rule out future political integration and to sell Europe primarily as an economic success story. The most one can say is that the rhetoric is rather more critical on the Tory side, but on substantive issues we still await a full-scale declaration of Euroscepticism from the Conservatives, such as a pledge that the UK will *never* join the Euro. The reason for this failure to fight openly on a pro- or anti-European platform is simple: Labour and Conservatives have both to appeal across the board to a collection of attitudes, running from strong Euro-enthusiasm to a desire to quit the EU. Unfortunately for those who prefer political clarity, neither of these options will ever attract enough voters to win an election. Hence this oblique, ambiguous discourse on Europe – which allows one voter to see scepticism where another finds hope – remains the order of the day.[29]

This applies even more inside the parties, where Europe is used as a rallying point for a whole range of discontents; it is a sort of proxy. In the Conservative Party, to be pro-European tends to be synonymous with a more Keynesian, consensual and social-libertarian approach to politics (what used to be called 'wetness'). It amounts to forgiving Edward Heath and recognising that Mrs Thatcher was less than a demigod. Within Labour, Europe was above all a delimiter of the Brown and Blair camps. It is quite possible that the beliefs of these two men on Europe (and indeed most of the range of public policies) are identical (both are Atlanticists, globalisers and market enthusiasts first and foremost). Yet they were locked in a power struggle of the most basic kind, which dare not say its name. Hence the necessity to disguise personal quarrels as policy. And what better an issue than Europe to fulfil this purpose? The outcome of this shadow-boxing was that Blair, for all his rhetorical enthusiasm, was totally outsmarted by Brown who, with his famous five tests for British entry to the euro, gained a right of veto over UK European policy. Here, at its most basic level, is the effect of Europeanisation on domestic politics. It is, however, an effect not on 'high' politics, but at the lowest level of everyday politics (*'la politique politicienne'*, as the French say). Europe became just another pawn in a personal power struggle.

Even the clothing of domestic issues in European guise is subject to internal party imperatives. The Conservative Party's 2005 election campaign clearly made much of asylum and immigration issues (though the immediate inspiration for this probably came from outside the EU, namely Australia, where the retaining of office by John Howard's Liberals was widely attributed to their skill at exploiting these themes, mainly through their director of communications, Lynton Crosby, who was promptly hired by Michael Howard!). It was easy to associate such questions with an anti-EU message, but the Conservatives had to be careful how they did it. Too much anti-EU rhetoric was likely to fuel a UKIP vote instead of retaining its own supporters. And in any case, Labour promptly adopted a harsher discourse and some improvised, severe-looking measures to head off any defection of its supporters on this issue. It seems clear from this that there is inevitably some blurring of domestic and European issues, but what is decisive is how the issue serves the party's internal needs. The content of the issue is less important than the way it is used. The case of the peripheral parties shows this from another angle. These forces have seized on parts of the European agenda, such as subsidiarity or multilevel governance, to reinforce, while sometimes slightly adjusting, their historic project.

As for the format and mechanics of the party system, one must agree with Mair, who sees little evidence to support the view that Europeanisation has changed either of these variables very much. Certainly, the format of UK party system is superficially changed with the upsurge of UKIP, but this may be more appearance than substance. UKIP has flourished – only been allowed to flourish – in the exceptional electoral circumstance of EP elections, that is to say in a contest where the gatekeepers (Labour and Conservative) relaxed the rules for reasons that have little to do with Europe and much to do with devolution and experimentation with insurance policies for the future (see above). But in first-order elections, and indeed in the upper tier of second-order contests (local government), where more punitive electoral rules reflect the fact that stakes are higher, UKIP's impact has been hitherto minimal; more accurately, the big two have restricted its impact. The number of parties in a system is one thing; the number of relevant parties another.

As to the mechanics of the system, the question is: has there been a significant shift in the axis of competition, with European issues coming to occupy a more central place? While conceding that the Conservatives seem to offer a distinct choice from Labour, Mair does stress[30] how 'contingent and partisan' these stances are and suggests that they derive mainly from an inability to find a difference with Labour on other substantive policy issues. We have suggested the fundamental hollowness of some Conservative posturing on these issues and we wonder if the Conservatives in government (as opposed to a party stuck in what was clearly likely to be a long period of opposition) would have behaved much differently from Labour. The Conservatives evolved towards more open scepticism in the European Parliament with the creation of the European Conservatives and Reformists group following the 2009 EP elections.

Mair's final point about possible 'depoliticisation' rested on the fact that EU politics was seen as remote from the citizens (the 'democratic deficit') and that much EU politics seemed to be about consensual bargaining, in which the sharp edge of political conflict and choice was removed. All political forces seemed thus to be making similar offers. These pressures came on top of various factors already inhibiting political interest and participation within national polities, leading to yet more citizen apathy. He suggested that a sharp Euro debate might be one way of reigniting interest. In that case, Britain would be a prime example. Unfortunately, as we have suggested, the Tory/Labour debate has always pulled its punches, for reasons suggested above. While the UKIP contribution is emotive and passionate, one would have to question whether it and its various echoes in the tabloid press really contribute to a serious debate at all; emotive slogan-mongering and the highlighting of minor irritants and examples of silliness within the panoply of EU legislation hardly amount to a serious argument about Britain's place, present and future, within the world system.

What these considerations suggest is that the two-level party system of the UK reflects the pressures of multilevel governance and wider factors, such as globalisation, as much as it does those of Europeanisation. Within the state-wide party system, it is clear that the sovereignist/integrationist cleavage has forced its way on to the agenda, as the rise of UKIP shows. But the principal axis of big party competition, the electoral system, continues to be managed collusively by the *frères ennemis* of Labour and Conservatives, despite some minimal concessions to proportional representation, which owe as much to developments inside the UK (the growing territorialisation of politics), as they do to any pressure from Europe.

In ideological or policy terms, it seems clearer that the Conservatives have been pulled in a more Eurosceptic direction, as a direct result of developments since Maastricht. Organisationally, Europe has brought them internal factionalism and complicated their relationship with transnational party instances. Labour's evolution is less clear, however. Blairite rhetoric about 'placing Britain at the heart of Europe' seems increasingly a smokescreen for the adoption of neo-liberal, transatlantic policy orientations, in both economics and international relations. These represent an acceptance by the party of the victory of neo-liberalism (Thatcherism, in its British form), but this is a force whose influence ranges far beyond the EU. Similarly, the party's chronic Atlanticism has never gone away as a result of its engagement with Europe. Quite simply, it has just surfaced more dramatically of late. The Iraq crisis showed that Labour will always choose America over Europe, but that will not surprise anyone who knows the party's history. In short, global pressures probably explain more about Labour's development of late than do European ones.

For the peripheral parties of the UK, Europeanisation has brought, in ideological terms, a much more flexible way of presenting their project. A 'Europe of the regions' allows these mainly left-of-centre forces to situate themselves flexibly, favouring more integration than mainstream parties, but sometimes in ambivalent ways (cf. their views on common foreign or security policies). In Northern Ireland, the direct impact of Europe seems at first sight small, yet the wider framework of governance that it embodies has undoubtedly helped political forces move towards arrangements based on some kind of consociational arrangement.

In short, the impact of European processes on the parties of the UK has been uneven; sometimes it is visible, sometimes less so; and Europeanising pressures always coexist with Atlanticist and global vectors, often in complex ways. There is no reason to believe that this situation will change in future.

Notes

1   The authors would like to thank Mirela Bogdani and Suzannah Lux for their help in gathering material for this chapter.

2   'Europeanisation' may be understood both broadly and more narrowly. Broadly speaking, it refers to the development of a wide range of international organisations, such as the European Union (EU), the Council of Europe (CoE) and even bodies such as the Office of Security and Co-operation (OSCE) in Europe, that are the creation of new frameworks of intergovernmental relations, governance and even new legal codifications of human and civil rights. The geo-political transformation of Europe following the collapse of the Soviet Union, has accelerated this wider Europeanisation. Europeanisation in the narrow sense has been at the core of these broad transformations, but it has also been facilitated by them. We should beware of simply concentrating on the narrower understanding.

3   We are reluctant to refer to this as a 'national system', since this term also applies to Scotland and Wales, which are, constitutionally, nations of the UK. The Welsh for instance have a *National Assembly* for Wales.

4   P. Webb and J. Fisher, 'The changing British party system: two-party equilibrium or the emergence of moderate pluralism?', in D. Broughton and M. Donovan (eds), *Changing Party Systems in Western Europe*, London, Pinter, 1999, pp. 8–29. See also P. Webb, *The Modern British Party System*, London, Sage, 2000.

5   M. Keating, *The New Regionalism in Western Europe: Territorial Restructuring and Political Change*, Cheltenham, Elgar, 1998. See also J. Loughlin *et al.,* (2004a) *Subnational Democracy in the European Union: Challenges and Opportunties*, Oxford University Press, 2004. In addition, see J. Loughlin, (2004b), 'The "transformation" of governance: new directions in policy and politics', *Australian Journal of Politics and History,* 2004, vol. 50 (1), pp. 8–22.

6   In 1999, UKIP took 7 per cent of the vote and four seats, in 2004, 16.2 per cent and 12 seats.

7   P. Mair, 'The limited impact of Europe on national party systems', *West European Politics,* 2000, vol.23 (4), pp. 27–51.

8   K. Reif and H. Schmidt, 'Nine second-order elections: a conceptual framework for the analysis of European election results', *European Journal of Political Science,* 1980, vol. 8, pp. 3–44.

9   The EP approved the Council proposal to modify the 1976 electoral law in June 2002. Earlier proposals of an integrationist nature (uniform system across the EU or compulsory proportions of 'transnational' candidates on lists) were watered down, to leave governments with considerable flexibility within the general parameters of the list system. Farrell and Scully rightly conclude that the new system will have 'minimal consequences' for the UK. The new system also reflects a consensus developed between Labour and the Liberal Democrats before 1997, which has enabled the introduction of limited PR to Scotland and Wales. This concession by Labour might also be regarded as an experiment with an eye to the future. If the majoritarian system were ever likely to disadvantage it seriously in the UK as a whole, then there would be a

tried alternative. See D. Farrell and R. Scully, 'The election and representative role of MEPs', Draft Paper, *Working Group on Democracy in the EU* for UK Cabinet Office, November 2002.

10 M. Holmes, 'The Conservative Party and Europe: from Major to Hague', *Political Quarterly*, 1998, vol. 69 (2), pp. 133–40. See also D. Collings and A. Seldon, 'Conservatives in opposition', *Parliamentary Affairs*, 2001, vol. 54, pp. 624–37.

11 D. Wring, D. Baker and D. Seawright, 'Panelism in action: Labour's 1999 EP candidate selections', *Political Quarterly*, 2000, vol. 71 (2), pp. 234–45.

12 McAllister and Studlar suggest that, even in the 1997 general election, the Referendum Party had cost the Conservatives some sixteen seats and the (then much weaker) UKIP a further two. I. McAllister and D. Studlar, 'Conservative Euroscepticism and the Referendum party in the 1997 British General Election', *Party Politics*, 2000, vol. 6 (3), pp. 359–71. For UKIP's effect on the Conservatives in 2004, see P. Taggart, 'The EP Election in the United Kingdom', *EPERN Briefing Paper*, no.14, Brighton, University of Sussex, 2004, p. 7.

13 D. Butler and U. Kitzinger, *The 1975 Referendum*, London, Macmillan, 1976.

14 Labour Party, *The New Hope for Britain*, London, 1983.

15 Liberal Democrats, *Making Europe Work for You* (EP Electoral Manifesto), London, 2004.

16 Green Party, *Real Progress: the Future is Green* (EP Election Manifesto), London, 2004.

17 P. Whiteley, P. Seyd and J. Richardson, *True Blues: the Politics of Conservative Party Membership*, Oxford, Clarendon Press, 1994.

18 M. Ball and R. Oulds, 'Freeing Conservative MEPs from the EPP: the strategy that should be at the heart of IDS' European policy', Bruges group website, 2004, http://www.brugesgroup.com/mediacentre.

19 The Conservatives now enjoy a vice-presidency of the group, a pro rata share of EP finance and staffing to deploy as they wish, the freedom to publish Eurosceptic material and to recruit incomers directly to the European Democrat fraction of the group, which they share mainly with the Czech ODS. See D. Hanley, 'Le PPE: bilan d'une législature, 1999–2004', Brussels, ULB- Les Cahiers du CEVIPOL, 2004–1, http://www.ulb.ac.be/soco/cevipol.

20 W. Messmer, 'Taming Labour MEPs', *Party Politics*, 2003, vol. 9 (2), pp. 201–18.

21 Wring *et al.*, 'Panelism in action...', p.243.

22 Messmer, 'Taming Labour MEPs', p.206.

23 E. Shaw, *The Labour Party since 1979*, London, Routledge, 1994.

24 This section draws on sources such as manifestoes and press releases from the parties themselves.

25 R. Scully, 'Going Native? Institutional and partisan loyalty in the European Parliament', in B. Steunenberg and J. Thomassen, (eds), *The European Parliament: Moving Towards democracy in the EU*, Oxford, Rowman and Littlefield, 2002, pp. 113–36.

26 J. Loughlin (2001), 'La Dimension Européenne de la Dévolution en Grande-

Bretagne', *Pouvoirs locaux*, 2001, vol. 49 (11), pp. 115–20.

27 R. Ladrech, 'Europeanization and political parties: towards a framework for analysis', *Party Politics*, 2002, vol.8 (4), pp. 389–404.

28 Mair, 'The limited impact...', pp. 27–51.

29 The surest proof of both parties' reluctance to fight openly on European integration is the fact that both took refuge in a referendum on UK membership of the Euro and on adopting the draft Constitution, rather than committing openly to a firm position on these issues. Labour was quite happy to see referenda in other countries derail the whole Constitutional project.

30 Mair, 'The limited impact...', pp.35–6.

chapter six | europeanisation and the party system in greece

Christoforos Vernardakis and Iosif Botetzagias

Introduction

Within a decade after the fall of the military junta of 1967–1974, Greece had witnessed the abolition of the monarchy, the country's (temporary) withdrawal from NATO's military wing over the Cyprus' invasion, the opening up of the political arena for the long persecuted Communist Party, the peaceful alteration of parties in government and, finally, EC membership. The Third Hellenic Republic grew and matured under the European Community's wing and most political researchers and commentators have stressed the important role Europe had played in consolidating the new regime.

How has this, quarter-of-a-century relationship with Europe influenced the Greek party system and individual political parties? We begin with an analysis of the systemic variables, trying to identify the influence of Europeanisation on cleavages and party competition. We then study the impact on the ideologies of individual parties, their organisation and policy stance. Overall, we find little evidence of any substantial influence on the party system and only minimal influence on individual parties. Our analysis, albeit showing that a dividing line over 'Europe' does exist – separating the two major parties and the rest – leads us to argue that this division has not yet substantially affected political competition, arguably because of the particular understanding Greek voters have of Europe.

Europeanisation and the Greek party system – cleavages and party competition

Currently, Greece has a single party government, the Panhellenic Socialist Movement (PASOK), which governed between 1981 and 2004, with a small break between 1989 and 1993. Staunchly anti-European back in the 1970s, PASOK is a social democratic party of the centre-left. It lost power in 2004 (40.5 per cent of the vote) and in the 2007 elections it dropped even further to 38.1 per cent. Following the 2009 elections, PASOK's electoral share jumped to 43.3 per cent.

The next most powerful party is the New Democracy (ND), a political party that occupies the centre-right ideological space. The ND won the September 2007 elections by 41.8 per cent, declining from its 45.5 per cent high point in the previous elections of 2004. The October 2009 elections showed that its electoral influence declined to 30.3 per cent.

At the wings of the political spectrum and to the right one finds the Popular Orthodox Rally (LAOS). The LAOS shares a number of common features with European extreme right parties, especially when it comes to issues of immigration and its 'nation-centred' political philosophy; it attracted 5 per cent of the voters in 2009. To the left, there are two parliamentary parties: the Communist Party of Greece (KKE), still adhering to traditional Soviet orthodoxy, registering around 7 per cent of voter preference in 2009 (a bit lower than its 2007 results); and the Coalition of the Radical Left (SYRIZA), a merger of new, radical and extra-parliamentary left groupings. SYRIZA secured 5 per cent of the vote in 2007 and 4.3 per cent at the 2009 election, although subsequent opinion polls suggest that its appeal has risen to over 10 per cent. It is widely projected that the next election (set for early summer 2012) will mark the entry into Parliament of the newly (2003) established Ecologists Greens (EG).

Historically, the main cleavage in the Greek political system is traced back to the civil war of the 1940s, the post-World War II conflict between the right and the (communist) left. The Greek civil war led to the creation of a state-in-emergency as well as to a host of prosecutions against the 'internal enemy'. The ideological-political animus of these prosecutions, starting in the early 1960s, led to the gradual altering of the original 'left-right' juxtaposition to a 'democrat-rightist' one. This novel framework allowed for the creation of a new, left, non-communist political party, the PASOK. Created soon after the fall of the military junta (1967–1974), PASOK was the political offspring of the communist left's crisis and the centrists' inability to change the workings of political power. Thus it was characterised both by a new political personnel as well as by a radical political discourse.

During its first period, which eventually led to its rise to power in 1981, PASOK had been staunchly anti-American and anti-European. The party was against Greece's membership to the EEC while it had opted against affiliating with the European Social Democracy, considering it but a 'Trojan horse of western imperialism'. Yet this anti-European stance withered over the 1980s and its gradual ideological and political realignment was important in changing Greek society's views towards Europe.

The moderation of the PASOK's actual position meant that together with the conservative ND they came to represent the greatest bulk of the Greek electorate. For the better part of the last twenty years, the party system had exhibited strong bipartite stability. The two power parties, the ND and PASOK, each representing a strong societal and ideological bloc, had secured the lion's share of the vote, adding up to 87 per cent in the 2000 elections. Thus the party system, albeit typically multipartite, in effect had been electorally bipartite.

Yet, as we have argued earlier in this section, the Greek party system is currently in a transitory phase, characterised by important changes and differentiations. We have evidence suggesting that the era of the two strong ruling parties is coming to an end. It is estimated that the ND and PASOK together will secure 70 per cent of the vote at the most in the next general election, far below their past scores. The reason is that societal alliances are radically changing, thus new political front-pieces will accommodate the new, emerging reality.

Europeanisation and Greek political parties

Ideology and policy stance

Do 'Europe' and the Europeanisation process play a role in the change described above? Studying the Greek political parties leads one to the conclusion that 'Europeanisation' has had a *mixed* influence. On one hand, for both power parties (the ND and PASOK) 'Europeanisation' has been a common ideological goal, as displayed by their manifestos. This common perspective had resulted, particularly since the mid-1990s, to a downgrading of their ideological and agenda differences as well as to a convergence of the economic and social policies pursued. On the other hand, the stance towards 'Europe' has not developed into a cleavage for Greek society, pushing political parties apart or internally dividing them, as has been the case in France, for example. The distinction between the 'big systemic parties' and 'small' ones is not one between 'pro-' and 'anti-' Europe in the Greek case. The 'European issue' has been neither visible nor allured to at the domestic party competition field, unlike other countries.[1]

That said, we should also note that at the diametric opposite of the ND's and PASOK's 'pro-European' view we find the communist KKE and ultra-conserv-ative LAOS; SYRIZA has lately become more critical of Europe. Yet, there are different reasons for each party's stance. The KKE, employing an anti-US and anti-imperialistic political discourse, considers 'Europe' to be subjected to US economic and military priorities. Thus, one can find anti-European elements in this party's political discourse; yet these are *secondary*. This is why, as we will show, the KKE's voters are characterised by a high ambivalence on the issue of Europe. The same political logic is more or less typical of LAOS. Thus, while the majority of the so-called 'Eurosceptics' are to be found in these two parties, these individuals do not constitute a clear majority of their voters. Further, and more importantly, the ideological-political make-up of either the KKE or LAOS is not founded on these Eurosceptics.

Moreover, SYRIZA's case is the most complex. In the past, the most impor-tant Greek New Left party, SYN, had been in favour of the country's European focus and had supported both politically, and on the floor of the Parliament all the ratifications of European treaties. Yet, a few years ago the SYN, with a number of different leftist groupings (Euro-communists, Maoists, Trotskyists, ecologists, autonomous, etc.) came together in creating a new coalition party, SYRIZA. This new party has been strongly critical of EU policies as well the proposed Lisbon Treaty, largely because of its overall opposition to neo-liberalism. The current economic crisis had only strengthened the party's critical stance.

Finally, the Ecologist Greens' Founding Conference (May 2003) failed to reach a general agreement on its 'Guiding Document on Europe' (the only one of all the topics debated that failed secure agreement) and delegated the issue to a new conference set for December 2003. Yet, this party was not anti-Europe, as had been the case for other European Green parties.[2] Furthermore, the EG has generally been in favour of monetary union, EU enlargement, the common European foreign and defence policies (although under certain qualifications), the creation of a federal EU without national vetoes and the adoption of a European Constitution. Such a positive pro-EU stance is bluntly connected to Greece's poor standing vis-à-vis the rest of Europe.[3] However, the Greek Greens have criticised their European counterparts. Of the various suggestions debated at the party's two Conferences (2003 and 2007), it was overwhelmingly approved that it is the Greek Green's objective 'to avoid any repetition of the criminal support to the [NATO] bombing of Yugoslavia in 1999, which opened the way to the "Coalitions of the Willing" and the military interventions in Afghanistan [2001] and Iraq [2003]', a course of action notoriously supported by the German Greens and their serving Minister for Foreign Affairs, Joschka Fischer.[4]

Organisation

Europe had different effects on different Greek parties' organisation. For example, some Greek parties have specialised sections or secretariats dealing with Europe, although not exclusively, but as part of the broader 'international relations' framework. Thus the ND has a Secretariat for International Relations and the EU, PASOK has a Section for Foreign Affairs-International Relations (headed by a serving Member of the European Parliament – MEP). Only SYN (the largest party in the SYRIZA coalition) has a specialised Department for European Policies – interestingly enough, distinct from the Department for Foreign Affairs. In comparison, LAOS and KKE do not have a specialised committee for EU affairs (or for any other topic for that matter).

Concerning the selection of candidates, party structures have retained a strong grip on the selection of Members of the European Parliament (MEPs). For elections to the European Parliament (EP), the whole country forms a single constituency with voters selecting a single party list. The party leadership has the final say concerning placement on that list, in effect deciding who gets elected and who does not. Especially for the two power parties, a term (or more) in Brussels has often been either a grooming period leading for the centre stage of national politics for younger aspirants, or an honorary way out for older party cadres.

For smaller parties, the European elections have been a welcome opportunity to increase their share of the vote and/or to overcome national debacles and wait to fight another (national election) day. The latter has been the case for both the SYN and LAOS. The SYN managed to elect two MEPs at the June 1994 European election, following its failure to get into the national parliament the year before, and was back into national politics by 1996. Similarly, LAOS, created in 2000 and narrowly missing the 3 per cent threshold in the March 2004 national election, had its president elected as an MEP in the European elections of 2004; the next stop was the national parliament in 2007. Also, other minor/extra-parliamentary parties have obtained positive results in the 'second-order' European elections.

Traditionally though, the European elections' political agenda has remained focused on national issues.[5]

At the national election of 2007, the Greek Greens secured their highest vote-share ever and overnight became a rising political force. Various opinions polls suggest they might both elect an MEP as well as make it into the national parliament. With the stakes rising, all candidates for the European election list of 2009 were allowed to circulate a brief introductory letter to party members, although references to Europe were largely absent. During the party's conference in December 2008, where the candidates' list was announced, the feeling was that both the selection procedure and the (ensuing) discussion were but the prelude to the next – and more important – milestone: the *national* elections. For the first time since the party's creation four years earlier, there were some feelings of resentment over the selection procedure and talk of 'opponents' neutralisation' via strategic voting. At the European election of 2009, the Greek Greens returned their first ever MEP (a seasoned activist), a development that furthered increased the relevance of European politics for the party.

National rivalries have not influenced the Greek parties' affiliation with political groups in the EP, perhaps attesting to the lack of significance some Greek political parties ascribe to such affiliations. However, quite expectedly, the ND sided with the European Peoples' Party (EPP), PASOK with the socialists' group, LAOS with the independence/democracy group and the EG with the European Greens. The KKE and SYRIZA, embittered former comrades who avoided any kind of co-operation in Greece,[6] are both members of the 'European United Left-Nordic Green Left', in the absence of any other alternative.

What does 'Europe' stand for? Turning to the voters

Obviously, the Europeanisation process influences parties through altering the public's (and voters') perceptions of Europe. In this section, we go into greater detail in analysing the Greek public's European views. Such an exercise allows us to better understand and account for possible influences on the Greek party system in general and political parties in particular.

In ideological terms, the Greek people have been 'pro-Europe'. According to the Eurobarometer surveys between 1995 and 2005, the percentage of those agreeing that 'Greece's participation in the EU is a good thing' stood between 56 and 70 per cent. Similarly, in a relevant question asking whether 'Greece has benefited from EU membership', the percentages are equally high, between 65 and 80 per cent.[7]

This stance is supported by national studies[8] exploring the Greek public's political opinions and behaviour. Thus Greek opinion of the EU has been 'positive', scoring between 60 and 75 per cent for the years 1996 to 2011. The country's participation in European Monetary Union (EMU), a strategic goal for both the ND and PASOK, has been supported by 64–72 per cent of respondents (14–20 per cent voted against it). In 2010, amid the current economic crisis, 63 per cent of Greeks were against leaving the Euro despite the fact that its introduction was considered to have a negative impact on the Greek economy (55 per cent). It is important to note that the EMU proponents covered the whole party and Greek political spectrum: according to surveys in 2000 – the year when Greece became officially an EMU member – PASOK voters were in favour by 78 per cent, the ND's supporters by 70 per cent, and even followers of SYRIZA by 71 per cent. Those that took a different view were the KKE's voters: only 36 per cent were in favour with 51 per cent opposed. As late as 2005, and despite the scepticism induced by the issue of the European Constitution, 73 per cent of Greek voters were in favour of Europe's political union (for the ND, voters totalled 82 per cent; for PASOK, 66 per cent; 74 per cent for the leftist parties (SYRIZA and KKE); and 65 per cent for the lesser political parties). Based on these surveys, one reaches the conclusion that 'pro-Europeanism' has been for a long time and so far is the dominant ideological stance for Greek voters.

However, one has to go beneath the surface, to look for the constituent parts of this attitude. In other words, one has to seek out the material preconditions, the dominant ideological and political characteristics, as well as the internal contradictions of this sweeping support for 'Europe'.[9] Based on the available data, we put forward three suggestions:

Greek society's 'pro-Europeanism' is directly related to expectations of economic development and political modernisation for the country. The results of an opinion poll in 1997 (VPRC 1997) showed that three out of the four 'main benefits' of the Greek EU membership are related either to the country's general economic situation or to the respondent's personal position, namely 'the country's economic development' (mentioned by 67 per cent of the respondents), 'raising the citizens' standard of living' (60 per cent) and 'curbing inflation' (50 per cent). However, those that thought EU membership had a positive effect on reducing unemployment rates were a mere 29 per cent. *A fortiori*, 59 per cent thought that EU policies actually had a negative influence on efforts to reduce unemployment (an issue we will return to later). Thus, the Greek public has been 'pro-European' to the extent that it anticipated – and largely achieved – a higher economic, material and consumptive standard of living due to the country's EU membership. The Greek society's 'pro-Europeanism', starting with the restoration of democracy in 1974 and reaching to the present, is closely related to expectations for economic development and for the withering away of all the symptoms of social backwardness. As a consequence, the current economic crisis has dealt a heavy blow to the image of the European Union in Greek public opinion: only 18% of citizens trust its policies concerning the Greek economic crisis, (against 76% who do not trust). This opinion holds across the political spectrum (77% of ND voters, 75% of PASOK voters and 95% among voters of leftist parties (KKE and SYRIZA). The dissatisfaction with the economic crisis and social policies implemented in the last two years has affected the core of the pro-European ideology in Greece.

This 'pro-European' feeling is directly linked to a feeling of insecurity, springing from issues concerning Greek-Turkish relations and the 'external threat to the country'. The fourth 'main benefit' of the Greek EU-membership according to the aforementioned survey of 1997 was 'benefits on foreign policy and defence' (54 per cent of respondents mentioned it). The Greek public considers the EU to be the de facto security umbrella against Turkey's 'threat'. This deep-seated psychological view helps us to understand the *prima facie* contradictory views of the Greeks concerning the Turkish bid for EU membership. According to research (VPRC 2005), although the Greek public was against Turkey becoming a full EU member (in favour: 28.8 per cent; against: 57.7 per cent; neutral/no opinion: 13.5 per cent[10]), at the same time they thought that in such a case 'Greece would be threatened less' (55 per cent agreeing).

This 'pro-Europeanism' also exhibits some strong 'nation-centrist'[11] elements, which hint to the existence of a latent 'Eurosceptic' tendency, not (yet) independently articulated, but nevertheless present at the very core of the Greek 'pro-European' views. The main evidence supporting this view is a strong feeling of threat that runs across Greek society and has to do with Greek national identity, i.e. 'Greekness' (*Helenekoteta*). In tandem with the economic and political benefits accompanying EU membership, the majority of Greeks also consider that the EU poses a threat to national identity. In other words, it is felt (and feared) that a 'denaturation' of the national identity following the inclusion to a broader socio-political context might be the necessary price for all other economic and political benefits. As shown in Table 6.1, this feeling is held by the majority of respondents.

Table 6.1: 'We run a risk to lose our national identity in Europe' (percentages)

	1998	1999	2001	2002	2003	2007	2008
Agree + Rather agree	52	58	62	51	53	51	45
Disagree + Rather disagree	27	22	22	28	30	26	38

Source: *VPRC (Yearly Political Behaviour Research)*

This feeling of the national identity 'being at risk' within a European context runs across the party system. Forty-five per cent of PASOK voters share this view, alongside 60 per cent for the ND, 66 per cent for the KKE, 40 per cent for SYRIZA and 80 per cent for the LAOS voters (data for the year 2004). It also runs across all social classes: 47 per cent of the upper social strata agree; 55 per cent of middle social strata; 46 per cent of the lower (yet relatively financially secured) strata;

and, finally, 55 per cent of the 'poor' (those social groups that are below or very near the official poverty threshold).[12]

Such data leads us to argue that 'pro-Europeanism' is a dominant ideology and choice for the Greek public, articulated on specific economic and political expectations and underpinned on notions of 'development' and 'security'. This ideology's strong influence has so far not allowed for a counter 'Eurosceptic' stance from the other end of the spectrum to emerge, in spite of (or rather because?) the fact that one can find 'Eurosceptical' dimensions *within* this very 'pro-European' stance. Finally, the importance of political parties and the traditional influence of the bipartite system have entrenched, at least to a certain degree, the ideological and political framework, leaving no space for a Eurosceptic party to emerge.

Yet, one cannot ignore the dynamics at play under the surface. Since this 'pro-European' feeling has had strong utilitarian and 'inward-looking' characteristics, there is a chance that in the future it could come under strong criticism, provided that the current, reinforcing framework withers. To the extent that the expectations for economic development exhaust themselves while a sense of national security becomes more commonplace amongst Greeks, it is probable that their views concerning Europe will change, or that other ideological dimensions will come also to the fore. As we have already mentioned, on the issue of unemployment – an important aspect of the social agenda – the European influence is not considered positive; in fact, quite the contrary. This is an important issue that relates to EU social cohesion policies and could, under certain conditions, lead to important realignments in the pro-Europe and Eurosceptic camps, by strengthening the existing 'nation-centrist' tendencies of the Greek public. One should also note that there are now more political parties available to accommodate such Eurosceptic views. The unfolding economic crisis facing Greece over the last two years has fed significantly into the EU criticism. The debt crisis has led the Greek government, under pressure from Europe, into introducing a number of extreme neoliberal policies (cutting wages and pensions as well as shrinking the social welfare. These policies, which were implemented under the directions of the IMF and the European Commission, did impact on the traditional Greek 'pro-Europeanism'. Thus, the dissatisfaction with the European Union has greatly increased, despite the fact that calls for leaving the Eurozone are still a minority amongst the Greek public (30%). It is obvious that the crisis is having, and will have, important repercussions on the Greek parties' and voters' views on Europe. Yet, due to space restrictions and the developing character of the events (in particular the creation of splinter and new political parties across the political spectrum, whose survival will be put to the test in the forthcoming national election (early summer 2012), we are not able to discuss with greater detail where this process may lead.

Conclusions

It is appropriate to link our conclusions to the general theme of analysing the 'Mair/Ladrech paradox' guiding this book. Mair has argued that Europeanisation has little (if any) *direct* effect on national party systems.[13] The Greek case confirms that this has been indeed the case. Neither the format nor mechanisms of the party system have been drastically altered by the Europeanisation process, as we have shown in the first section of this contribution, save for the brief period prior to Greece's accession in the early 1980s. At that time, the rising PASOK was staunchly anti-European, rhetorically equating the EC with NATO and appearing as the guarantor of national interests vis-à-vis the ruling conservatives' supposed 'subordination' to the West.

However, once in power in 1981, PASOK proved to be a pro-European (albeit grudgingly) political party, while over the years both the socialists and conservatives converged towards a very similar pro-European position. Here we find evidence of Mair's *indirect* influence of Europeanisation on party systems. The constraints (or obligations) following EU-membership have shaped both the ruling parties' policy options, which had been justified by and had referred to the widely acceptable European framework of 'doing business'. Thus, and in accordance with Ladrech's view[14] of 'policy/programmatic [EU-induced] change', both PASOK's and the ND's 'grand visions' for a major renovation of the Greek polity ('modernisation' for the socialists and 're-establishing the state' for the conservatives) were modelled on European-inspired 'good practices' and defended on the grounds of helping Greece's social and political convergence with the rest of Europe.

Our analysis shows that organisational changes have been small and rather inconsequential. This has to do with the fact that any of the ideological differences between Greek political parties over Europe are only secondary and do not constitute a prime dividing line. Nevertheless, this broad-stroke description misses some of the telling differences that render support to Ladrech's (2002) claim for the differentiated sensitivity of individual parties to the process of Europeanisation. This is particularly relevant to the minor Greek political parties. Apart from serving (at least, for some of them) as an electoral springboard into national politics, scepticism over Europe has been, differentially, accommodated into their ideological arsenal. Thus for the KKE, the European level has been used as another facet of US hegemony; for SYRIZA it was the domain where neo-liberal policies are forged; while for LAOS it was a possible threat to national identity. For the (extra-parliamentary) Ecologist Greens, the Europeanisation process has had the most important effect: it has offered the party much needed visibility as well as providing the only, to date, framework for arranging the intra-party power configuration. In the absence of national relevance, the European dimension has been a rallying point while the relevant positions (e.g. MEP candidates, international delegates and so on) had been the only source of leverage to be managed and/or controlled.

Has Europeanisation contributed to the Greeks' depoliticisation? Surely the citizens do turn out to vote in European elections in large numbers (albeit lower than national elections, yet still much higher than the European average). Yet it would not be an exaggeration to say that, for the Greek people, European politics are but the continuation of national politics by other means. This is primarily because European issues have not caused any major shift in the axis of political competition. Despite the (bloc of) parties' differences over Europe, which we have referred to, both the pro- and the anti-European feeling has not yet emerged as the characteristic feature of any single political party. To that extent, Mair's view only partly fits with the Greek reality. The 'issue of Europe' does *not* figure in national elections, as one would have expected due to either a 'realistic/traditional' or to a 'strategic' (i.e. aiming at 'depoliticising' the voters) course of action by individual parties; yet, *neither* does it figure in the European elections.[15]

The reason for this is that for the Greek political power parties, 'Europe' had been a strategic choice, a choice that both contributed to the citizens' well-being and, perhaps more importantly, was 'shielding' the country against external threats. EU membership has offered the country much needed leverage in its external relations, traditionally vis-à-vis Turkey and, more recently, the FYR of Macedonia. This frame of mind is particularly apparent in the case of Cyprus's EU-candidacy (and eventual membership), which has been promoted by the Greek (and Cypriot) political elites as the only viable way of resolving the 'Greek Cypriot/Turkish Cypriot' problem – by turning it into a 'European Cyprus-Turkish' one.

Set within such a framework, the Greek public have come to accept this rationalisation and, accordingly, never seriously questioned the wisdom of EU membership or policies. And the existence of such a hegemonic discourse, ascertained that Europeanisation could have had no unsettling effects for either the Greek party system or the parties themselves. Additionally, the sustained influx of EC funds made sure that the rhetoric had been coupled with tangible evidence.

This combination has so far insulated the Greek party system from the Europeanisation effects. However, it now seems that the expectations of economic development, which have been the motor of the Greek 'pro-Europeanism', are gradually withering. Issues of social cohesion are coming to the fore, spearheaded by calls to fight unemployment. On this particular issue, Greeks have felt that EU-membership has not offered them enough. To date, this negative view had been counterbalanced by the other benefits offered. Yet nowadays we are witnessing the closing of that first historic circle: having achieved economic development in the 1980s and 1990s, the demands of the social agenda have now changed and issues of unemployment, poverty and social cohesion are coming to the front of the stage.

The Greek party system is also changing: it is moving away from the historic dividing line of the 'right' and 'anti-right' (which had been synonymous to the antithesis between the ND and PASOK) to a juxtaposition between systemic and anti-systemic parties. The former consists of the two power parties, the centre-right ND and the centre-left PASOK. The rapprochement of those two powerful parties is characterised not simply by their 'pro-European' ideology, but also, as we have argued, by their acceptance of the EU's strategic governance options: although they advocate different 'managerial' approaches, these are nevertheless politically sanctioned by the existing EU 'orthodoxy'. Emerging from the other end of the spectrum are the Greek leftist parties and the LAOS. This camp argues that the policies promoted by the EU should be transcended, advocating active state intervention and curtailment of the free market dynamics. The latest fiscal crisis has reinforced these tendencies for the Greek political system, with the social agenda becoming a dividing line for the political forces.

Another, albeit secondary, agenda refers to environmental issues, a topic particularly prominent for SYRIZA and the Greens, who refer to it as part of their broader social and redistributive political goals. Keeping in mind that these issues also feature prominently amongst EU priorities, one could speculate that, in the years to come, the Europeanisation process will have a greater impact on the Greek political system and parties than it has exercised so far.

Postscript March 2012: the Greek party system in turmoil

The ongoing fiscal crisis facing Greece has had serious repercussions for the Greek party system. While a detailed analysis of the current situation is clearly out of the scope of this chapter as future developments can only be guessed at this stage, we offer a brief account of what has occurred over the past few months. We realise that by the time you will be reading these lines a great deal would have changed – and most likely in a radical way- since the forthcoming national elections (due for May 2012) are widely expected to reshuffle the Greek party system. Thus, the following lines are but a snapshot of the, rapidly changing, Greek political landscape.

In early November 2011, the beleaguered PASOK ruling government got herself into fresh trouble when PM George Papandreou announced his intention to hold a referendum on whether the country should accept the EU/IMF new bailout proposal (which came with new and harsher austerity measures). Faced with strong reactions, Papandreou was ready to drop his proposal if the opposition parties would join the Socialists in a coalition government. On November 10, PASOK, ND and LAOS agreed on a 'National Utility' government headed by former European Central Bank vice-president, Lucas Papademos. The new government's main goal was to approve the new bail-out deal and lead the country into fresh elections (originally envisaged for mid-February 2012).

In early February 2012, LAOS withdrew from the government, after refusing to support the proposed deal. While PASOK and the ND eventually approved it on February 13, scores of their MPs resigned in protest, declared themselves 'independent', or voted down the deal- and were subsequently expelled from their respective parties. These expulsions led to the creation of two more new parties. On the centre-right, *Anexartitoi Ellines* (Independent Greeks, established on February 24) brings together a number of former ND MPs and party cadres. On the centre-left, *Koinoniki Symfonia* (Social Deal, established on March 14, 2012) is chaired by two former ministers of the PASOK government. Thus, two more new parties were added to a quickly growing list, including (most importantly), the centre-right *Dimokratiki Symachea* (Democratic Coalition, a ND splinter-party established in November 2010) and the centre-left *Dimokratiki Aristera* (Democratic Left, a SYRIZA splinter-party established in June 2010). It is worth noting that while only 5 parties made it into the Parliament following the 2009 election, currently there exist 10 parties and a number of independent MPs.

The dead reckoning for the current Greek party system will occur at the next election (May 2012). While many talk about a 'melt-down' of the traditional parties (especially PASOK and ND), no clear projections can be made at this point, save that it is well unlikely that any single party will ensure the parliamentary majority. As a final note, we present the various parties' share of votes at the last national elections (October 2009) and their projected share-of-the vote at the time of writing.[16] The figures are quite telling.

	In **bold** are the parties represented in Parliament at the time of writing	Vote share, % (October 2009)	Projection of vote share, % (March 2012)
		A party needs > 3% of the vote to elect any MPs	
Left	**KKE**	7.54	12.5 (±0.8)
	SYRIZA	4.60	12.0 (± 0.8)
	Ecologists Greens	2.53	2.5 (±0.4)
	All Greek Citizen's Chariot	Splinter Party	1.5 (±0.3)
	Democratic Left	Splinter party	11.5 (±0.8)
	Social Deal	Splinter party	< 1.0
	PASOK	43.92	12.5 (±0.8)
	ND	33.48	22.5 (±1.0)
	Democratic Alliance	Splinter party	2.0 (±0.3)
	Independent Greeks	Splinter Party	11.0 (±0.7)
Right	**LAOS**	5.63	3.0 (±0.4)
	Hrisi Avgi (Golden Dawn)	0.29	3.5 (±0.4)

Note: The Left-Right positioning of the various parties is indicative. We opted for including the Ecologists Greens and *Hrisi Avgi* since, at the time of writing, they look likely to elect MPs.

Notes

1. G. Ross, 'Europe becomes French Domestic Politics', in M. Lewis-Beck (ed.), *How France Votes*, New York, Seven Bridges Press, 2000, pp. 87–114. See also, C. Belot and B. Cautrès, 'L'Europe, invisible mais omniprésente', in B. Cautrès and N. Mayer (eds), *Le nouveau désordre électoral: Les leçons du 21 avril 2002*, Paris, Presses de Sciences Po, 2004, pp. 119–41. See also, B. Cautrès and V. Tiberj, *Une sanction du gouvernement mais pas de l'Europe: Les élections européennes de juin 2004, Paris*, Cahiers du CEVIPOF, no. 41, 2005.

2. E. Bomberg, 'The Europeanisation of Green Parties: exploring the EU's impact', *West European Politics*, 2002, vol. 25 (3), pp. 29–50.

3. *Prassini Politiki* , 2003, vol.6, no.37.

4. *ibid.*

5. Y. Mavris, 'The European Elections of June 13, 2004: the second round of the national elections', *Political Science*, 2005, 1, pp. 89–101 [in Greek]. See also, M. Mendrinou, 'European elections and minor political parties in Greek politics', in C. Vernardakis (ed.), *The Public Opinion in Greece 2003*, Athens, Savallas, 2004, pp. 13–40 [in Greek]. See also, E. Teperoglou and S. Skrinis, 'The second-order elections model and the European Election of June 13, 2004 in Greece', *Hellenic Review of Political Science*, 2006, 27, pp. 126–47 [in Greek].

6. See M. Boudourides and I. Botetzagias, 'Networks of protest on global issues in Greece 2002–3', in D. Purdue (ed.), *Civil Societies and Social Movements: Potentials and Problems,* Routledge/ECPR Studies in European Political Science, London, 2007, pp. 109–123.

7. In a 2005 opinion poll (VPRC 2005) 46 per cent thought that 'Greece benefits from the current EU policies' (32 per cent were against while 22 per cent hold the middle position and/or gave no answer).

8. V-PRC (*Yearly Political Behaviour Research*) 1996–2011.

9. C. Vernardakis, 'Pro-Europeanism and Euro-scepticism in Greece: ideological dimensions and political representations', in C. Vernardakis (ed.), *The Public Opinion in Greece 2005–2006*, Savallas, Athens, 2007, [in Greek]. See also, C. Belot, 'Les logiques sociologiques de soutien au processus d'intégration européenne: éléments d'interprétation', *Revue internationale de politique comparée*, 2002, vol. 9 (1), pp. 11–29.

10. The Greeks have been traditionally hostile to the Turkish bid for membership. Back in 1999, 43 per cent were against (31 per cent in favour), while in 2004, 54 per cent were against (34 per cent in favour).

11. According to Mayer and Roux (p.98) the concept of 'nation-centrism' allows us to delimit the ideological practices of (social) inclusion or exclusion of different societal groups on the basis of culture and not their racial (national) character. N. Mayer and G. Roux, 'Des votes xénophobes?', in B. Cautrès and N. Mayer (eds), *Le nouveau désordre électoral: Les leçons du 21 avril 2002*, Paris, Presses de Sciences Po, 2004, pp. 97–117. See also, M. Baimbridge, B. Burkitt and M. Macey, 'The Maastricht Treaty: exacerbating racism in Europe?', *Ethnic and Racial Studies*, 1994, vol.17 (3), pp. 420–41.

12. This classification is based on an index of social integration, including vari-

ables such as the respondent's income, educational attainment, employment and position, property assets as well as possession of consumerist items.

13. P. Mair, 'The limited impact of Europe on national party systems', *West European Politics*, 2000, vol. 23 (4), pp. 27–51.

14. R. Ladrech, 'Europeanisation and political parties: towards a framework for analysis', *Party Politics*, 2002, vol. 8 (4), pp. 389–403.

15. Thus, in the latest Eurobarometer survey dealing with the European elections of 2009, Greeks (and Cypriots) top the EU-27 list by claiming that the main criterion in the forthcoming election would be the 'candidates' position on national issues' (33 per cent vs. 16 per cent of the EU-27 average). Special Eurobarometer 299, 'The 2009 European elections', http://ec.europa.eu/public_opinion/archives/ebs/ebs_299_en.pdf [accessed 20 January 2009]. The reader should note that for the Greeks, 'national issues' are the external affairs issues (such as the Cyprus problem, the national minorities' issues, the problems with Turkey and FYR Macedonia). If the researchers wished to investigate the importance of 'national *aka* domestic' issues for the Greek public, then their particular choice of language is rather inappropriate for the Greek context.

16. VPRC opinion poll, March 2012, available in Greek at: http://www.vprc.gr/uplds/File/teleytaia%20nea/Epikaira/Graphs_Political%20Conjuncture_Mar2012.pdf

chapter seven | the spanish party system and european integration – a consensual europeanisation[1]

Rafael Vázquez-García

Introduction – Spain in Europe

The death of Franco in 1975 saw the commencement of a successful transition – led by the desire of the majority of Spaniards – to rejoin the family of Western democratic nations, especially the increasingly powerful European Community (EC).[2] While Franco's regime was isolationist, authoritarian, highly centralised and repressive of national minorities, the new Spain would be European, democratic and decentralised.[3] In this sense, the Spanish Constitution, which was approved in December 1978, reflected these aspirations and associated compromises. In the words of Loughlin and Handy (2006):

> The democratization of Spain was a preparation for entry into Europe and, at the same time, the prospect of Europeanisation was a powerful stimulus towards democracy. Most Spaniards at the time of Franco's death were very keen to reconnect with the rest of Europe and wished to put the past behind them.[4]

Even before the accession, Spanish political elites identified national interests with European interests. As some historians and scholars have remarked, the newly-created social democratic state was constructed in part around the notion of the myth of Europe, which epitomised everything that was modern.

Entry into the EC in 1986 was supported by key sectors of Spanish society: the army, the church, trade unions and political parties. Thus, Spain's European vocation exerted a powerful unifying influence over political life: 'Throughout the years since its accession into the European Union, Spain was both an ardent supporter of integration and a major beneficiary of its largesse, largely through Structural and Cohesion Funds.'[5]

During Prime Minister Felipe González's terms in government, Spain held two presidencies of the Council of the European Union. In 1989, González pushed forward issues of the so-called 'Social Europe' leading up to the Charter of Fundamental Workers' Rights. This was quite a prestigious and important achievement for the Spanish Government, which wanted to become an active player both in the European integration process as well as on the world stage. As Closa has indicated, the existence of a democratic state in Spain is almost unthinkable outside of its incorporation into European integration. Most importantly, its membership to the EEC guaranteed greater political and social stability. The successful result can be understood as a symbiosis between integration and democratisation, both of which were supported by public opinion as well as political forces.[6]

Europeanisation and the Spanish party system

Nowadays, the political cleavages in the modern Spanish party system are two-fold: the left-right cleavage, and the territorial cleavage. The left-right cleavage is still important in contemporary Spain, but expresses itself in much less stark terms than in earlier periods. National politics is in fact dominated by two large political blocs, led by the leftist *Partido Socialista Obrero Español* (PSOE) and the conservative *Partido Popular* (PP). However, these are now essentially centre-left and centre-right, which, in many aspects, leaves little to differentiate their policies except for individual rights and welfare, as well as nuances on Spanish membership. For Loughlin and Hanley, 'This centrist orientation of the two parties harmonizes well with the mood of the country and the extremes of both right and left are relegated to the political wilderness.'[7] As a crucial dimension of the party system itself in the case of both Greece and Spain, these patterns took shape rather quickly since adopting – almost from the very beginning – a very clear logic of competition, pitting one large right-wing party against one large left-wing party.[8]

The state-wide party system, therefore, can be defined as one of moderate bipolarism. Since the first democratic elections, Spanish voters have decided between the PSOE, a moderate social democratic party, (in power from 1982 to 1996, and 2004 to 2011), and a moderate conservative party, be it the *Unión de Centro Democrático* (UCD) during the first two general elections (1977, 1979), or the PP – formerly *Alianza Popular* – (1996 to 2004). Under normal circumstances, the government can presently be formed by the PSOE or PP. If neither party wins a clear majority (more than 50 per cent of seats in the low chamber), the regional-nationalist parties come into their own, as occurred after the elections in 1993 and 1996, with *Convergència i Unió* (CiU) and *Basque Nationalist Party* (PNV), and to some extent in 2004 and 2008 with several parties playing an important 'pivotal' role.

The acceptance by the *Partido Comunista Español* (PCE) of 'Eurocommunism', as well as the absence of an extreme right-wing force, did not eliminate a polarised multiparty system, but drastically reduced the possibilities.[9] In other words, the Spanish electorate has not only tended to vote for just a few parties, but also for moderate ones. Since the 1970s, when most voters initially chose centre-right parties (such as the UCD), the majority has since switched to the centre-left (such as the PSOE) and, later still (1996–2004), to parties such as the PP, which fluctuate between the right and centre-right. Democratic parties have covered almost the entire parliamentary spectrum, whilst the extremist parties have obtained minimal support.

Spain remains a country of geographical contrasts that overlap nationalist, linguistic, and cultural cleavages. Traditionally, the economic dynamism of the country has been situated in the north, specifically in the Basque Country and Catalonia, while the south has been underdeveloped economically. Important sections of the population in both regions, at the elite level as well as that of the masses, consider themselves to be 'stateless nations' and simply not a part of the Spanish nation. Furthermore, like most states that combine a central government with sub-national institutions endowed with specific degrees of autonomy, Spain does not have a one-party system, but several. In addition to a recognisable state-wide system of parties, there exists in every autonomous community a regional party system, whose actors may well include state-wide – or their regional branches – as well as exclusively regional parties.

The case of the Spanish party system is notable for its *consensus* in favour of European membership and integration – both throughout the Spanish population and across the political spectrum – while there is comparative *lack of debate* within Spanish society on the question of European integration.[10] Yet, popular support for the integration process has been invariably high and visible since 1986[11] and confidence in European institutions has remained remarkably strong during the last few decades.[12] Public opinion polls taken at regular intervals since 1986 have consistently revealed that the proportion of the Spanish public who favourably evaluate EU membership has exceeded 50 per cent, while the proportion of those regarding EU accession as a negative development has run at between 10 per cent and 15 per cent. Unlike voters in France and Netherlands, Spanish citizens voted clearly in favour of the European Constitution (77 per cent) during the February 2005 referendum. However, political support for European integration has always been somewhat lower among citizens than among the political elite.[13]

As has been demonstrated, political culture in Spain is deeply imbued with an awareness of the significance that the European dimension has held since 1975. MacLennan emphatically asserts that 'a very significant characteristic in Spain was the absence of Euroscepticism or proposal of alternatives to European integration'.[14] Thus, no significant opposition to European integration made progress in Spain, as suggested by the fact that, except for marginal right-wing parties, no parties have used Eurosceptic discourse. In Spain, as in Italy, Europe was to remain identified with liberty, modernisation and prosperity.[15] In contrast to Greece and Portugal, the consensus in Spain in favour of European integration among state-wide parties has always been absolute. The UCD and PP have agreed with European ideals since the beginning, thus the 'Europeanism' of Spanish socialists did not need to undergo a similar process of evolution as it did to some extent in Greece or Portugal.[16]

Europeanisation and Spain's individual parties

In this section, it is relevant to distinguish between state-wide political parties (UCD, PSOE, AP-PP, and PCE-IU) and peripheral parties, all of which are nationalist (CiU, PNV, and ERC).

State-wide parties – ideology and policy stance

The Union of the Democratic Centre (*Unión de Centro Democrático* (UCD)) was the first party in power after Franco's death. It always maintained European integration as a priority and, like most political groups coming from the Francoist regime, *Alianza Popular* (the future PP) being one example, defended the right to participate as a full member in the political and economic dealings of Europe. The European project fitted very well within the internal party programme, which was focused on democratic principles associated with a market economy and few interventions from the state.[17]

The Spanish Socialist Workers' Party (*Partido Socialista Obrero Español* (PSOE)) and the other national democratic and socialist organisations supported the idea of European membership from the beginning, even during their period of political exile. The PSOE is generally considered to be the most European of Spanish political parties and European integration provided the party with a major framework for policy throughout its first period in power from 1982 to 1996. For more than a century 'the party has viewed Europe as being the solution to Spain's chronic historical problems of economic backwardness, authoritarianism and international isolation'.[18] Under the leadership of Felipe Gonzalez (beginning in 1974), the PSOE abandoned its Marxist rhetoric and all pretensions to socialist revolution by accepting the capitalist system.[19] As soon as it reached power, the party's main objective was to consolidate Spain's recently established democracy and transform the country in order to secure a place amongst Europe's leading group of countries. Many of the EU's national social democratic parties aided this transformation, most notably Germany's SPD (Social Democratic Party). In response to a survey conducted among leading political scientists in Europe, Leonard Ray remarked that the PSOE has always been the most enthusiastic and pro-European national political organisation, even before Spain's entry into the EEC. What is more, the PSOE, along with nationalist parties in Catalonia, has continually demonstrated the lowest levels of internal dissent towards European affairs.[20]

From 1982 to 1986, the PSOE introduced an ambitious economic plan in order to prepare the Spanish economy for the competitive characteristics of EC membership. By initiating dramatic industrial reform and important cuts in social spending, they aimed to liberalise the domestic economic regime and adapt it to European laws. The consequent accelerated liberalisation of the Spanish economy and modernisation of their economic structures following Spain's integration into the EC resulted in the progressive internationalisation (and Europeanisation) of domestic politics under socialist rule.[21]

Gonzalez's policy was clearly pro-European, but with more emphasis on economic modernisation and social cohesion within Europe than on federal construction.[22] Between 1986 and 1991, the economy was quickly opened up in accordance with the terms of the Act of Accession and, by 1987, a new concept of the socialists' roles in the common integration process were introduced through the *Nuevo Compromiso Europeo* (New European Commitment). The new agreement included redefining certain classic liberal principles to signify more labour market flexibility, more effectiveness and a demand for modernisation, while always referring to the social dialogue and consensus politics among actors, the defence of general interests and the maintenance of social welfare. Finally, between 1992 and 1996, Spain's economic policy was dominated by the government's (then controlled by the PSOE) efforts to meet the Maastricht convergence criteria for economic and monetary union. The government adopted privatisation in order to improve public finances and stock market flotation of public companies was greatly intensified. Also, EU integration served the PSOE both as a point of reference as well as providing it with political justification for unpopular policy decisions. At the same time however, the dilemma of simultaneously balancing the demands of the liberal economic framework provided by the European project and the more traditionally social democratic emphasis on public investment in welfare and social cohesion was acute.

Beyond economic policy, European integration had a remarkable influence on the PSOE's foreign and security policies. Regarding foreign policy, EU membership offered the PSOE the opportunity to further develop Spain's relationship with the two areas traditionally associated with Spanish foreign policy, the Mediterranean and Latin America. Furthermore, Spain has declared to support of the integration of the Western Balkans and Turkey into the EU. With respect to security policy, the PSOE was finally able to transcend Spain's historical international isolation by joining the EC and accepting the country's responsibilities within NATO. 'With Spain's entry into the Western European Union in 1988, the PSOE had brought the country's security arrangements in line with EU norms, enabling Spain to participate fully in the framework of European security.'[23] Throughout the past few years, a discourse has emerged concerning globalisation and its consequences and supporting a mutually-binding, pacifist Europe, with a strong and active citizenry, and defending a culturally-shared identity as a response to globalisation.

Analysis of Euro-manifestos from 1986 to 2004 clearly demonstrates the PSOE's continual support of the supranational level as the most effective for managing the majority of public policy issues. This is particularly true in the case of foreign affairs, defence issues, crime reduction, and judicial and environmental policies. With regard to social and employment policies, an evolution can be observed from a shared responsibility among multiple levels of government (supranational, national and sub-national) until the mid-1990s, to exclusively European level management. Conversely, the involvement of the national state is stronger with regard to immigration policy.

Alianza Popular, which later changed name to the *Partido Popular* (the Popular Party (PP)), was the closest group to Franco's regime. However, despite its origins, Alianza defended European integration and inclusion in the European Economic and Monetary Union as priorities in policy. Since the first national democratic elections in 1977, and despite the heterogeneous groups within the party, Manuel Fraga, the former minister during Franco's regime, was able to secure a solid commitment to Europe.[24] Henceforth, the PP has progressively increased its support for the European project and made its position clearer towards community affairs. However, there still remains some degree of internal dissent (especially by those who strongly support national sovereignty), which has been present over the last two decades.[25]

Entry into the European Community was presented as a great achievement for the party, although, for party members, it was important that the EU remained a union of national states and not a federal construction where national positions prevail. The PP has been in power from 1996 to 2004, during which time it strongly supported the European Union through pragmatic discourse. It asserted, however, that transfers of political domains in favour of transnational institutions should be limited to those that reinforce individual country's rights at the same time.[26] The PP is, undoubtedly, the party most impermeable to EU influences concerning national public policy. Although it has increasingly accepted a stronger European presence in its management of national issues, the party still tries to maintain power in favour of the Spanish state or, at the very least, disposed towards combined actions between Spain and the EU.

Prime Minister Aznar's first term in government also improved the participatory mechanisms of autonomous communities in Europe by creating the post of Autonomic Attaché in Brussels. Until 1993, party and policy positions pertaining to Europe focused on the defence of national privilege and a rigid opposition to political integration. However, its stance on European affairs became more optimistic as the important benefits that Spain derived from being an EU member state became apparent. Therefore, by 1996 the objective to achieve economic integration served as a justification for cuts in public expenditure and the creation of a budgetary austerity programme. The result was a shared position on European affairs with the PSOE, though, unlike the socialists, the PP favoured a non-federal Union with strong states and clearly recognised national rights for citizens.[27]

Spanish communists (PCE), by accepting Eurocommunism, have defended the adhesion of Spain to the EEC since their 8th Congress in 1972. Even before Franco's death, the PCE had distanced itself from Moscow and, as a consequence, was among the first of the European communist parties to develop the theory of Eurocommunism. The PSOE has been the dominant party of the left in Spain since the country's return to democracy, but its victory in the 1982 elections saw the first decline in the PCE vote, with many voters opting for a more modern left-wing alternative. In 1985, the PCE initiated a debate that focused on the need to form a leftist alliance, the result of which was the formation, in April 1986, of the *Izquierda Unida* (United Left (IU)). Apart from the PCE, the IU was formed by six other small parties and non-affiliated individuals.[28] Generally speaking, the Spanish Communists have never opposed European integration following Franco's death, despite objecting to some EU economic policies. Although the first criticisms arose around 1986, the economic crisis in the early 1990s led the IU to oppose both the Treaty of Maastricht in 1992 and the EU Constitution in 2005 (though not the Treaty of Amsterdam in 1997).

As previously noted, the IU is the only national Spanish political party to display real criticism of the economic and monetary integration project with the EU and, consequently, the party soon discovered that criticism of the European project was essentially committing electoral suicide. The IU's strategy in opposing Maastricht in 1992 and the EU Constitution in 2005 underlies what may be described as 'federalist maximalism' rather than Euroscepticism, reflecting a vote and coalition-seeking strategy.[29] Opposition to the Maastricht Treaty formed a part of the IU's strategy, including the use of soft, economics-based Euroscepticism. Since the opposition of the IU leadership to Maastricht was not wholeheartedly supported by rank and file members, this policy, like others related to European integration, must be seen as a tactical ploy to distinguish the party from the PSOE, its nearest ideological rival. Similar to the PSOE, the IU has clearly favoured the supranational level of government to conduct the majority of public policy decisions since 1986. However, it still confers an important role on the national state when dealing with social and employment policies, while environmental conservation requires the collaboration of all levels, led by European consensus.

Peripheral parties – ideology and policy stance

In recent years, we have witnessed growing literature on an under-studied party family, the regionalist political party.[30] Since European integration decreases the necessity for traditional large states, making smaller, more homogeneous states more viable,[31] the EU may be an unwitting ally of sub-national groups against central governments, thereby encouraging regionalist parties to be Europhiles. Many see a role for the EU in a revival and transformation of minority nationalism and some prospect for a European solution to long-standing questions on nationality.[32] Jolly (2007) says:

> Thus, for regional political entrepreneurs, European integration increases the credibility of demands for greater autonomy, ranging from independence to devolution to cultural rights, and therefore their parties' credibility. In return, this factor provides incentives for regionalist political parties to be pro-European Union or Europhiles.[33]

Contesting the centre-periphery cleavage, regionalist political parties should be more supportive of European integration precisely because the EU threatens national sovereignty.[34] Furthermore, the EU may be a friendlier environment for sub-national groups because it is multicultural, with no single dominant or pan-European identity.[35] Although there are important differences among minority nationalist parties on EU issues, commitments to post-sovereigntist conceptions of power sharing involving EU, state and sub-state authorities in many of those parties sustain common demands.[36] Thus, European integration implies a variety of changes that constrain the emancipation of 'nations without states' and the expansion of their main representatives, the ethno-regionalist parties. Hence, it comes as no surprise that, from the beginning of this process, some main ethno-regionalist parties opposed European integration due to the perspective of the widening of the gap between regional populations and supranational decision-making centres. However, 'as the Europeanisation of decision-making expanded and accelerated, paradoxically their Eurosceptic position gradually evolved into a rather strong Europhile stand.'[37]

Catalonian nationalists of the CiU defend the European Union as a whole as well as its economic dimension through the Economic and Monetary Union (EMU). In line with other regionalist and nationalist parties in Europe, the CiU observes the process of European integration as positive, since the process is perceived as eroding the absolute sovereignty of the member states and, in this way, opening up possibilities for the sub-state level of government. Moreover, Europe has always represented modernisation and openness compared with the involution, centralism and 'rejection' of the Spanish state. An important component of contemporary Catalanism is that of Europeanism. The vision of a 'Catalanised Spain' shared by the conservative Catalan Party of the early twentieth century, *Lliga Regionalista*, was transformed during the Franco regime into that of an 'Europeanised Catalonia'. Catalonia has acted as a 'bridge between Spain and Europe'.[38] The 'Europeanism' of contemporary Catalanism echoes a long tradition in Catalanist discourse, which has seen Catalonia as an integrally-European culture. Thus, the CiU has always been a strong supporter of European integration, especially through the Catalan government, the *Generalitat*, which has been at the vanguard of the European regional movement. The CiU is in favour of the most advanced programme for European integration, including the single currency and common foreign and security policies, but accompanies this with demands for the strict application of subsidiarity and a guaranteed role for regional interests. Therefore, the CiU supports the idea of shared sovereignty between the various levels of government involved in Europe, with equal respect for the language and identity of all the nations of the EU, whether they enjoy the recognition of statehood or not. At the practical level, the CiU has encouraged the Spanish state to enable Catalonia and the other autonomous communities to play a more important and direct role in EU policy making, especially in those areas that concern the policy competence of the regions in Spain. The CiU was a firm believer throughout the 1990s that globalisation and European integration were leading to the decline of the nation state.

The symbolic discourse of Europeanism has had less resonance in the Basque Country than in Catalonia, since there is a weaker historic basis for it. However, the PNV was converted to the cause of European integration by its contacts in the Christian Democratic International and by 1949 had modified its independence policy to call for national autonomy within a federal Europe. The PNV has been the voice of moderate Basque nationalism for well over a hundred years and has headed the regional government ever since autonomy was granted to the Basque Country in 1980. It clearly supports the EU Treaty and favours all measures of integration, including the single currency, but with an obvious emphasis on defending a Europe of nations as opposed to the only official Europe of states.[39] The ultimate goal of the PNV is clearly national independence within the EU, although this is expressed as a long-term aspiration rather an immediate aim.

The Republican Left of Catalonia (*Esquerra Republicana de Catalunya* (ERC)) takes a more radical stance, supporting Catalan independence, but this is a long-term aspiration linked to changes in Europe. The ERC's vision is of a Europe of the Peoples, in which the existing states fade away and small nations and regions take their place. Matters such as defence or currency would be handled by a European government, while other matters would be dealt with locally. The ERC supports the EU for two basic reasons:

1. Europe has always been an important element of Catalanism (in a similar way to the CiU); and

2. the ERC recognises the inevitability of European integration in political, economic and social terms.

Additionally, the party demands the establishment of a European federation, with a strong European government accountable to the European Parliament (EP). Therefore, the process of decentralisation in favour of regions will be inevitable. The ERC also supports the unique nature of Catalonia and seeks to establish it as a separate electoral constituency for European elections.

With the exception of marginal right-wing parties, all political parties supported the Spanish membership of the EU. Accordingly, it is useful to sum up the nuances of the debate between political parties on EU membership. To begin with, the PSOE was supportive of the membership of the EU before the break-up of the right-wing authoritarian regime – such as the Spanish communists, the PCE (1972). The PSOE showed the lowest level of internal dissent along with regionalist Catalonian parties. The PSOE saw many advantages for Spain: Europe is a solution to economic backwardness, authoritarianism and international isolation. It would allow the consolidation of democracy, the liberalisation of the economy and benefit the mechanism of financial redistribution. In contrast, the PP (the closest party to the Franco regime) supported progressive Spanish membership after the dictator's death. The internal dissent is important and owes much to the strength of national sovereignty. Accordingly, the PP promoted the idea of a union of national states. In opposition, the Basque PNV has defended national autonomy within a federal Europe. In addition, the ERC proposed the Europe of the Peoples. The PNV, the ERC and the CiU support European integration because they perceive it as an important means of eroding member states' sovereignty and providing new possibilities for regions.

Organisation

Regarding organisation, the starting point is that, historically, parties have been interested in transnational activity of some kind since almost their creation.[40] Thus, national parties have organised their representatives along transnational lines, according to party family, within these bodies.[41] With the entry into the EU, organisational changes in Spanish political parties have been twofold. First, perhaps less significant and in reference to the internal organisation, it seems that there are no substantive transformations in the process of Europeanisation except the creation of European (International) Affairs offices within the party.[42] More importantly, the second organisational change relates to external organisation. In this sense,

Spanish political parties have made considerable efforts to integrate themselves into European political groups, especially in the European Parliament. They have made possible a stronger cohesion of partisan structures, as well as more capability for community co-operation when acting as an instrument to improve positions on European integration, both inside federal groups as well as in national parties.[43] This is because the majority of Spanish political parties are members of transnational party federations in the EU. Therefore, in spite of the growing importance of EU politics, there is no position devoted exclusively to EU issues in the structure of political parties in the central office. Moreover, the party representative in the transnational party federation usually shares this role with other positions, e.g. the International Secretary.[44] The parties analysed have created some advisory groups that work on EU issues, but it is interesting to remark that even these specialised advisory groups are integrated within a wider advisory group devoted to foreign and international affairs and relations.

Simultaneously, and with regard to economic resources, it must be emphasised how Spanish EU membership and EP politics have entailed an additional source of funding for Spanish parties. They frequently use EP funds for organising workshops or seminars related to EU issues and, on occasion, for hiring personnel (in Spain and at the EP). In addition, some parties (such as the IU) also retain part of the salary of their MEPs. This pattern of funding implies that the main source of funds for EU-related party activity is not national party organisation, in spite of the extensive public subsidies received by Spanish political parties, but the funding and resources that come from the EP.[45] Finally, and before the analysis, it is interesting to note how the Europeanisation of party politics has implied that EP elections increasingly act as a barometer to measure the national political situation. Attitudes towards European integration are indeed capable of influencing choice at national elections,[46] although some analyses demonstrate that national voting remains the main focus for those citizens who have little interest in European affairs.[47] There is also evidence that public opinion helps shape elite preferences concerning the EU and vice versa.[48]

Conclusion

Entry into the European Economic Community in 1986 was supported by all sectors of Spanish society, from the army and the church to the trade unions and political parties and, of course, the citizens, who are among the most pro-European people in today's European Union. The process of integration presumed the adaptation of national party programmes to new European challenges as well as organisation on both national and supranational levels in a process called 'Europeanisation'. This is because most of the Spanish political parties are members of transnational party federations in the EU. In contrast to Greece, Portugal and other European countries, the consensus in favour of European integration among state-wide parties has been absolute since the beginning, spanning the entire ideological spectrum, from the UCD and the *Alianza Popular* (conservative parties close to the Franco regime) to the IU (former communists) and even most of the peripheral regionalist-nationalist parties, which simultaneously perceived the EU as a chance to transform minority nationalism and promote sub-national groups against central governments.

So, there is some evidence for the Europeanisation of individual parties; however, the Europeanisation of the party system is almost non-existent. As Mair has pointed out, European integration has had virtually no effect on the format of national party systems. Although policy making is increasingly supranational in character, politics is still primarily a national affair.[49] Thus, the Spanish party system has not experienced a great impact from its entry into the EEC. Despite all the parties that have joined different transnational and European federations – as well as their respective EP political groups – the internal dynamics have remained more or less intact, thus producing a fairly homogeneous attitude towards most European affairs. The main differences concerning Europe can be explained by national cleavages, such as the traditional left-right (mainly between the PSOE and the PP) and the centre-periphery (with the PP confronting nationalist parties such as the CiU, the PNV and, especially, the ERC).

However, some changes can be emphasised at the individual level of the party system. There has been a strong and clear development of pro-European attitudes among almost all political organisations, although some important differences can be pointed out. Thus, while the PSOE has developed more engaged and unconditional pro-EU values, the AP-PP (the main reference for Spanish conservatives) has maintained some suspicions (at least until the mid-1990s) although is currently a hardline supporter of the EU, but from the viewpoint of national sovereignty. The communists of the IU, a more factionalised party with some groups opposed to EU economic and political criteria, have appeared more distrustful with regard to Europe, especially against the free market and the lack of democratic legitimacy in the decision-making process. The nationalists of the CiU, the PNV and the ERC have seen Europe as a platform to expand the limits of the nation state in order to obtain recognition of their specific singularity as a nation within a supranational sphere.

It can be said, therefore, that the Spanish party system as a whole – as well as individual parties – have expressed a high level of Europeanism, due in part to the perception that Europe guarantees democracy and economic development. In any case, the party system has not changed to a great extent since 1986, having maintained the same historical cleavages. However, it is also true that Europeanisation has had an effect on party programmes and manifestos in national and European elections and, at the same time, on the internal structure of parties, especially through their inclusion in the European federations of political parties.

Finally, it can be added that, as in most countries, and following Mair's thesis, the progressive Europeanisation of Spanish politics has strengthened the prevailing tendency to depoliticisation. Despite the outstanding consensus towards European integration, and the positive image of Europe among Spaniards,[50] there is quite limited participation and interest in European issues. Europe is seen as necessary and beneficial, but too far removed from national citizens. As has been stressed, public opinion perceives that the most important issues are still dealt with on the national level. The EU is considered as a source of income and a common market, but not as a shared political idea.

Moreover, political support for European integration has always been somewhat weaker among citizens than among the political elite.[51] Spanish political parties, aware of the importance of increasing the engagement of citizens in EU politics, were strongly involved in the campaign for the European Constitution Referendum in 2005. Both the governing Spanish Socialist Workers' Party (PSOE) and the main opposition, the People's Party (PP), campaigned for a 'yes' vote. However, due to the widespread apathy surrounding the constitutional treaty and ignorance of its contents (in a government poll, 90 per cent of voters admitted to having little or no knowledge of its provisions), turnout was only 42 per cent of the electorate – by far the lowest in any election since the restoration of democracy in the late 1970s.

Notes

1. The author would like to thank Katie Calhoun for her help in the language revision for this chapter.
2. J. Avilés, 'España y la integración europea: partidos y opinión pública, 1977–2004', *Espacio, Tiempo y Forma*, vol. 16, 2004, pp. 409–423.
3. A. Richards, 'Spain. From Isolation to Integration', in R. Tiersky (ed.), *Europe Today. National Politics, European Integration and European Security*, Boulder, Rowman & Littlefield, 1999.
4. J. Loughlin and D. Hanley, 'The Emergence of the Spanish Party System: Historical Background and Contemporary Realities', in D. Hanley and J. Loughlin (eds), *Spanish Political Parties*, Cardiff, University of Wales Press, 2006, p. 5.
5. M. Farrell, 'Spain in the new European Union', in Balfour, S. (ed.) *The Politics of Contemporary Spain*, London, Routledge, 2005, p. 216.
6. C. Closa, (ed.) *La Europeización del sistema político español*, Madrid, Istmo, 2001.
7. Loughlin and Hanley, 'The emergence...' p. 11.
8. F. Casal, 'Sources of Party System Institutionalization in New Democracies. Lessons from Southern Europe', Paper presented at the 58th PSA Annual Conference. Swansea, UK, 2008.
9. J. J. Linz and J. R. Montero, *The party Systems of Spain: Old Cleavages and New Challenges*. Madrid, CEACS Working Paper 138, 1999.
10. P. Kennedy, 'The Spanish Socialist Party', in D. Hanley and J. Loughlin (eds.) *Spanish Political Parties*, Cardiff, University of Wales Press, 2006, p. 24.
11. I. Szmolka, 'Veinte años de pertenencia de España a la Unión Europea: actitudes de los españoles ante el proceso de integración comunitaria', *Cuaderno Opiniones y Actitudes*, 2007, 57, Madrid, Centro de Investigaciones Sociológicas.
12. A. M. Ruiz, '*The European Identity of Spanish Citizens: Trends, Meanings and Consequences. A Quantitative Analysis*', Working Paper Online Series, 72, Madrid, Universidad Autónoma de Madrid, 2007.
13. J. Diez, *Framing Europe. Attitudes to European Integration in Germany, Spain, and the United Kingdom*, Princeton, Princeton University Press, 2003.
14. J. C. MacLennan, *Spain and the Process of European Integration 1957–85*, London, Palgrave, 2000.
15. G. Benedetto and L. Quaglia, 'The comparative politics of communist Euroscepticism in France, Italy and Spain', *Party Politics,* 13, 2007, pp. 478–499.
16. B. Alvarez-Miranda, *El sur de Europa y la adhesión a la Comunidad. Los debates políticos*, Madrid, Centro de Investigaciones Sociológicas, 1996.
17. Avilés, 'España y la integración..., p. 410.
18. Kennedy, 'The Spanish Socialist Party', p. 64.
19. P. Heywood, *Marxism and the Failure of Organised Socialism in Spain*, Cambridge, Cambridge University Press, 1990.
20. L. Ray, 'Measuring party orientations towards European Integration: Results from an expert survey', *European Journal of Political Research*, 36, 1999, pp. 283–306.

21. O. Holman, *Integrating Southern Europe. EC Expansion and the Transnationalization of Spain*, London, Routledge, 1996.

22. M. A. Quintanilla, *La integración europea y el sistema político español*, Madrid, Congreso de los Diputados, 2001.

23. See Kennedy, 'The Spanish Socialist Party', p. 69.

24. Carlos López, 'Europeísmo y oposición: Alianza Popular y la adhesión de España a la CEE (1976–1985)', *Cuadernos de Historia Contemporánea*, 29, 2007, pp. 279–296.

25. Ray, 'Measuring party...', p. 303.

26. Avilés, 'España y la integración...', p. 412.

27. Aguilera de Prat, C.R. *Partidos políticos e integración europea*, Barcelona, Institut de Ciències Polítiques i Socials, 2008, p. 94.

28. L. Ramiro, 'Electoral Competition, Organizational Constraints and Party Change: The Communist Party of Spain (PCE) and United Left (IU), 1986–2000', *Journal of Communist Studies and Transition Politics,* 20, 2004, pp. 1–29.

29. Benedetto and Quaglia, 'The comparative politics...', p. 493.

30. G. Marks, C. Wilson and L. Ray, 'National Political Parties and European Integration', *American Journal of Political Science,* vol. 46, 3, 2002, pp. 585–94; see also L. Hooghe, G. Marks and C. J. Wilson, 'Does Left/Right Structure Party Positions on European Integration?', in G. Marks and M. R. Steenbergen (eds), *European Integration and Political Conflict*, Cambridge University Press, Cambridge, 2004, p. 95–99.

31. A. Alesina and E. Spolaore, *The Size of Nations*, Cambridge (MA), MIT Press, 2003.

32. M. Guibernau, 'Nations without States in the EU: the Catalan Case', in J. McGarry and M. Keating (eds.) *European Integration and the Nationalities Question*, London, Routledge, 2006; M. Keating, *Plurinational Democracy: Stateless Nations in a Post-Sovereign Era*. Oxford, Oxford University Press, 2001; and J. Llobera, 'The future of Ethno nations in a United Europe', in Wicker, H. (ed.) *Rethinking Nationalism and Ethnicity*, Oxford, Berg, 1997.

33. S. K. Jolly, 'The Europhile Fringe? Regionalist Party Support for European Integration', *European Union Politics,* 8, 2007, pp. 109–130.

34. G. Marks and C. Wilson, 'The Past in the Present: A Cleavage Theory of Party Response to European Integration', *British Journal of Political Science* 30, 3, 2000, pp. 433–59.

35. P. Lynch, *Minority Nationalism and European Integration*, Cardiff, University of Wales Press, 1996.

36. See Keating, *Plurinational Democracy...*, 72–83; see also A. Bourne, 'Europe, Constitutional Debates and the Spanish State of Autonomies', *Perspectives on European Politics and Society*, 9, 3, 2008, pp. 283–300.

37. L. de Winter, *The Impact of European Integration on Ethno Regionalist Parties*, ICPS Working Paper Series, 195, Barcelona, 2001, p. 6.

38. A. Dowling, 'Convergència i Unió, Catalonia and the new Catalanism', in S. Balfour, (ed.) *The Politics of Contemporary Spain*, London, Routledge, 2005.

39. G. Jáuregui, 'Basque Nationalism, Sovereignty, Independence and European

Integration', in J. McGarry and M. Keating (eds) *European Integration and the Nationalities Question*, London, Routledge, 2006, pp. 240–242.

40. D. Hanley, *Beyond the Nation State: Parties in the Era of European Integration*, Houndmills, Palgrave, 2008.

41. A. Kreppel, *The EP and the Supranational Party System: A Study in Institutional Development*, Cambridge, Cambridge University Press, 2002.

42. Aguilera de Prat, *Partidos políticos...*

43. P. Román, 'Partidos, programas e integración europea. La europeización del sistema de partidos español', in C. Closa (ed.) *La europeización del sistema político español*, Madrid, Istmo, 2001.

44. L. Morales and L. Ramiro, 'Spanish Political Parties and Europeanisation', Paper presented at Budapest ECPR General Conference. Hungary, 2005.

45. L. Morales and L. Ramiro, 'Spanish Political Parties...', p.107.

46. G. Evans, 'European Integration, Party Politics and Voting in the 2001 Election', in L. Bennie, C. Rallings, J. Tonge and P. Webb (eds.), *British Elections and Parties Review*, London, Frank Cass, 2002. p. 98; See also M. J. Gabel, 'European integration, voters and national politics', *West European Politics*, 23, 4, 2000, pp. 52–72.

47. Aguilera de Prat, *Partidos políticos...*, p. 48.

48. C. J. Carrubba, 'The Electoral Connection in European Union Politics', *Journal of Politics*, 2001, 63, 1, pp. 141–58.

49. P. Mair, 'The Limited Impact of Europe on National Party Systems', *West European Politics*, 2000, 23 (4): 27–51.

50. In the Standard Eurobarometer 69 (Spring 2008) Spain's membership in the EU has been positively evaluated by the Spanish population: two thirds (68%) of the interviewees said that being a Member State of the EU has been "good" for Spain. Only 8% of the group said that being a member of the EU was "bad", a much lower percentage than the EU27 average of 14%. European Commission (2008) *Standard Eurobarometer 69. Spain National Report* (Spring 2008).

51. M. Jerez-Mir, J. Real and R. Vázquez-Garcia, 'Identity and representation in the political elite vs. public opinion perception: a comparison between Southern and Postcommunist Central-Eastern Europe', *Europe-Asia Studies*, 2009, vol. 61, no. 6, pp. 943–66.

chapter eight | the europeanisation of poland's political parties and party system

Jean-Michel De Waele and Anna Pacześniak

Introduction

In Poland, as in the rest of central Europe, the priority of most political elites, after the system change, was 'the return to Europe' identified with the entry into the political, economic and military structures of the West. The accession to NATO and the EU was considered to be the main political challenge to which all the other actions must be subordinated, a viewpoint shared by both the centre-right and centre-left governments. Almost all actions taken by the successive parties in government aimed at 'Europeanisation',[1] namely to accommodate individual economic sectors to the requirements set by the European Commission and to adapt to the *acquis communautaire*.

As a result, subsequent governments had marginal flexibility. The aspiration to become a member of the EU made it practically impossible for political and social discussion on the shape of many public policies (e.g. health, transport, education, environmental and research policy). In this situation, the political parties focused on ideological and historical debates instead of working on and enforcing different policies. In spite of appearances, the ruling elites' focus on the integration process of the EU held back the Europeanisation process of Polish political parties for years.

The Europeanisation of the Poland's party system

The evolution of the Polish party system after 1989

Before analysing the core topic, we need to frame the common tendencies observed in Poland's party landscape.[2] First, there was a degree of instability in the party system and political parties following the downfall of Poland's 'peasant democracy' in 1989. Only two parties have self-described themselves as social democratic – the Democratic Left Alliance (*Sojusz Lewicy Demokratycznej* (SLD)) and peasant activists from the Polish Peasant Party (*Polskie Stronnictwo Ludowe* (PSL)), and have, from the beginning of the 1990s, been constantly present in the Polish Parliament.[3] The party landscape has stabilised in recent years compared with earlier times when the dominant feature of the Polish party system was permanent change.[4] At the beginning of 2000, two parties joined the party system: the centre-right Civic Platform (*Platforma Obywatelska* (PO)) and the conservative Catholic Law and Justice Party (*Prawo i Sprawiedliwość* (PiS)).

Secondly, the structural weaknesses of the Polish parties are a fact worth noticing. The number of party members is low. The agrarian party, PSL, has 143,000 members, while the others parties have considerably fewer: the SLD has 70,000 members, the PO 32,000 and the PiS 20,000. With the exception of the agrarian party, political parties are weakly embedded on the ground. With no exceptions, all the parties felt they had good relationships with non-governmental organisations (NGOs). However, the situation meant that one of the traditional functions of a party, namely communication and information exchange between the rulers and the ruled, was fulfilled only to a limited degree.

Thirdly, Polish political parties are poorly and weakly linked to society. They have not established stable connections with the electorate, so it is difficult to consider their relations with the constituency in terms of party loyalty. They do not control the separated segments of society. This is a result of the limitations/disabilities of existing parties and from the lack of a homogenous and consolidated political identity of social groups. Those groups can be defined as social categories, but not as political ones. In such a situation, the parties do not have the capacity to genuinely represent those groups and adopt a proper 'potential voter perspective'.[5] Few voters in Poland have at their disposal distinctive forms of group and party loyalty. In the previous political regime, the creation of such party identification was impossible because party pluralism was non-existent. Therefore, during the period of system transformation, the parties faced the dilemma of a floating electorate characterised by unstable electoral behaviour, a reluctance to identify with a particular party, symbol or ideology.[6] The weak membership of political parties is also influenced by general distrust towards the party institution, the high level of political alienation and the fact that parties originate on a basis of advocacy of particular values, and not around defined interest groups.[7]

In Poland, it is very hard to describe which party represents which social interests. The social democrats are neither a working class party, nor a party of those employed in the public sphere. The centre-right PO is supported by teachers and clerks, as well as by private enterprises, executive staff, blue-collar workers and farmers. The only clear differentiation of voters is one based on geographical location. The west of the country is more tolerant and modernised, contributing to greater support for the PO (earlier for SLD). However, the eastern and major part of the country remains the bastion of the Catholic, conservative and Eurosceptic parties: the PiS won the two last parliamentary elections (2005 and 2007).

It is also worth noting that Polish political parties are wrestling with a problem of the 'professionalisation' of their political elites. The parties are not distinct as almost all try to occupy the centre of the political spectrum. They neglect activity on the ground and instead focus on the creation of a media image. This stems from a lack of stable forms of identification with other social groups and the lack of a developed membership structure that allows the potential electorate to gain access. As a result, the parties have looked for alternative ways of promoting political strategies, mediatisation and the professionalisation of electoral campaigns. Polish parties frequently take advantage of help provided by specialist organisations and experts in the field of electoral market research. Many of these activities already occur in other countries in Western Europe, but they are used to a greater extent in the 'new democracies'.

Poland is becoming more congruent with Western European countries and this is apparent in relation to its socio-political cleavages.[8] Referring to Rokkan's model, the centre/periphery division does not play any political role in Poland. However, the Polish political scene is structured by the city/countryside division (with a deep-rooted peasant movement in an agrarian area), and by the religious division (the Catholic Church in Poland is in an indisputably strong position; the businesses of the non-believers are represented by SLD). Slowly, the socio-economic (class) division is becoming more visible, which for the first fifteen years was barely visible, especially in the context of the deep changes taking place in Polish social structures. For years, the citizens did not realise who were the winners and losers in the economic transformation and privatisation process. The neo-liberal model that affected all political parties was seen as something obvious, as a necessity for a quick move from a centrally-planned economy to a free-market model. The differences between the political parties with respect to economic and social policies were not marked. That is why the conflict between the left and right wing was not analysed in the context of socio-economics. The social democrats, who after 1989 were in power twice, were implementing the same economic policies as their political adversaries from the right. As mentioned above, the preparations of Polish accession to the EU have played a significant role in the continuity of policies implemented by subsequent governments. Nevertheless, in the last few years, social issues have been raised more often in political debate. Questions arise about the division of profits derived from economic growth, while there is an increased awareness concerning who lost and who gained following the transformation. The socio-economic division is slowly playing a role in the Polish party system.

To summarise, more than two decades after the system change, the Polish party system operates in a slightly altered way. There has been a move to the classic socio-political divisions and similar tendencies displayed in Western party systems. To make the picture clearer, it is worth mentioning the division between communists and anti-communists, which was typical for central European systems. Over the course of time, this division had become dated in all the countries of the region, but in Poland such acceptance has been much slower.

Successive stages of the European debate in the Polish party system

In order to analyse the phenomenon of the party system's Europeanisation, it is useful to follow the way European integration emerged (or failed to emerge) as an issue for inter-party competition, how it changed the logistics of party competition and co-operation – by encouraging or preventing domestic actors from aligning with particular political forces – and even prompted the emergence of new parties around the 'Europe issue'. In Poland, there has been no relevant party originating and deriving from the European integration dimension. We do not aim here to describe short-lived parties and ephemeral political existence.[9] In this section, we focus on the first-mentioned variables and submit for analysis the stages of the European debate in the Polish party system.

The analysis of the European debate in Poland centres on three successive stages:

1. an initial enthusiasm, which occurred when there was a low level of knowledge about the EU;
2. the fears that emerged over the costs of integration and the potential threat to national business; and
3. a sense of normalisation after accession to the EU, the result of holding discussions similar to those conducted in other member states.

These stages proposed by us represent a simplification, but indicate an evolution of how the EU was perceived and discussed in Poland.

Enthusiasm

The system transformation initiated in 1989 quickly aroused Polish aspirations to full integration with the Western world. Under the slogans, 'return to normality' and 'return to Europe', a symbolic breaking of bonds with the USSR took place. This paved the way toward the West, to which Poland in its collective memory, historical mythology, and political and social culture belonged for years. A desire of a 'return to Europe' was not wholly defined and directed. In this period of time, Europe did not only mean membership of the EU, as Western political elites wrongly interpreted; for Polish citizens, Europe meant something more. People expected a democratic political system, a confirmation of belonging to Western values, of starting a market economy and of security guarantees by the international security structures. In short, Poland was searching for a total break from Moscow's past and for recovering its historical place in the Western and Christian world. Barely anyone differentiated between the EU, the United States, the West, NATO, capitalism and the free market. All these terms were used interchangeably and all the political actors were defending this vision. Even the post-communists quickly abandoned ideas about a third way of development between the East and the West. They quickly turned to a position of being followers of Polish accession to the EU and NATO.

The political consensus on the issue of Poland's return to 'normality' was extremely broad. After the downfall of the previous regime, negotiations with the EU quickly began. Polish elites presented the EU as a club for countries with a high standard of life and the accession as a reward for a period of transformation, hard but worth the effort. Wealth, consumption and freedom were important goals; problems, difficulties and sacrifice in the context of European integration were not mentioned.

The fears

The opening of accession negotiations changed the climate of European debate in Poland. There were many technical problems that stemmed from the need to adjust Polish law, the economy and social system to the requirements of the European Commission and *acquis communautaire*. It became clear that Europe represented not only a benefit, but also costs that were previously underestimated and passed over. Europe lost its charm by becoming a concrete creation and society at large, and the ruling elites, quickly understood that negotiations with Europe meant that Poland would have a very limited range of freedom.

Two factors additionally complicated the way Europe was perceived:

1. In Poland – as in all other countries – politicians used the EU in order to justify a number of unpopular decisions and difficult reforms. The responsibility for any lasting problems was shifted on to the EU.

2. The centre-right wing PO became a problem. During the most difficult period of accession negotiations, the PO was in opposition to the centre-left wing government and began to defend Polish sovereignty. With the motto 'Nice or death', this theoretically pro-European party set the tone for government, weakened by many scandals, and criticised from all sides, by pro- and anti-European groupings. The Prime Minister, Leszek Miller, toughened the tone and hardened the position towards the EU. Fears and objections to Europe gained legitimisation from all important political parties.

The intensity of Eurosceptic discourse depended on which party used it: whether it was the populist-peasant Self-Defence of the Republic of Poland (*Samoobrona*), the traditional social values, Catholic faith, and the concept of Polish national sovereignty from the League of Polish Families (*Liga Polskich Rodzin* (LPR)) or the Kaczyński brothers' Law and Justice Party. At the same time, the Polish Peasant Party and the Civic Party displayed a strongly ambiguous attitude towards the EU. In such an atmosphere, even social democrats from the Democratic Left Alliance, viewed as post-communists, had to show that they were defenders of Polish identity and sovereignty equal to the other parties.[10]

In order to understand the atmosphere of that time better, it is worth mentioning the arguments promoted by the contemporary elites. They threatened that:

– the European Union would put barriers on the east border and, therefore, there would be no entry for Belarusians, Ukrainians, or Russians;

– the directives from Brussels would be sent via e-mails directly to each officer, omitting ministers and department directors, which would eliminate national administration; and

– some regions would be obliged to be under protection and would become backwaters.

Other potentially dire consequences included Polish energy being put into someone else's hands; there would be an expansion of bureaucracy and corruption would rage; religion would disappear from schools; and children would be brought up as European citizens. On the one hand, the EU was accused of being a sluggish, limp behemoth that was bound to collapse at any time. On the other hand, it was a terribly efficient conspiracy, a Hydra from whose tentacles no decent Polish patriot would leave alive. Accession to the EU was meant to be a catastrophe for moral and religious civilisation. The EU would make Poland introduce abortion on demand, allow euthanasia, give homosexuals permission to marry and adopt children. The EU was compared with Sodom and Gomorrah; Brussels to Moscow. It was predicted that the country would collapse as did Ancient Greece and the Roman Empire as a result of a slackening of morals and acceptance of deviation. The kingdom of atheism would come into existence because in the EU there is no place for Christianity. Children would be incited to rebel against their parents, wives against their husbands.[11] This idea was the most distinctly expressed by the Catholic *Sunday Weekly* (*Tygodnik Niedziela*), which wrote at the end of year 2001:

> We will be in a community where there will be no boundaries and people will mix. We will go to strangers, strangers will come to us, they will teach us their language, they will buy our lands for foreign money. They will plant foreign culture and religion. Not much that belongs to us, what homeland is, what Polish is, what piety is, what is close to the Holy Mother's heart will survive. Our homeland will cease to exist.

At this stage, there was a need to look for a support of an institution that had authority among most of the Poles, namely the Catholic Church. For most of the commentators, the contemporary social democratic president, Aleksander Kwaśniewski, had made a settlement with the church hierarchy to obtain its support for Poland's integration with the EU. In exchange, he promised to respect points of ethics and legislation (e.g., concerning the acceptability of abortion).

In this unfavourable political climate, on the 7th and 8th June 2003, the accession referendum took place. Only 58.85 per cent of the electorate voted (in order for the results to be valid, 50 per cent of votes were needed); of these 77.45 per cent were in favour of the accession of Poland to the EU. The analyses of public opinion from this period indicate that the greatest opposition towards the EU was expressed by citizens of villages and small towns, and people of low education.[12]

Normalisation

Joining the EU on 1st May 2004 was a planning accomplishment, but soon the discussion turned into a debate about the future of the EU. The same questions being asked by other member states were also an issue for Poland, namely: does the EU need a constitutional treaty? Should Poland stand for or against the Treaty of Lisbon? Where are the boundaries of the EU? The normalisation period could be further divided into two sub-periods. The first corresponds to the coming to power of the Law and Justice party of the Kaczyński brothers (2005–2007) thanks to the support of Eurosceptic parties in an atmosphere of political instability and suspicion. The second period began with the success of the Civic Platform during the 2007 parliamentary elections.

Victories for the Kaczyński brothers in 2005 (Lech won the presidential elections and Jarosław became leader of the Law and Justice party in parliamentary elections) were not the consequence of their Eurosceptic views, but rather of the fears of voters who were threatened with a perspective of ultra-liberal reforms proposed by the Civic Platform. The social and national discourse presented by the Law and Justice party seduced a part of the Polish electorate, but to perceive the results of the 2005 elections as proof for the Euroscepticism of Polish society would be erroneous. During those campaigns, the issues concerning Europe and the EU were marginal topics. Paradoxically, despite this fact, the results and the subsequent politics of the Kaczyński brothers led to Poland's isolation in the EU.[13]

In the parliamentary elections of 2007, the most Eurosceptic parties (the Self-Defence and the League of Polish Families) lost their parliamentary representation and the Law and Justice party returned a reduced vote. The big winner (and similar to the results of the European elections in June 2009[14]) was the Civic Platform, which was evolving into a pro-European party while still showing ambivalent attitudes towards the EU. Polish society had also changed to a more pro-European stance. The most visible change concerned the farmers, who benefited from the agricultural politics partnership and money from the EU. Surveys illustrated that public opinion was becoming more favourable towards European politics. There were new affiliations and political groupings in the European Parliament: the Civic Platform, together with peasant activists from Polish Peasant Party, aligned with the Group of the European People's Party (Christian Democrats). In 2009, the Law and Justice party joined forces with, among others, the British Conservative Party, to form the European Conservatives and Reformists (ECR).

The Europeanisation of the parties' policies

Twenty years after the system transformation that initiated a build-up of the Polish party arena, four main political parties operate: the left-wing Social Democrats, the agrarian Polish Peasant Party, the liberal-conservative Civic Platform and the conservative Law and Justice grouping. Until 2007, two other parties had their representatives in the Parliament: the national-conservative League of Polish Families and the populist Self-Defence, which is hard to classify. In the spring of 2006, they entered a cabinet coalition with the Law and Justice party. In terms of attitudes toward European integration, we can divide them into three groups: pro-European parties, Eurosceptic parties and indecisive parties.

This classification, although partly arbitrary, is based on an analysis of the content of political programmes and the public speeches of leaders and members of parties. The classification by political researchers, such as Benoit and Laver, as well as Rohrschneider and Whitefield, based on their study conducted in Poland in the pre-accession period, puts the political parties in order from the most to the least pro-European as follows: the Civic Platform, the Democratic Left Alliance, the Law and Justice party, the Polish Peasant Party, the Self-Defence, and the League of Polish Families (see Table 8.1). For Benoit and Laver,[15] the scale ranges from 1 (opposes joining the EU), to 20 (favours joining the EU); for Rohrschneider and Whitefield,[16] the scale ranges from 1 (nationalist, anti-EU), to 7 (internationalist, pro-EU).

Table 8.1: Expert surveys on Polish party position on EU integration in the period 2003–04

	Benoit/Laver (2003–04)	Rohrschneider/ Whitefield (2004)
Civic Platform	18.4	6.6
Democratic Left Alliance	18.3	6.4
Law and Justice	12.5	4.0
Polish Peasant Party	9.8	3.6
Self-Defence	3.6	1.2
League of Polish Families	1.5	1.0

Observations of the Polish political arena during the next few years lead us to a slightly different conclusion. We find that the most pro-European parties are the Democratic Left Alliance and the Civic Platform. In a group with ambivalent views of the EU is the Polish Peasant Party, whereas the Law and Justice party, the Self-Defence and the League of Polish Families are Eurosceptics.

Pro-European parties

The Democratic Left Alliance (*Sojusz Lewicy Demokratycznej* (SLD)) was formed in 1991 as an electoral coalition comprising various parties and groupings clustered around the Social Democracy of the Polish Republic (*Socjaledmokracja Rzeczpospolitej Polskiej* (SdRP)), the direct organisational successor to the Polish United Worker's Party (*Polska Zjednoczona Partia Robotnicza* (PZPR)). During subsequent parliamentary election campaigns, the SLD consolidated more and more groupings (1991: 13, 1993: 28, and 1997: 33)[17] and, in 1999, the SLD was transformed into a single, unitary party.

At first, the programmes of left-wing groupings clustered around the SLD treated European issues marginally. At the beginning of 1990s, the SdRP was against the dissolution of the Warsaw Treaty, which was a kind of guarantor of USSR business in the region.[18] However, the SLD won the parliamentary election and was the main governing party between 1993 and 1997. The party felt obliged to reaffirm Poland's commitment to EU integration, rhetorically and through its liberalisation reform agenda, because of two incentives: to enhance its democratic credentials and its belief that EU integration is a guarantee to economic development accompanied with 'a social-market, open and loyal Europe'.[19] The integration with the EU was considered by the SLD to be a top priority.

The Democratic Left Alliance wrote in its programme that 'Poland ought to be led to the EU accession as soon as possible and on conditions which would allow our country measurable and long-term profits'.[20] Obtaining membership was perceived as a chance to promote Poland, by overcoming backwardness in socio-economic development through quicker economic growth, by modernising agriculture, and improving the infrastructure and security. It is worth mentioning that the SLD, unlike other Polish actors, never saw EU enlargement as a gift for Poland or as payment for historical injustice or Polish service. For the 2004 European Parliamentary elections, the SLD prepared a programme document in which it highlighted integration as a chance for the realisation of social-democratic values: solidarity, equality, freedom, justice and democracy.[21]

The Democratic Left Alliance is a supporter of federalist concepts of European unification and, in this respect, is an exception among other Polish political parties. However, it is worth highlighting that the party changed its position concerning the European Constitution. When Leszek Miller was the head of the party and also the Prime Minister, the party was against renegotiating some regulations of this document. Such an attitude represented a dispute with the Civic Platform, the Law and Justice party and the League of Polish Families about who is a better defender of Polish business, which arose from a situation on the domestic political scene.[22] After the change of party leadership and the dismissal of Miller as Prime Minister, the SLD suddenly declared its support for the EU Constitutional Treaty.

The next pro-European party is the Civic Platform (PO). It was formed in January 2001 as a liberal-conservative party to capitalise on former finance and foreign minister Andrzej Olechowski's relative success as an independent candidate in the 2000 presidential election (17 per cent of votes, the second highest score after Aleksander Kwaśniewski). The Civic Platform is a party that is based on centre programme propositions. After the parliamentary election in 2007, the Civic Platform formed a Coalition Government with the Polish Peasant Party (*Polskie Stronnictwo Ludowe* (PSL)), with Donald Tusk becoming the Prime Minister.

Since the beginning, the PO has consequently been in favour of a linear tax, a reduction of the country's economic interventions, especially in respect to concession and regulatory entitlements of public administration. In relation to the EU, this party was perceived as pro-European even though one of its leaders was the author of the motto 'Nice or death', as an expression of opposition concerning a proposition to change the rules for counting votes in the EU Council. The events connected with accepting the EU Constitutional Treaty nuanced the image of the PO as a pro-European party.

In the Civic Platform's programme (2001), the EU exists as a stable element of affirmative reference for processes under way in contemporary Poland. Positive phenomena connected with EU structures were being pointed out; a tax system, higher employment rate in small and medium-sized enterprises, banking standards and public service institutions.[23] The EU, according to the PO, is a project similar to Europe of Homelands, based on conservative values and respect for the sovereignty of individual member countries. The PO absolutely objects to federalist conceptions.

The undecided parties

The Polish Peasant Party (PSL), during the first years of transformation period, was seen as a post-communist formation operating on the left side of the political spectrum; however, de facto, it is a centre party. It was formed in 1990 as the organisational successor to the former communist satellite, the United Peasant Party (*Zjednoczone Stronnictwo Ludowe* (ZSL)). It appeals to traditional peasant movements, Catholic ethics and the need for regulation of the market economy, in so far as it should take into account small businesses in villages and agriculture.

When the Polish Peasant Party formed the coalition government with the Democratic Left Alliance (1993–1997), it was regarded as the party with the strongest doubts about Polish entry to the EU. It claims to defend the interests of Polish farmers. It was concerned that Polish agricultural practices were incompatible with EU rules and, thus, criticised the government as well as the EU itself for hammering out disadvantageous accession conditions for Poland. While this Eurosceptic party did not reject accession publicly, some politicians went further by claiming that European integration constitutes a danger to Polish national values such as Catholicism and patriotism.[24]

After the 2001 parliamentary elections, the party joined (for the second time) the cabinet coalition with the pro-European Democratic Left Alliance (SLD), which considerably quickened and ultimately finalised the accession process. The SLD, 'careful' with the Polish Peasant Party on EU issues, placed itself in a difficult political situation. According to programme documents of the Polish Peasant Party, from 2001, integration for Poland means mainly a chance for improving the economy, education, development of agriculture and an improvement in general life conditions. The peasant activists highlighted that the Polish value of cultural accomplishments and traditions can contribute to the European structures. The Polish Peasant Party pointed out the importance of an independent development of Polish culture and for joining the EU on a partnership basis, and establishing the rules of membership on equal rights with countries that were already member states.[25]

The Eurosceptic parties[26]

Law and Justice (PiS) is a right-wing conservative party formed in 2001 by Jarosław Kaczyński to capitalise on the popularity of his twin brother, Lech, the Justice Minister. The party's name indicates a conservative programme orientation and its chief slogans are 'repairing the country' and 'cleaning the politics'.

The PiS's position with respect to EU accession was not entirely clear. This rather Eurosceptic party describes itself as 'Euro-realistic'. Since the very beginning, the party had problems with the EU and presented an ambivalent position. In the pre-accession period, it held a very different position from the Democratic Left Alliance or the Civic Platform, but it did not want to be associated with radical anti-European circles. In December 2002, when the accession talks entered the final phase, the PiS assumed that Poland would not access the EU on the 'up-to-now' negotiated conditions. However, it highlighted the fact that, if Poland remained behind, it could not receive any financial support. Constant analysis and multiple identities are typical of the European discourse of the PiS, which hedged its position concerning accession with multiple restrictions. Integration with the EU was, according to its programme, less important than preserving the country's national identity in the united Europe.[27] In its view, the main advantages of accession were: increased prestige in Europe and around the world; equal status with other democratic European countries; a revision of the Yaltan order and the existing post-communist balance of power in Europe (and battle for Europe's unity); and improved competitiveness of Polish goods and services together with an increased inflow of new foreign investments. For these reasons, the leaders of the PiS were in favour of accession.[28]

The Law and Justice party was heavily involved in discussions on the EU Constitutional Treaty project. The party's leader, Jarosław Kaczyński, found this project proof of 'Europe's hegemony', in which the biggest countries, especially the German-French tandem, would dictate conditions. During this period, the PiS hardened its sceptical position towards the EU, but tactics were dictated by a battle in the Polish party arena for the voters of the League of Polish Families.

After the accession, and while exercising power between 2005 and 2007, the PiS adopted the shrewd tactics of a 'win-win' stance: whenever Poland gained something, such as a multi-billion Euro structural funding, then the successful negotiation by the Polish Government was thanks to the Law and Justice party. Besides, Poland deserved such treatment because of historical treasons committed by the West. If, however, the EU 'rebelled' and refused to give something or demonstrated dissatisfaction, this was also fine because one could say then, 'look, haven't we said that the Union is infected with the virus of liberalism, not loyal and Christian enough'.

The two other Eurosceptic parties left the Polish political arena and it is worth noting that they were important actors, especially in the context of the accession period and between 2006 and 2007, when together with the PiS, they created a Coalition Government. The League of Polish Families (LPR) – which until 2007 occupied the extreme right wing of the parliamentary arena – was always resolutely against EU integration. The party was formed in the run up to the 2001 parliamentary election as a coalition of right-wing and clerical-nationalist parties. Its programme leaflet was entitled 'In the name of the defence of Polish political and economic sovereignty' and related to resignations and potential renegotiation of the association contract between Poland and the EU, a common national property policy and a change of constitution. The LPR postulated protection of native production by increasing national subsidies, setting customs barriers, restricting an inflow of foreign capital and strict control of existing foreign investments. It was also in favour of protecting traditional Catholic values, the Polish family way of life and unborn life (i.e., firmly anti-abortion).

In the LPR's leaflet, the accession to the EU was described as a new German colonisation. There were threats of loss of sovereignty, a buy-out of Polish lands, deteriorating relationships with the United States, the bankruptcy of most Polish companies and eight million unemployed. Some were convinced that the Polish Government would not be able to lead an independent monetary policy, since joining the Eurozone was immediate and obligatory and that, once a member, it would be very difficult to leave the EU. The EU was considered a 'Masonic godless idea' established in the interest of Germans who 'hate Poles and it is not a secret'.[29] After two years in the EU, the LPR 'proved' that the Polish political position was dramatically weak. Even though, they could not question the fact that Poland did receive money from structural funds, politicians complained that it was three billion Euros less than was promised. The LPR lost all EU parliamentary seats after the European elections of 2009.

The Self-Defence, another Eurosceptic party, was set up in 1992 as both a political party and farmers' union by Andrzej Lepper, one of the most controversial figures in Polish politics who first came to prominence as a leader of radical farmers' protests against debt foreclosures. The party appealed to all dissatisfied social groups. During the negotiation period for accession, the Self-Defence presented itself as totally anti-Europe. It proposed to seal the borders, to restore high subsidies for production and to develop native production, which was supposed to suffer from the accession to the EU. On the topic of accession (May, 2003), the Self-Defence party made it views very clear:

> Its finale is the act of capitulation signed by the government of the Republic of Poland in Athens on 16th April, 2003, called the Accession Treaty. The rules of this war, as any other, are merciless – the winner takes all – banks, lands, industrial plants and real estate. The effects of that war are perceived by the whole Polish nation.[30]

The Self-Defence tried to criticise the EU mainly from an ideological viewpoint (nation as the highest good) and economic position (negative system transformation). In the party leader's opinion, the integration processes were leading to extermination and, in a short period of time, they would lead to the devastation of the economy. After the 2007 parliamentary elections, the party practically disappeared and in the 2009 European elections, the Self-Defence obtained a share of the vote of 1.46 per cent.

Quantitative analysis of political manifestoes

Apart from qualitative analysis of political parties' election programmes and the degree of their Europeanisation, it is useful to pay attention to the amount of space devoted to issues connected with the EU in those documents. Based on research carried out by Szczerbiak and Bil (see Table 8.2), we may assume that:

- there does seem to be a broadly upward trend as far as the amount of space devoted to European policy in party programmes was concerned, with all six political groupings surveyed devoting as much or more (or as little) space in their 2007 programmes as they did in 2001, but the trend is not a linear one;

- even if some commentators were talking about the parliamentary election of 2001 as representing a kind of 'Eurosceptic backlash',[31] 'Europe' was not a particularly salient issue in the 2001 campaign;
- Poland's relations with the EU played virtually no role in the 2005 parliamentary elections and did not feature very prominently in most party programmes or on their campaigns[32];
- European issues had a somewhat higher profile in the 2007 parliamentary election campaign, partly because the Law and Justice-led foreign and European policies of the government were extremely controversial, both in Poland and among its EU partners[33];
- the increase in space devoted to EU policy often simply reflected changes in the overall length of the party programmes;
- there was no obvious link between support for or opposition to European integration and the amount of space devoted to European policy in party programmes;
- EU issues had become more prominent in other sections of party programmes that, prior to Polish accession, might have been regarded as primarily or solely the domain of domestic politics.[34]

Table 8.2: Space devoted to the EU policy in 2001, 2005 and 2007 in the Polish party election manifestoes[35]

Party	2001	2005	2007
Civic Platform	None	None	16 paragraphs
Democratic Left Alliance	3 paragraphs	3 paragraphs	11 paragraphs
Law and Justice	1 paragraph	20 paragraphs	16 paragraphs
Polish Peasant Party	2 sentences	5 short paragraphs	2 sentences
Self-Defence	None	1 sentence	None
League of Polish Families	2 sentences	3 paragraphs and 2 sentences	1 short paragraph and 2 sentences

Conclusion

Eastern European party systems (including the Polish system) are more fragile and fragmented than those of the West; party competition is more open than in the West and the profile of the parties is less crystallised. Therefore, the impact of the EU integration process on the parties is widely expected to be greater than in the West.[36] The focus of political parties on the issue of national sovereignty and the fact that the prestige conferred by the association with western political structures can be a larger electoral asset than in the West, may also strengthen the impact of the EU.[37]

Many scholars find that EU accession had little direct impact on Polish party politics and the party system. The Polish case confirms Mair's postulate (see page 3) according to which European integration had little influence on the mechanics and the format of party systems. The Polish party systems are built on a number of factors including: the national dynamics that were influenced by a communist legacy; the capacity of political parties to build themselves as modern and efficient organisations; and as a means to answer to the demands and hopes of the population. The impact of European integration itself had little impact on the party system. However, as demonstrated, the weak domestic political and economic autonomy influenced party programmes and ideological debate. Referring to Rokkan, it can be estimated that there is no cleavage between pro- and anti-European stances in the Polish party system. Europe was used by the various political parties in order to build their identities. It is important to distinguish between a legitimate debate on Europe and the existence of a structural cleavage that would give birth to political parties whose objectives would be to fight against European integration – but this is not the case for Poland.

Mair considers also that European integration reinforces domestic depoliticisation (see page 3). The Polish case seems to confirm his hypotheses. However, one has to be cautious with countries in central Europe since the lack of historical perspective complicates the analysis and weakens the conclusions.

It is true that European issues attract very little interest from Polish voters: the 2001 polls showed only between 4 per cent and 7 per cent of respondents considered that it was an important issue, but it was very low on the list of issues that would impact on their vote[38]; later polls confirmed this observation. However, there are many other factors which, to us, confirm the progress of the Polish system and the Europeanisation of the political parties. During the last twenty years, the Polish political system has undergone fundamental changes. The number of parties decreased – in 2007, four parties had representation in the Seym (Polish Parliament), whereas in the 1991 poll there were as many as twenty-seven parties and two civic committees. It is hard to say how the political arena would look if Poland had not negotiated accession to the EU. Similarly, it is difficult to differentiate between the influence of Europeanisation and other factors that have shaped or modified the Polish party system.

In all the countries of central Europe, one can see the indirect impact of the EU on political parties – confirming Ladrech's observation (see page 3). The vision of the political elites consisted of doing what Brussels expected in order for their country to be seen as a good candidate for EU membership and, after, to be a good member state to be accepted by the old European democracies. However, one cannot ignore the fact that during the two last decades there has been a complete transformation of the Polish political world in terms of the reconstruction of the party system, the political parties and the political institutions. In addition, it is important to remember the considerable anxiety regarding Polish security issues and the inhospitable attitude displayed by Russia.

The Europeanisation of the ideology/policy stance of the Polish political parties needs to be clarified. At the beginning of the democratic transformation, the policies of the new political parties were westernised in response to the expecta-tions and requests of the big European party interests (social democratic, Christian democrat, liberal, and conservative). The external legitimacy provided by these Europarties was important to the Polish political parties as they faced numerous internal competitors. Both the 'European label' and visits from EU political lead-ers provided domestic credibility. This external factor was crucial for Polish social democrats as they attempted to distance themselves from the image of commu-nism's legacy.

Nevertheless, it seems clear to us that the influence of European integration is visible, both when it comes to the whole system as well as its actors. A few factors provide evidence:

1. Despite the fact that the debate on European integration failed to create either a new socio-political division or any important political party, the attitudes to the EU were used by parties to consolidate and strengthen their political identities, even when their position towards the EU was evolving (as in case of the Civic Platform).

2. The period of negotiation and accession moved other political issues aside. This had a negative effect on national politics and on the diversification of politics offered by the parties. However, it also brought positive effects as it did not allow authoritative shortcomings and demagogic promises. This aspect of Europeanisation is often neglected in the analysis of Polish democratic consolidation.

3. The connection of the Polish parties with the Europarties' structure (Eu-ropean party federations and European parliamentary political groups) influenced the process of their institutionalisation. It is noticeable that parties adapt programmes and organisation to European standards. Polish political parties found their place in EP political groups and played more or less significant roles. During the 2004–9 term, the PiS was at the core of the political group known as the Union for Europe of Nations (UEN) and, after the 2009 elections, the PiS linked with the British Conservatives to establish a new political group – the European Conservatives and Reform-ists (ECR). The important position of the Civic Platform in the Group of the European People's Party (Christian Democrats) was confirmed by the election of Jerzy Buzek as European Parliamentary chairman. The role of the Democratic Left Alliance and the Polish People's Party in the Group of the Progressive Alliance of Socialists and Democrats in the European Parliament (S&D) and the Group of the European People's Party (Christian Democrats) is more modest and determined by its smaller representation.

4. It is impossible to explore thoroughly the subject of the Europeanisation of political parties without mentioning the Europeanisation of the society from which those parties derive. Numerous signs indicate that Polish society is currently becoming Europeanised and modernised. The analysis of these manifestations is not the aim of our chapter, but it is worth mentioning the demographic tendencies or decrease in participation in religious practices.

In Poland, there was much public debate over issues, such as the rights of sexual minorities, *in vitro* fertilisation, euthanasia and the legalisation of soft drugs, which in western European democracies were discussed some time ago. This questions the link between the Europeanisation of Polish society and Polish political parties.

Notes

1   It is interesting to indicate the peculiarity of embracing Europeanisation in Polish scientific literature. The application of a term 'Europeanisation' diverges from capturing this issue in western literature and applies either:
*   to its narrow understanding (and not necessarily the most important from the point of view of political science, e.g. in cultural dimension): see Piotr Mazurkiewicz, *Europeizacja Europy. Tożsamość kulturowa Europy w kontekście procesów integracji. (Cultural identity of Europe in the context of integration processes)*, Warszawa, Studium Generale Europa, 2001; or
*   it concerns only a part of the issue, e.g. the analysis of the Europeanisation of public administration : see Irena Lipowicz, *Europeizacja administracji publicznej. (Europeanisation of public adiministration)*, Warszawa, Wydawnictwo Uniwersytetu Kardynała Stefana Wyszyńskiego, 2008; or
*   it concentrates on a chosen sector of politics: see, for example, Anna Pacześniak, Rafał Riedel, *Transfer unijnych wzorców instytucjonalnych na przykładzie prawodawstwa w zakresie równouprawnienia płci w Polsce. (Transfer of EU Institutional Patterns – Europeanisation of Gender Law in Poland)*, Wrocławskie Studia Politologiczne, no. 10/2009.
In Polish literature on the subject, Europeanisation is understood in a sociocultural perspective and means transmitting characteristics of Europeans features, cultures and European countries or giving European features. In economical texts, the Europeanisation category is employed to describe the economic internalisation processes constrained to European scale which relies on, for instance internationalisation of national enterprise activity. In Polish journalism of the 1990s, many authors continuously used the term 'Europeanisation' in order to describe the adaptation processes present in all spheres of life, or even wider – everywhere where the fragments of crude (post-) socialistic reality were assimilating to standards known from Western Europe. However, it did not make a contribution to the precision of scientific conceptual instrumentation. In Polish literature on Europeanisation, this term is used mainly by J. Ruszkowski who understands it as a transfer of values or standards from European level to national level; moreover, their implementation and the effect caused by it. This understanding corresponds to the use of this term in western European literature and simultaneously relates to a common way of defining Europeanisation. See Jerzy Ruszkowski, *Wstęp do studiów europejskich. (Introduction to the European studies)*, Warszawa, PWN 2007.
2   J-M. De Waele, 'Le système politique polonais entre spécificité et convergence', in J-M. De Waele (ed.), *La Pologne et l'intégration européenne*, Bruxelles, Editions de l'Université de Bruxelles, 2003, pp. 15–32.
3   Exactly the SLD–Alliance of Democratic Left exists as political party from 1999. Before, in the aftermath of the Round Table negotiations and of the defeat of the PZPR in the semi-democratic elections of June 1989, the PZPR delegates decide, during the XI Congress (27–30 January 1990), to dissolve the communist party and to create a new one. The social democratic vision, with the approbation of the democratic rules and the renouncement to communist references, ends to the formation of Social Democracy of Poland

(SdRP). Only a few number of the former communist party's members joined the new organisation. Moreover, the heir party benefits from the organisational structures and the financial means of its predecessor. But, confronted by hostility, the SdRP is at the origins of the creation of a wider electoral alliance (SLD – Alliance of Democratic Left), including among others the OPZZ trade union and various associations stemming from the former regime. The SLD is transformed into political party in 1999, whereas the SdRP auto-dissolves.

4   J.-M. De Waele, *L'émergence des partis politiques en Europe centrale*, Bruxelles, Editions de l'Université de Bruxelles, 1999.

5   P. Kopecky, 'Developing Party Organizations In East-Central Europe', *Party Politics*, vol. 1 (4), 1995, p. 519.

6   A. Antoszewski, R. Herbut and J. Sroka, 'System partyjny w Polsce (Party system in Poland)', in A. Antoszewski, P. Fiala, R. Herbut and J. Sroka (eds), *Partie i systemy partyjne Europy Środkowej (Parties and political systems in the Middle Europe)*, Wydawnictwo Uniwersytetu Wrocławskiego, Wrocław, 2003, p. 129.

7   A. Antoszewski, *Wzorce rywalizacji politycznej we współczesnych demokracjach europejskich (The patterns of political rivalry in the european democracies)*, Wydawnictwo Uniwersytetu Wrocławskiego, Wrocław, 2004, p. 185.

8   J-M. De Waele (ed.), *Les clivages politiques en Europe centrale et orientale*, Bruxelles, Editions de l'Université de Bruxelles, 2004.

9   Only one new party has been formed in Poland directly as a result of the EU issue, and that was prior to the EU accession. The Polish Agreement (*Porozumienie Polskie* – PP) emerged in 1999 after seven clerical-nationalist deputies broke away from the governing Solidarity Electoral Action grouping the previous year because of their opposition to Polish membership of the EU. This small fraction provided the main focus for opposition to the EU membership in the Polish legislature during the second part of the 1997–2001 Parliament. The party's leader, Jan Łopuszański, ran as a candidate in October, 2000 presidential election on the slogan 'Europe – Yes, the EU – No', and made opposition to the Polish EU accession as his dominant campaign theme. However, the party never really took off and Łopuszański won in 2000 with only 0.79 per cent of the vote.

10   A. Szczerbiak, 'Opposing Europe or problematizing Europe? Euroscepticism and eurorealism in the Polish party system', in P. Taggart and A. Szczerbiak (eds), *Opposing Europe? The comparative party politics of euroscepticisme*, vol. 1, pp. 221–41.

11   M. Janicki, 'Strachy na Lachy', *Polityka*, no. 19/2006, p. 28

12   T. Zarycki , 'The polish enlargement referundum', in Jean-Michel De Waele (ed.), *European Union accession referundums*, Brussels, Editions de l'Université de Buxelles, 2005, pp. 95–113.

13   H. P. Gaisbauer, 'Euro-scepticism revisited: Poland after EU accession', *Perspectives on European Politics and Society*, 2007, vol. 8, no.1, pp. 55–72.

14   The European parliament election in Poland 7 June 2009, A. Szczerbiak, http://www.sussex.ac.uk/sei/documents/no_36_epernep2009poland.pdf

15   K. Benoit and M. Laver, *Party Policy in Modern Democracies*, Expert survey scores of policy positions of political parties in 47 countries, 2004–2005,

http://www.tcd.ie/Political_Science/ppmd/PPMD_11apr2006.pdf

16 R. Rohrschneider and S. Whitefield (eds), *Public Opinion, Party Competition and the European Union in Post-Communist Euro*, New York, Palgrave Macmillan, 2006.

17 W. Jednaka, 'Hasła encyklopedyczne (Encyclopeadic terms)', in M. Żmigrodzki (ed.), *Encyklopedia politologii (Encyclopaedia of political sciencei*, t. 3, Zakamycze, Kraków, 1999, p. 244.

18 M. Jeziński, *Marketing polityczny a procesy akulturyzacyjne. Przypadek III Rzeczpospolitej (Political Marketing and Acculturization Processes: The Case of a Republic of Poland III)*, Wydawnictwo Uniwersytetu Mikołaja Kopernika, Toruń, 2004, p. 224.

19 T. Łoś-Nowak, 'Contemporary government attitudes towards the EU', in K. Cordell (ed.), *Poland and the EU*, New York, Routledge 2000, p. 18.

20 S. L. Demokratycznej, *Deklaracja ideowa SLD*, 1999.

21 S. L. Demokratycznej, *Manifest Europejski*, 2004.

22 M. Migalski, *Czeski i polski system partyjny. Analiza porównawcza (The Polish and Czech Party Systems: Comparative Analysis)*, Wydawnictwo Sejmowe, Warszawa, 2008, p. 225.

23 The Civic Platform, *Nasz program. Normalni ludzie. Normalny kraj. (Our Programme. Normal People. Normal Country)*, 2001.

24 T. Petrova, *Differential Impact of EU Enlargement on First and Second Wave Applicants: Europeanizing Political Parties In Poland and Bulgaria*, CDDRL Working Papers, no. 65, June 2006, http://cddrl.stanford.edu

25 P. S. Ludowe, *Czas na zmianę... Program społeczno-gospodarczy*, 2001.

26 A. Szczerbiak, 'Polish Euroscepticism in the run-up to the EU accession', in R. Harmsen and M. Spiering (eds), *Euroscepticism: Party Politics, National Identity and European Integration*, Amsterdam and New York, Rodopi, 2004

27 P. i Sprawiedliwość, *Prawo i Sprawiedliwość. Program*, 2001.

28 M. Jeziński, *Marketing polityczny a procesy akulturyzacyjne. Przypadek III Rzeczpospolitej*, Wydawnictwo Uniwersytetu Mikołaja Kopernika, Toruń, 2004, p. 236.

29 Janicki, 'Strachy na Lachy', p. 28.

30 The Self-Defence leaflet, May 2003.

31 For instance: J. Reed, 'Election results may deal a blow to Poland's EU hopes', *Financial Times*, 25 September 2001.

32 A. Szczerbiak, 'Europe and the September/October 2005 Polish Parliamentary and Presidential Elections', *European Parties Elections and Referendums Network Election Briefing*, no. 22.

33 J. Cienski and S. Wagstyl, 'Twins are remaking Poland', *Financial Times*, August 2006.

34 A. Szczerbiak and M. Bil, 'When in doubt, (re-) turn to domestic politics? The (non-) impact of the EU on party politics in Poland', *European Parties Elections and Referendums Network*, Working Paper, no. 20, May 2008.

35 ibid.

36 P. G. Lewis, 'EU enlargement and party systems in Central Europe', *The Journal of Communist Studies and Transition Politics*, 2005, vol. 21, no. 2, pp.

171–99; J. Bielasiak, 'Party competition in emerging democracies: represen- tation and effectiveness in post-communism and beyond', *Democratization*, 2005, vol. 12, no. 3, pp. 331–56.

37 Z. Enyedi, 'The "Europeanisation" of Eastern Central European Party Sys- tems', Paper prepared for the POLIS Plenary Conference 2005, Workshop 8: Party Systems and European Integration, http://www.epsnet.org/2005/pps/ Enyedi.pdf

38 A. Szerbiak, 'After the election, nearing the endgame: The Polish Euro-debate in the run up to the 2003 EU accession referendum', *Sussex European Insti- tute Working Papers No. 53* and *Opposing Europe Research Network Working Paper No. 7*, May 2002, Brighton, pp. 11–18.

chapter nine | the romanian party system's europeanisation: an open bet

Sorina Soare

Introduction – in search of the lost time

On the smoky ruins of the communist regime, the allegiance to Moscow has rapidly been replaced by a broad consensus for Europe.[1] In this context, 'European integration and democratization were processes that were likely to advance together'.[2] In Romania, sceptical discourse on Europe is rather absent and the EU still enjoys one of the highest levels of social support in the region.

The impact of EU-led changes upon parties and party system mechanisms and format has been relatively insignificant and the Romanian party system has been impervious to the EU's influence. From the early 1990s, the Romanian party system was divided between the communists and the anti-communists; the latter based on the historic parties.

The ex-communist camp was composed largely of the National Salvation Front (FSN), together with the Great Romania Party (PRM), the Labour Socialist Party (PSM) and the National Unity Party of Transylvania (PUNR). Despite common origins and initial convergences in terms of national-populist discourse, the political trajectories of those parties rapidly diverged. The FSN adopted the concept of social democracy while the PRM became a nationalistic party; the two other parties 'disappeared'.

The anti-communist camp centred on established parties, in particular the Christian Democratic National Peasant Party (PNŢCD), the National Liberal Party (PNL) and the Romanian Social Democratic Party (PSDR). Two new parties integrated the anti-communist 'club'. First, the Hungarian Democratic Alliance (UDMR), which represents the interests of the Hungarian community and, second, by the mid-1990s, the Democratic Party (PD), which splintered from the FSN and progressively integrated the 1996 historic anti-communist Coalition Government. The PD merged with the Liberal Democratic Party (PLD) to form the centre-right Democratic Liberal Party (PD-L).

Following the 2000 elections, the intolerance between the communists and the anti-communists evaporated. A traditional democratic left-right divide became more visible. The PNŢCD disappeared and the PSDR merged with the Social Democratic Party of Romania (PSD). For a while, the PNL remained the only representative of the old parties, reinforcing its economic liberal discourse. The PSD progressively monopolised the left of Romanian politics. The PD's political realignment to a people's party moved it towards the centre-right, openly challenging the PNL liberal discourse. The small Conservative Party continues, being a symbiotic ally of the PSD. The PRM softened its nationalistic discourse and initiated a political realignment process similar to the PD transformation. The UDMR, with its Hungarian base, became a 'pivot' party; its consistent electoral results reinforced its political attractiveness.

The Group of the European People's Party (Christian Democrats) refused to accept the PRM representatives in its parliamentary group because of its nationalistic stance. This refusal only enhanced its nationalistic programme.[3] Since 2004, the PRM faced competition from the New Generation Party, which has contested the PRM primacy on nationalistic and populist discourses.[4]

The Romanian party system's superficial Europeanisation

In the early 1990s, Romania was considered to be 'the least promising in terms of creating a democratic system' within the region.[5] Despite the initial reticence, diplomatic relations with the European Union (EU) were restored, starting in 1990. In 1993, the so-called 'Europe Agreement' provided an official framework for both political dialogue and economic relations with the EU. During the debates on the Association Agreement, the Romanian negotiators were quick to emphasise the importance of these moves. No political party contested the potential integration and there was no relevant resistance to the relations between Romania and the EU. The party in government had particular reasons for enthusiasm – after two years of international boycott,[6] the signing of the treaty was seen as the end of Romania's ostracism. The PDSR hailed the signature of the 1993 Europe Agreement as a proof of European recognition of its commitment to gradual integration into the Community. On the eve of the 1996 elections, the PDSR initiated the intra-party agreement brokered by President Iliescu himself. The so-called 'Snagov Pact' committed all the parliamentary parties to support the EU accession. The relevance of the EU accession was described by Adrian Năstase, former President of the Chamber of Deputies, as being 'to such an extent crucial to Romania that we could consider it to be an internal factor of our development'.[7]

Following the Helsinki European Council's decision in December 1999, Romania started negotiations with the EU in February 2000. By February 2005, Romania was considered to have fulfilled the general conditions for EU membership and, with 497 'yes' votes, the European Parliament (EP) declared its support. The Accession Treaty was officially signed on April 2005. On this occasion, the main political leaders emphasised the importance of the signature and underlined the consensus behind the preparation of the accession process. E. Dinga, Minister of European Integration, compared the historic day of the 25th April with the creation of the national unitary state on the 1st December 1918. M. Bela (UDMR) underlined that 'the Accession Treaty is due to all the previous governments' and 'after fifteen years we can finally affirm that we have swept away the past and we are finally in Europe'.[8] This moment was also emphasised by M. Geoană (PSD), who said that the signing of the Treaty is 'the result of the work of all the Romanian citizens for the fulfilment of the accession criteria. They are the ones who have pushed the politicians since 1990 to bring Romania into the West and back into Europe'.[9] D. Voiculescu (Conservative Party (PC)) stated that the signing of the Accession Treaty is 'greatly to the incontestable merit of the overall political class'.[10] The entire political spectrum laid emphasis on the consensus behind this historical event and, for a moment, political differences gave way to shared enthusiasm.

Within this landscape, the surveys have regularly pointed out the Romanian population's outstanding support for EU membership. In the 1990s, the popular support for EU was stable at around 80 per cent of the population. Significantly, by 2002, 76 per cent of citizens considered that Romania could obtain major advantages from the integration process, while only 6 per cent of the population were sceptical.[11] On the eve of the accession, a strong majority continued to support EU integration.[12] Nevertheless, in the aftermath of the EU enlargement, criticisms were raised, mainly from rural entrepreneurs against the EU norms. Recently, small-scale dairy farmers and sheep farmers protested against the EU food safety standards. Since 2007, a degree of Euroscepticism has spread across Romanian society, which could provide support for ultra-nationalist politicians. Small parties, such as the National Initiative Party (PIN), structured their programmes to criticise EU requirements, although with insignificant electoral impact. On the eve of the 2009 European elections,[13] the farmers' criticisms, the fears of the business community and the current economic crisis could easily have become triggers for increasingly Eurosceptic positions. Based on this brief historical overview, three stages of the Europeanisation of the Romanian party system can be found – and these are discussed below.

Proto-Europeanisation – Europe envisaged as a land of democracy (1990–1993)

While in the rest of Eastern Europe, the democratisation wave swept communist parties away from the first political scene, the Romanian Communist Party (PCR) indirectly stayed in power while the FSN rapidly monopolised the political arena. Under various labels, the original FSN turned out to be the undoubted winner of the December 1989 events. The FSN won the first free elections with more than 66 per cent of the vote against a motley opposition of the old parties, which won only 10 per cent. The lack of transparency of the FSN's origins, the accusations of *coup de Palais*, FSN's support for the miners' violent irruptions in the capital city (Bucharest), its highly nationalistic statements and hesitations regarding the market economy were envisaged as signs of a reluctance to change.

In a period during which the intellectuals' involvement in political life was common currency, their discourses depicted the 'return to Europe' as indicative of the reminders of Romania's quintessentially European heritage. In this context, the democratisation issue polarised the political system, pitting ex-communist against anti-communist. During this proto-stage of 'Europeanisation', 'democratisation' and 'westernisation' (including accession both to the EU and NATO) were seen as having the same meaning. Thus, all the parties embraced Europe and the project of European integration as an essential ingredient of their political communication. Consequently, Europe has never been a topic of debate. This 'proto-Europeanisation' was exclusively limited to a war of symbols. Anti-communists were automatically entitled to display their pro-European 'label of quality' without any proof of ideological or programmatic commitment to the EU cause. An automatic interconnection was in operation and being pro-Europe was envisaged as a synonym of 'pro-democracy' and 'pro-market'. However, the ex-communists were denied this label, since they had to prove their 'redemption' and their support for democracy and market economy.

External Europeanisation – broad consensus and lack of debate (1993–2006)

In the second stage, Europeanisation became an elite-based process. Parties were caught in a rhetorical trap that forced them to approve the enlargement in order to acquire a national reputation of being democratic and acquiring the European status of partners. Significantly, the civil society was the major absentee at this stage. Once again, the ex-communists and the anti-communists battled for recognition as legitimate partners to their EU counterparts. As Romanian political parties sought membership of their international and European groups, an unexpected alliance emerged, with the European Socialists accepting the post-communist parties in preference to the historic social democratic party. This move could be interpreted as a cynical one since the ex-communist grouping had the larger number of seats in the Romanian Assembly. The fierce debates of the 1990s did not focus directly on Europe, but on how the national parties were granted recognition from Europe.[14] Eventually, both groups integrated into their appropriate European party federations. Significantly, the EU still did not feature in the domestic debate.

Initially, the EU had an impact on the Romanian party system by affecting the mechanics. In brief, the collaboration with the European federations of parties can be seen as a catalyst for the diminution of the ideological distance.[15] The collaboration between the centre-right government that came to power in 1996 and the UDMR was motivated not only by marginal electoral results, but also by the external/European consensus raised by this collaboration. In 1996, the commitment to please EU authorities pushed the government to rapidly prepare and sign the bilateral Treaty of Neighbourhood between Romania and Hungary.

However, the EU issue has never been a central dimension of the Romanian parties' identity. On the contrary, EU commitment was seen as a natural stance. This explains why even parties such as the populist PRM were 'contaminated' by the mainstream pro-European policy consensus. In 2006, C.V. Tudor, the PRM leader, spoke enthusiastically about EU membership: 'I think our life will be better after the accession'.[16]

Until 2007, the Europeanisation of the Romanian political arena was exclusively limited to a process of external adjustments.[17] As a direct consequence, EU prescriptions were automatically adopted at the national level; no real alternative option was ever mentioned. EU pressure in terms of adaptation linked to the Copenhagen criteria (which endorsed the market economy and democratic standards) encouraged all parties to support the changes required by the accession process.

Initial internal Europeanisation – from taboo to open debate (2007– present)

The third stage corresponds to the post-accession period. The democratisation process was no longer at stake. EU membership has regularly been held up as proof of the democratic quality of the political system and the networks of socialisation with the European party federations were by now consolidated.

The EU continues to be envisaged as 'an unidentified' political objective for national political life. For the Romanian parties, Brussels is still very far away from the political corridors of Bucharest, but a burgeoning internal Europeanisation can be identified. The Romanian delegation in the European Parliament brings together both long-term politicians (such as A. Severin (PSD), R. Weber (PNL), D. Dăianu (PNL), M. J. Marinescu (PD-L)) and younger politicians, some of them demonstrating a strong interest in EU affairs.[18]

In this context, as observed by Agh,[19] the EU effect on parties has to be distinguished between an external effect and an internal one. In the Romanian case, Europe has been an issue exclusively for the governing politicians who socialise with their European counterparts to the exclusion of the rest of society.[20]

Europeanisation and individual parties

From the early 1990s, Romanian parties chose to 'fit' the prescriptions of the European Union without a real debate. The dynamics of the national political system influenced the development of individual parties. Their attempts to join their European counterparts induced a strong consensus on EU values. In terms of individual parties' ideology and policy stances, the parties were fully committed to the EU. By referring to the current parliamentary parties, we can observe that they tend to encompass the EU as a provider of credibility for their policies.

Europe – a programmatic benchmark

As an example of their European commitment, most of the major parties declared their loyalty to Europe in their constitution. In this category:

- the PSD 2006 statute mentions that it 'is a leftist and progressive modern party, a national party with European vocation, a member of the Party of European Socialists' (art. 3–1);
- the PNL 2008 statute mentions that it is 'a liberal party, member of the European Liberal Democrat and Reform Party' (art. 6–1); and
- the PDL statute exclusively mentions the party's commitment to 'the Romanian active participation in the European construction and the fulfilment of the commitments linked to the membership status' (art. 6. 3–e).

The only party that does not openly mention its EU vocation is the small Conservative Party.

The absence of public debate plus the lack of coherent policy statements on the EU by Romania's political parties encouraged the Romanian Academic Society (SAR) into action. In 2007, it published the results of some research,[21] and this emphasises the parties' consensus on seeing the EU as profitable for Romania. With the exception of the Hungarian Democratic Alliance (UDMR), which supports a federal Europe, the other parties are in favour of the current EU format refined by the Lisbon Treaty and agree to further prerogatives of the European Parliament (EP). Regarding the reform of the EU regional policy and, in particular, of the EU structural funds, all the parties are committed to the current arrangements. In brief, behind the consensus on the EU, the SAR points out that the left-right divide does not really influence the position of parties on Europe. The Romanian parties could present a solid national position in the EP – with the exception of the UDMR.

Romania held elections in 2007 on accession and taking seats in the EP. It attracted a mixture of candidatures ranging from former ministers, such as Florin Frunzăverde (head of the PD list), Renate Weber (head of the PNL list), long-term politicians such as Adrian Severin (PSD), technocrats such as Daniel Dăianu (PNL), and also newcomers such as Gigi Becali (PNG president), Gabi Luncă (a Roma singer), or the anti-communist pastor Laszlo Tokes.[22] The election provided a platform on which new aspirants developed debates on EU topics, but these failed to stimulate much public interest.

Because of overlap with the referendum for a new electoral system, the European elections failed to mobilise the electors and the turnout was only 29.5 per cent. The referendum to change the electoral system was invalidated as it failed to attract the necessary 50 per cent turnout. In this context, the political campaign was overshadowed by the national conflict between the Prime Minister backed by Parliament and the President. The debate almost ignored such political issues as the Lisbon Treaty – the main topic on the European agenda. Various European foundations and the EU delegation in Bucharest energised political debates on European topics, but they remained peripheral to the political campaign. In the context of the *Mailat* case, linked to a Roma accused of sexual crime in Rome, the main topics were 'freedom of movement' and the European labour market.

Significantly, the party programmes were elusive on EU topics and concentrated on issues of national interest. The Democratic Party's (PD) campaign was labelled 'Popular in Europe, democrats in Romania', emphasising the party's membership of the European People's Party (EPP). The Social Democratic Party (PSD) campaign focused on social issues and presented two correlated mottos: 'For a stronger and more equal Romania' and 'You make the offer'. The PNL campaign was inward looking as illustrated by their mottos: 'I promote Romania. What about you?' or 'We promote Romanians, Romanian products and values'. The Hungarian alliances adopted two mottoes: 'Together for Europe' (for the Romanian community) and 'The new dismount', an allusion to the creation of the Romanian princedoms. In all the political programmes, European slogans were noticeable, but the major political statements had a more national slant.

Total commitment to the EU started to unravel immediately after the historic January 2007 accession. In 2008, the European Commission's report on justice and the fight against corruption was critical and said that the reform 'was uneven'.[23] Romania's failure to dispel doubts about its capacity to fight corruption was a strongly criticised point at the domestic level. In a clash between the Prime Minister's party and the President's party, the Justice Minister, Tudor Chiuariu, openly claimed that there had not been enough time for the European reviewers to get a complete image of how things had evolved in the country. However, the President's supporters were more positive, considering the report as objective and balanced. As in the early 1990s, the European issue once again became a bargaining chip in the political competition and the Commission's comments were thus exploited in an internal clash between former allies, the PD-L and the PNL.

With the exception of these clashes, the parties' programmes remained impervious to the EU. By taking into account the 2008 political programmes, a common observation can be underlined. EU standards were regularly emphasised as indicators of results and measures of credibility, but there was caution on detailed application. Thus, the political programme[24] of the PSD and PC pointed out a commitment to Europe, saying: 'We have initiated the integration process and we have concluded the accession negotiations'.[25] The programme formally referred to Europe, despite not having a real debate. The left's commitment was confirmed by the acceptance of European standards of education, research, health, economic development, and the European agriculture policy. Regarding the economy, the PSD and the PC were committed to guarantee a higher rate of absorption of EU funds and Romania's integration into the Eurozone by 2014. In brief, the PSD+PC political programme considered the EU standards as a measure to evaluate domestic governmental performance.

The 2008 political programme of the National Liberal Democratic Party (PDL) emphasised the importance of EU membership as a precondition for increasing living standards.[26] In terms of national identity, the PDL programme laid emphasis on the notion of 'constitutional patriotism' and declared that 'the Romanian national identity doesn't stand out against the European one'. The rest of the political document tended to refer to the EU and measurable targets or objectives such as sharing European living standards, learning from success stories like Greece, Spain or Portugal.

Similar to the PSD+PC programme, the PDL electoral manifesto spoke of insufficient improvements in institutional modernisation and warned that additional efforts were urgently needed to achieve the European benchmarks. It also pointed out the various benefits linked to EU accession and the positive impact of the financial support available to new member states. The PDL emphasised the goal of transforming Romania into one of the most competitive European economies while the PSD+PC programme also insisted on the European social model.

A difference in emphasis was nonetheless present in the PNL's electoral programme placed under the historical motto 'By ourselves'.[27] The 'European affairs' were developed in the first chapter of a detailed document. By referring to the EU norms and benchmarks, the PNL programme focused more on EU topics. In accordance with the Lisbon Treaty, the programme indicated the necessity to increase the co-operation between the national parliaments and the European Parliament. The PNL laid emphasis not only the EU benchmarks, but also on the national needs and expectations in the perspective of the Lisbon Treaty. The social dimensions of the EU standards were subordinated to the need for economic competitiveness. The PNL believed that EU enlargement would resolve problems related to the Republic of Moldova and Ukraine. On the Common Agriculture Policy, the PNL insisted that Romania had to conform to the security norms and benefit from the direct European payments. While the other parties tended to contain the EU debate to an index of benchmarks, the PNL took a visionary approach to Europe.

The political programme of the UDMR, with its Hungarian minority, reflected the position of the Alliance for Transylvania[28]: 'our goals are a strong decentralization, reform of the educational and healthcare system, the sustainable development of Transylvania, of the infrastructure and naturally, the enlargement of minority rights'. The UDMR programme was consistent with the general approach of the EU in the Romanian political arena. The EU was, once again, encompassed as a benchmark, interpreted in a sectoral logic: autonomy and minority rights. In order to legitimate its position and avoid being labelled 'separatists', the UDMR regularly used EU norms in support of its policies.[29]

Weak internal Europeanisation

The final step looks at the way the 'Europe' issue is reflected by the parties' internal organisation. The key question is to observe whether these systemic patterns have influenced internal dynamics or whether the EU has been the catalyst for a deeper transformation of the party organisation. Beyond limited changes in terms of the parties' internal democratisation, they remained impervious to the EU impact. Significantly, the Romanian parties' selection procedures for the European parliamentary candidates confirmed the tendency to recruit outside the party or to include on the lists names of recently recruited members. Significantly, the PDL list for the 2009 elections included candidates who joined the party on the eve of the European campaign.[30] The only reason for this odd method seems to be that candidates were chosen for their electability rather than their commitment to the EU.

In brief, when it comes to the impact of the EU on the internal parties' organisation, we can agree with the conclusion of Lewis, and state that the Romanian parties' Europeanisation has been 'something of a cosmetic process that left the internal roots of the party organization largely unchanged'.[31]

Conclusions

The European Union has provided considerable visible pressure on the new democracies – and Romania is no exception. Twenty years after the fall of the Ceauşescu regime, the Romanian political arena has changed profoundly. The status of 'EU member state' was envisaged as the end of a journey through a tortuous tunnel towards EU accession. From the very beginning, Europe had been the guiding star of Romania; the entire political spectrum gathered in a consensual logic in order to support the accession process. No real debate has ever been launched on EU accession. Europe was an unmentionable topic and each criticism was seen as political heresy, hampering the national objectives. From this point of view, the Europeanisation of the party system is exclusively seen as an extension of the democratisation process. At an individual level, the political parties have undergone a long process of external Europeanisation.

At no time was there an anti-European party in Romania, but the EU's indirect impact on the Romanian political arena cannot be denied.[32] First, the indirect EU effect can be seen in terms of stabilising the party system. Romanian parties rapidly understood that any political instability was not well received by Brussels and they were committed to guarantee a progressive stabilisation. Every time the spectre of anticipated elections haunted the political arena, the EU became an invisible arbiter. The 'EU-indirect effect' can also be seen as intrinsic to the complete allegiance of the Romanian political elite to the EU accession process. The EU had become a 'model of emulation'[33] for the political parties and important progress, such as the inclusion of the UDMR in the 1996 and 2000 coalitions, is directly linked to the EU's indirect impact.

The external Europeanisation of the parties throughout their international recognition may have been superficial, but it nevertheless allowed the transfer of values and policies required for the membership in the various European federations of parties. The decriminalisation of homosexuality is another eloquent example of policy adjustment in response to social networking in various European Parliamentary groups.

In reference to the Mair/Ladrech paradox (see page 3), the Romanian parties and party system remain consensual about Europe, which directly contributes to a 'depoliticisation' of the topic and creates pockets of 'Europeanised' elites, mainly linked to circles of Members of the European Parliament. The major parties with government experience, or parties like the PRM that held some prospect of entering government at the beginning of 2000, have been strongly in favour of enlargement and nearly all are committed to continuing European involvement. The consensus about Europe hampers a real Europeanisation beyond the limited circle of elites.

Such a situation renders the impact of EU-led changes upon the Romanian political arena as superficial and testifies for the weak public and political scrutiny of European politics. In addition, the nature of the Romanian political arena and the absence of a European debate within parties, social movements and even the media have limited the relevance of the European issue at the domestic level. As such, it is additionally claimed that, although there is evidence for depoliticisation in Romania, the EU is not the cause since it has never been an internalised framework, a channel through which political debates were triggered and public concerns represented.

Notes

1   G. Pridham, 'EU enlargement and consolidating democracy in post-communist states – formality and reality', *Journal of Common Market Studies*, 2002, vol. 40 (3), pp. 953–73; G. Pridham, *Designing Democracy: EU Enlargement and Regime Change in Post-Communist Europe*, Basingstoke, Palgrave, Macmillan, 2005; M. A. Vachudova, *Europe Undivided: Democracy, Leverage, and Integration After Communism*, Oxford, Oxford University Press, 2005; F. Schimmelfennig and U. Sedelmeier (eds), *The Europeanisation of Central and Eastern Europe*, Ithaca, NY, Cornell University Press, 2005.

2   P. G. Lewis, 'Changes in the party politics of the new EU member states in Central Europe: patterns of Europeanisation and democratization', *Journal of Southern Europe and the Balkans*, 2008, vol. 10 (2), pp. 151–65.

3   The PRM MEPs join the Identity, Tradition, Sovereignty group in the European Parliament in 2007. Following Italian MEP, Alexandra Mussolini's declarations against Romanian immigrants in Italy, the PRM withdrew from the group that formally ceased to exist on 14 November 2007.

4   The 2008 electoral failure pushed both the PRM and the PNG into extra-parliamentary opposition.

5   M. E. Fischer, 'The new leaders and the opposition', in D. N. Nelson (ed.), *Romania after Tyranny*, Boulder, Westview Press, 1992, p. 45.

6   T. G. Gallagher, 'The West and the challenge to ethnic politics in Romania', *Security Dialogue*, 1999, vol. 30, (3), pp. 293–304

7   A. Năstase, 'Politics in transition', *Central European Issues*, 1995, vol. 1 (1), p. 14 quoted by M. Ram, *Romania's Reform through European Integration: The Domestic Effects of European Union Law*, Kokkalis Program on Southern and East-Central Europe, 2001, http://www.hks.harvard.edu/kokkalis/GSW1/GSW1/20%20Ram.pdf.

8   Official declarations quoted on the internet page – Permanent Representation of Romania to the European Union ue.mae.ro/index.php?lang=ro&id=31&s=2437&arhiva=true.

9   'Dezbateri parlamentare. Sedința Senatului din 25 Aprilie 2005. Mircea Geoană - semnarea Tratatului de aderare a României la Uniunea Europeană, 25 Aprilie 2005, Luxembourg', http://www.cdep.ro/pls/steno/steno.stenograma?ids=5856&idm=2,02&idl=1.

10 Declaration from Dan Voiculescu's Internet site, http://www.danvoiculescu.ro/omul-politic/declaratii/declaratie-privind-semnarea-tratatului-de-aderare-a-romaniei-la-uniunea-europeana-.html.

11 Gallup Survey for the Eurobarometers, 6–28 March 2002, http://www.gallup.ro/romana/poll_ro/releases_ro/pr021111_ro/pr021111_ro.htm.

12 Based on a Gallup survey on the urban population, the most positive effect of EU integration is linked to an increase in quality of Romanian products in order to compete with EU market requirements. The worst effect was considered to be linked to an increase of taxes. Despite this general consensus, 68 per cent of the business community considered that EU integration will have a negative impact on the Romanian SMEs. 'Mediul socio-economic din România în perspectiva integrării în UE', *Gallup Survey*, March 2006, http://www.gallup.ro/download/Prezentare_Gallup-UNPR_2006.pdf. Similar opin-

ions were reported by the 2006 Rural Euroraboremeter: 'Almost one quarter of the inhabitants of Romanian villages endorse the EU integration and two thirds expect a life improvement afterwards', *Eurobarometrului Rural 2006*, Fundaţia pentru o Societate Deschisă, http://www.osf.ro/ro/publicatii.php?cat=4#.

13 The Eurobarometer survey on 'The 2009 European elections: expectations of the Europeans' testifies for the growing Romanian electorate disinterest in EU, ec.europa.eu/public_opinion/archives/ebs/ebs_303_fiche_ro.pdf.

14 The process of 'acquaintance' and progressive socialisation with the EU federations of parties has been the main source of Europeanisation of the Romanian parties. In 1987, the well-known leader of the Romanian Farmers' Party (PNTCD) asked Jean-Marie Daillet for membership in the EU of the Christian Democrats and on 6th December 1996, the EPP Political Bureau delivered the PNTCD, the status of observer. Three years later, after having flirted with the ELDR, the Hungarian Minority Alliance (RMDSZ) also received the EPP status of observer. At the 1996 20th Socialist International Congress from New York, the Democrat Party (PD) and the historical social democrats (PSDR) received the status of consultative members. Three years later, in Paris, they received full status. During the 2001 San-Domingo SI meeting, the heir of the FSN (the Social Democrat Party – PSD) received the status of consultative member. Two years later, it received full membership. Parallel to it, on 4 March 1998, the European Socialists accepted PD and PSDR as observers and, during the 2001 PES Congress in Berlin, the PSD received a similar status. In April 1999, the liberals (PNL) became full members of the ELDR. In 2005, the PD shifts allegiance and integrates the EPP by adopting a popular identity. After flirting with the PPE, PRM eventually joins the ITS group.

15 By 2000, the PSD ceased to be considered an anti-system party. The PSD pro-European positions were not the only reasons behind the dismantlement of its ostracism. The party undertook a deep process of programmatic chiseling and internal reorganisation. Its commitment to EU accession, transformed the PSD into one of the most Europhile Romanian Parties.

16 Interview quoted by Nadia Dincovici, 'Clasa politica, despre beneficiile aderarii', *Cronica Română*, 29 December 2006.

17 See the conditionality mechanism, H. Grabbe, *The EU's Transformative Power: Europeanisation Through Conditionality in Central and Eastern Europe*, Basingstoke, Palgrave Macmillan, 2006.

18 *Activitatea europarlamentarilor candidaţi la alegerile din 25 noiembrie 2007*, Institutul de Politici publice, Bucharest, 2007, 27 pp. Significantly, Ramona Mănescu (ALDE) won the 2008 price for Education for her interest in young generation involvement in EU decision-making.

19 'The Europeanisation of ECE Social Democracy: the case of HSP in ECE context', Paper prepared for the ECPR Joint Sessions of Workshops, Uppsala, 2004, p. 10 quoted by P. G. Lewis, 'Central European Party Systems in the Context of EU Enlargement', in A. Agh (ed.), *Post-Accession in East Central Europe: The Emergence of the EU 25*, Budapest: Hungarian Center for Democracy Studies, 2004, p. 252.

20 Hough defines this process as a 'process of moving policies, programmes, ideas or institutions across time and space'. D. Hough, 'Learning from the

West: policy transfer and programmatic change in the communist successor parties of Eastern and Central Europe', *The Journal of Communist Studies and Transition Politics*, 2005, vol. 21, (1), p. 7.

21 'Poziţionarea partidelor autohtone faţă de probematica europeană. Partidele româneşti faţă cu Europa', SAR Polocy Brief, no. 28, 2007, http://www.sar. org.ro/index.php?page=articol&id=233.

22 During the 2009 EP elections, the situation changed as, for instance, Frunzăverde, Daianu, and Luncă are not MEPs while Weber, Severin, Becali and Tokes confirmed their position as MEPs. This change might be explained by the following reasons: losers of the national 2008 elections (ex-ministries) and new comers queuing for the June 2009 elections; financial incentives (MEPs standard salary), the limited space for political promotion at a national level or a growing interest in EU affairs.

23 *Report from the Commission to the European Parliament and the Council on progress in Romania under the co-operation and verification mechanism{sec*(2008)2349, Brussels, 23.7.2008.

24 Programul politic de guvernare al alianţei PSD +PC 2008–2012. 10 angaja-mente pentru România, www.psd.ro

25 Mircea Geoană PSD President, «Introduction», Programul politic de guver-nare al alianţei PSD +PC 2008–2012, 10 angajamente pentru România, p. 3.

26 *Programul politic al Partidului Democrat Liberal* 2008, p. 4.

27 PNL Program de guvernare (2009–2012), 2008.

28 Impreună pentru Transilvania (modernizare si autonomie). Programul elec-toral al UDMR 2008

29 S. Gherghina and G. Jiglău, *Ce caută România in UE? (What is Romania Doing in the EU?)*, Timisoara, Bastion, 2008.

30 Based on the Public Policies Institute Report, of the nineteen out of the thirty-six observers that represented Romania in the EP before the 2007 elections, the candidates rated with a low level of involvement (D. Sârbu (PSD), M. Ridzi (PD), S. Busoi (PNL) and the entire PRM delegation) were re-proposed by their parties. Their position on the electoral lists didn't take into account their commitment to EP activities. ('IPP a întocmit clasamentul celor mai ac-tivi europarlamentari-candidaţi', *Gândul,* 17 Noiembrie 2007). The national headquarters controlled the lists, taking into account more the internal balance of power and less the involvement in the European arena.

31 Lewis, 'Changes in the party...', p. 154

32 See similar conclusions developed by R. Grecu, 'EU Enlargement and the Romanian Party System', in P. G. Lewis and Z. Mansfeldová (eds), *The European Union and Party Politics in Central and Eastern Europe,* Basingstoke, Palgrave Macmillan, 2006, pp. 227–9.

33 J. Sloam, 'West European social democracy as a model for transfer', *Journal of Communist Studies and Transition Politics*, 2005, vol. 21 (1), p. 68.

chapter ten | the strange case of the 'european parties'

Stefano Bartolini

Introduction

Historically, the rise of the state is associated with a transformation of collective action from localised to centralised, from spontaneous to planned, from reactive to proactive, from ephemeral to enduring. Similarly, the shift in the location of institutional power related to European integration can be accompanied by corresponding changes in the direction of the efforts of mass politics. European political parties (parliamentary groups as well as party federations) are at the core of this potential change and their evolution is crucial component. However, when analysed as structures of representation and of conflict resolution, European political parties display considerable peculiarities. In this chapter we discuss these peculiarities, taking the lead from the three main perspectives that characterise the classic literature on parties and party systems:

1. A *genetic* perspective, focusing on the process through which social and cultural divisions are politicised into a set of oppositions and organisations.

2. A *morphological* perspective, focusing on the format and the alignment of the party system and the way these affect the performance and the stability of the institutions.

3. A *representation* perspective, focusing on the extent to which elected political elites are representative of and responsive to the distribution of identities, interests, values and preferences of the voters and of public opinion in general.

Genetics – national parties and the formation of Europarties

In the European Parliament (EP), the wide diversity of national parties coalesces into fewer families of European parties to form 'Europarties' (this term refers to both European party federations and European parliamentary groups when no distinction is necessary). The development of Europarties is quite surprising if one considers:

- the diverging attitudes toward the integration process of national political parties that coalesce into a single European party family; and
- the unfriendly environment in which they operate.

Diverging attitudes – the integration process of European party families

The attitudes of national political parties toward the integration process can be viewed as rather permanent national geopolitical features (north–south; Catholic–Protestant; early arrivals–latecomers) or of changing institutional roles (government and opposition). Most interpretations, however, underline a *partisan* or *genetic* model, whereby orientation to the European Union (EU) is related to the dimension of competition prevalent at the national level. The orientation of national parties to the EU is seen as depending on their position on the left-right cleavage, on the authoritarian-libertarian cleavage, or on a GAL (Green, Alternative, Libertarian) versus TAN (Traditional, Authoritarian, Nationalist) opposition. This approach convincingly documents the common elements of the parties on the TAN wing – nationalist, populist right-wing radical – as the most clearly-defined group of Eurosceptical parties, while it is less convincing when dealing with other party families and with the economic dimension of integration.[1]

Left parties are generally regarded as opposed to excessive market competition and welfare retrenchment. To explain the recent growing social democratic support for integration, the argument is that this is the only way to reconquer the market control lost at the national level. But additional variables are necessary to explain further differences within the social democratic family (linkages with trade unions, levels of state spending, early arrival/latecomer, etc.). Within the denominational party family, most continental catholic parties favour further integration, while protestant parties are more reluctant. But even continental catholic parties need to be divided in sub-categories, with social Catholics being more supportive and right-wing Christian democrats less supportive (and growingly so). The very heterogeneous orientation of the liberal family is interpreted with reference to the different historical cleavages generating it: the urban-rural cleavage (British and German liberals); the state-church cleavage (Italy, France, Spain, the Netherlands and Belgium), and the historical centre-periphery cleavage (Scandinavia, including Finland, Welsh and Scottish liberals). The majority of the conservative parties are in favour of enhancing economic competition and free trade through the EU, but many fear too much EU interference and regulation. Therefore, the conservative party family requires a crucial subdivision between neo-liberal and nationalist conservative. Further distinctions are then discussed, adding groups such as 'Scandinavian conservatives', and 'post-authoritarian conservatives' (*New Democracy* in Greece and *Alianza Popular* in Spain).

A different partisan-genetic approach maps party orientation to the EU, starting from an objective definition of the EU's main features: centralisation, bureaucratisation and economicism, as opposed to national and regional independence, resistance to market economy, and globalisation. These features can then be related to four historical domestic cleavages:

1. economic left versus right (the right more supportive of supranational market);
2. the centre versus periphery (the centre more supportive of integration);

3. the urban versus rural (urban groups more supportive of European integration);

4. ecology versus growth (growth more supportive of economic integration).

Conservative parties should be pro-integration because their genetic orientation is pro-market, urban, and growth oriented. The social democrats' 'imprint' is urban, favourable to growth but opposed to the market and defensive of welfare, and this should result in a general positive orientation with, however, strong internal tensions. Liberal parties should be in favour of European integration the more their historical origin is pro-market, urban and growth oriented, but there should be strong internal tensions when the origin is not urban. Left parties and the greens, being anti-market, ecological more than growth oriented and urban, should have a negative attitude; rural/centre parties should consequently have a rather negative view.[2]

In conclusion, partisan and genetic interpretations require significant contextual specification when applied to European party family variations. They also substantiate the extent to which European issues reshuffle the historical roots of national parties. These perceptive analyses show the difficulty of interpreting the alignment on the integration issues of European party families via the national bases of the parties that compose them.

The unfriendly environment

The institutional and political environment of the Europarties is not particularly favourable to their development and consolidation for a number of reasons. First, key social actors enjoy today far more avenues of access to the EU decision-making centre than they did at the national level before representative government. With state representation in the Council, sub-national territorial representation in the regional institutions, corporate representation in the Brussels lobbying activities, it is unlikely that relevant interests regard Europarties as a privileged or preferred avenue of influence.

Secondly, historically, national parties were established either by way of organisational penetration from the centre to the periphery (opening braches, penetrating other organisations and elite groups, etc.), or the other way around of organisational penetration from periphery to the centre via incorporation in coalition at the centre of locally-entrenched elites and groups, as cross-local alliances of a traditional type. The complex cultural infrastructure of Europe and the solid entrenchment of national parties clearly exclude the possibility of organisational penetration from the EU level to the national one. Therefore, the prospects of Europarties are dependent on the solution of the vertical and horizontal problems of co-operation related to the incorporation of the peripheral (national) political elite into a supranational coalition. These coordination problems are absurd within the EU. Organising parties across territories and levels is likely to create centres of autonomy within party organisations and push towards the *stratarchic* and *indirect* type of parties. The likely incongruity among levels increases the acuteness of coordination problems.

Thirdly, the institutional and political environment of the Europarties is not particularly favourable because the EU's institutional environment on which the Europarties depend looks quite unfriendly to them. Among the positive incentives favouring the formation of Europarties one can mention the following: the introduction of direct elections in 1979; the generalisation of forms of proportional representation; the growth in competencies of the European Parliament (EP); the material resources and political advantages (financing, positions within the EP) offered by membership in one of the main EP groups; and the accrued influence of the large and inclusive Europarty on the Intergovernmental Conference negotiations and in general on EU policy formulation.

However, the list of negative incentives is longer – Europarties are 'unconstrained' by the disciplinary requirements for executive formation, composition, and tenure. They have no 'constitutional' powers and are bound by legislative powers. Treaty norms impose large majorities, which forces major groups to coalesce and prevents differentiation of voting choices. The need to support the overall institutional influence of the EP in the continuously evolving institutional architecture of the EU makes partisan alignments secondary. The membership enlargement de-structures internal patterns of behaviour and alliances. Europarties have limited sanctions capacity on individual Members of European Parliament (MEPs), but sanctions against national subgroups are impossible. Neither the parliamentary groups nor the parties' federations control EP candidate selection. Career and/or re-election of a MEP are not dependent on her/his vote, work and participation within the parliamentary group.[3]

All these elements could explain why neither group consciousness nor group stability is high in the EP. New groups composed of different parties have emerged at each election; splits and mergers are frequent, and the switching of group affiliation and the continuous arrival of new members de-institutionalises alliances and alignments.

Morphology – the surprising 'aggregation' into Europarties

Notwithstanding the unfavourable context outlined above, Europarties are seen to be growing in strength. A number of studies conclude that European parliamentary parties show a growing degree of voting cohesiveness. Research based on long-term roll-call analysis suggests a growing left-right alignment of coalitions and voting patterns.[4] Moreover, there is a tendency for national parties to aggregate into a small number of parliamentary groups and party families. In spite of the high number of national parties gaining representation in the EP, the number of groups has remained fairly stable. The number of 'one-party' groups has not increased over time and the percentage of MEPs belonging to a one-party group has declined. Therefore, EP party groups have so far had an astonishingly high capacity to incorporate new members and to limit the 'fragmentation' of the European party system.

On the extreme political right, the difficulties of international co-operation among nationalist parties might make it difficult to strengthen parliamentary groups. On the contrary, the growing competition between the European People's Party (EPP) and the Party of European Socialists (PES) brought about a growing logic to incorporate smaller groups and unaffiliated national parties. On the left, the collapse of communism has made more salient and visible a left-right divide in many European party systems and has helped strengthen the PES group – now the Group of Progressive Alliance of Socialists and Democrats (S&D). On the centre-right, the trend is even more significant: the 1986 admittance of the Spanish *Partido Popular* (PP) and the exchanges among the centre-right forces of the EPP, the European Democrats group, the Liberal Democrats and Reformists, the European Democratic Alliance, and the Union for Europe suggest that a multi-group split of the centre-right increases the power of the socialists.

The joining of the EPP by the British and Danish Conservatives (and, later, other secular conservative parties such as the Italian *Forza Italia*) was particularly surprising – even unlikely – given differences in ideological and representative factors. On the economic dimension, the social Catholicism of many Christian parties is at odds with the neo-liberal free market ideology of the conservatives. The differences in social and agricultural policy are significant. On the religious and value dimension, one could hardly find a more difficult relationship than that between the secular (and Protestant) conservative parties and the Christian/Catholic profile of most EPP members. On the European integration dimension, again it is difficult to imagine a stronger contrast than that between the pro-integrationist views of many founding Christian parties and the sceptical traditions of the British Tories and Danish conservatives. On the political level, it is not easy for those Christian parties with strong ties with Christian unions to accept the class-based anti-unionism of the conservatives. Yet, this 'unholy' alliance took place. A thorough analysis of the merger suggests that it was motivated by the common goal of maximising anti-PES parliamentary influence, and the EPP concern to relate to prospective governing parties (ND in Greece, PP in Spain) and to conservative parties in new member countries.[5]

It is puzzling that so ideologically heterogeneous alliances were achieved in the EP, which offers only a slight advantage to the economy of electoral scale. Scholars of national party politics may be bewildered by the ease of these alliances, considering how difficult things prove at the domestic level, where the prize for electoral size is very high (control of the executive and legislation).

These achievements can be interpreted as sign of the strengthening of the incipient left-right alignment, but they leave open the door to different interpretations. If the advantages of large coalitions in the EP are too small to justify large and heterogeneous political alliances, it may be that the costs too are irrelevant. These alliances had no palpable perspective of electoral reward/punishment in either the European or national elections. The respective electorates remained uninformed and unaware of the alliances, and were not asked to ratify them. Therefore, ideological constraints were more easily overcome. The differences over the economic, religious and European dimensions can be overcome because the EP is so invisible to the public at large and inconsequential for domestic alignments, so that no actual costs are foreseen in exchange for the advantages (even if limited).

In the EP, the lack of ideological intensity allowed compromises and alliances to be made without generating costs back home. In this sense, these alliances were instrumental marriages made possible by the low visibility of the EP politics. Therefore, from this point of view, the increase in alliances and the general expansive logic of European parliamentary groups could be read as a sign of weakness of the EP. This expansive logic reached a kind of limit with the creation of the European Conservatives and Reformists Group (ECR), composed mainly by the British, Czech and Polish Conservative domestic parties.

In addition to the lack of ideological constraints, the strengthening of the Europarties can also be explained by the considerable assistance and effort of top-down institutionalisation offered by the other EU institutions. This effort is mainly focused on strengthening the extra-parliamentary parties, the weak party federations.[6]

Since explicitly mentioning their function in the Treaty on the European Union (TEU), Europarties have continued to seek more explicit public recognition, legalisation, and public funding. The Nice Treaty has added the short but important sentence that the Council establishes the statute of the 'political parties at the European level' and the rules concerning their public financing (art. 191). The EP Constitutional Affairs Committee Final Report of 27th March 2000 on the Europarties statute and the debate surrounding and following it are important indicators of the effects of institutionalisation from the top of the Europarties. The final regulation,[7] approved in November 2003, set demanding conditions for the recognition of a European party. These deal with the aim to constitute a parliamentary group, the commitment to adopt a common electoral programme, the respect of the fundamental constitutional principles enshrined in the TEU, the commitment to spell out organisational provisions, a written statute, be democratically-legitimised and accountable, and have periodic meetings, consultative and management communications, democratic and transparent procedures.[8] This regulation immediately fostered the doubling of new European parties, from the four present in 2003 to the eight that were actually financed in 2004 on the basis of the new rules.

European parties commit themselves to use statute and financial reporting to inform and solicit the participation and the support of the citizens. As a result of the need to formalise both the conditions of financing and of operational survival, the organisation of political parties may experience a further institutionalisation, moving to a more hierarchical and authoritative model at the EU level.

In conclusion, the European parliamentary groups and party federations showed a tendency to become more inclusive and cohesive and to structure along a left-right alignment. This tendency is difficult to explain given the lack of inter-linkage between European and national electoral markets and the unfriendly institutional environment of the EP and European elections. It can be interpreted as resulting from the weakness of ideological constraints to alliance formation in the EP, combined with the institutions of the EU attempt to develop legitimising institutions, capable of fostering participation, support and recognition by the citizens. The Council and the Commission offered support and institutional recognition of the Europarties in exchange for indirect popular legitimacy, control and the exclusion of anti-EU sub-elites, and the necessary discipline required for the efficient working of Parliament. This attempt at top-down institutionalisation of a European 'party system' may be successful in the long run. Much depends on whether Europarties are (or will) be able to perform the function of 'informing and soliciting the participation and the support of the citizens' that they claim for themselves. In turn, this rests on how much these parties will shape and represent the attitudes of European citizens toward the European Union.

Representation – Europarties and the mass public

Do Europarties represent citizens, reflect public opinion, and can they improve the dissemination of information, competence, participation, etc.? The debate on the structuring of public attitudes concerning the European Union has evolved around three closely-connected issues:

- whether those attitudes are sufficiently salient to become important for voters;
- whether national and European parties and elites are in tune with their voters' attitudes on EU issues and institutions; and
- what are the dimensions along which such structuring takes place?

Salience

The *salience* of European issues divides observers as to the level of their importance for political behaviour at the elite and mass level. Through evermore frequent ratification referendums, European elections, debates about membership enlargement, wider publicity and media coverage of the Intergovernmental Conference (IGC), implications of EU legislation for everyday life and economic activities, and the actuality of the single currency, public opinion is today more directly involved in the integration process than ever before. This growing salience is indirectly witnessed by the fact that, over time, national political elites have been more and more busy convincing their domestic audiences that the benefits of further integration are greater than the costs. This is also indicated by the growing number of anti-EU breakaway groups and factionalism, manifested in political parties and relevant voter-party differences on a ratification referendum.[9]

However, a direct challenge to the salience of integration issues is made by those studies that suggest referendum outcomes and second-order European elections are affected by popular feelings about the incumbent governments, parties and leaders, and by the institutional context of the choice.[10] According to this view, the level of information and competence about the EU and the treaties is insufficient to justify the claim of their direct significance. Voters react to the EU question mostly on the basis of domestic issues and then on the perceived unity of their parties on such matters. This thesis is mainly supported by a strong correlation between negative support for government and anti-EU votes. However, this finding can be read to provide a different outcome: those who are worried by further steps in integration deem the incumbent government responsible for supporting them.

In tune

Observers and experts are divided over the extent to which representative elites adequately represent their voters' opinions. Studies based on the 1989 and 1994 European Parliamentary elections concluded that, on the whole, party voters show a similarity of position,[11] although most parties were perceived to be more in favour of EU integration than voters actually were. Ten years later, a similar study documents that considerable proportions of the European electorate have preferences on major European issues that are not represented by the positioning of their respective parties.[12] Other studies have documented that a mass-elite agreement is high on broad ideological dimensions, such as left-right and pro- or anti-integration, but when individual issues are considered (e.g. border control and common currency), the discrepancy between voters and their party representatives is considerable. The position of those voters who are sceptical or opposed are largely ignored in the representation channels. These authors suggest that voters are insecure about the outcomes of specific EU policies and therefore tend to prefer the status quo. In this view, political representation in the European Union might be deficient as regards specific EU policies, but it functions well as far as the grand directions of public opinion are concerned.[13] Yet, a different legitimate interpretation is that voters have more precise opinions about specific policies (common currency, enlargement, liberalisation/privatisation), while they tend to give generic answers to general questions concerning integration.

On the whole, the literature suggests that parties are more supportive of integration than their voters are, and that they reflect quite well voters' preferences on very general attitudes toward integration, but less so when issues are made specific. If Europarties sufficiently differentiate their positions, voters are offered the choice of moving to the party that best satisfies their preference (with the exception of the more extreme positions, which may require specific anti-integration parties to satisfy such preferences). If all parties develop a similar profile on the integration issue, the politicisation of such issues cannot be re-absorbed by inter-party realignment, but may trigger more conspicuous changes.

Dimensionality

The *dimensionality* of the attitudes toward the EU divides observers as to whether a left-right dimension or a more complex dimensionality (including a pro- and/or anti-integration or even other dimensions) prevails in the EP and with the general public, and how much these dimensions correlate with one another. Several research studies have concluded that for national parties, Europarties and voters, the addition of a second dimension to the dominant left-right is necessary, which is generally labelled 'nationalist versus supranationalist', or 'integration versus independence'.[14] Moreover, with the reconciliation of some left parties with, and the growing opposition of some right wing parties to the integration process, the two dimensions have become more independent one from the other.[15] Within the EP, roll call data and survey interviews have been used to show that a left-right alignment is the most important one, followed by the grouping around pro- and anti-integration.[16] Parliamentary groups are regarded as not ephemeral, but characterised by a common ideology, leading to cohesive roll call behaviour whenever facing those issues that reproduce the left-right dimensionality prevailing in national politics.

However, as soon as these studies move from issues that are similar ('isomorphic') to national ones (market regulation, welfare and social policy, environment, etc.) to issues pertaining to the 'constitutive' dimension of EU politics (membership, competences, institutional design), the within parliamentary groups' cohesion and the between parliamentary groups' dimensionality collapses. On constitutive issues, national differences weaken dramatically the cohesiveness available on isomorphic issues. Any attempt by the Europarties to take a clear stand on these problems would simply tear them apart and there is little chance that they would organise and compete by structuring opinions on the integration dimension. It is very difficult to organise the EU-level party system along lines that allow voters in European elections to have a meaningful say about the membership, competences and institutional design of the EU project. If EU constitutive issues became dominant in European politics, existing Europarties would find them divisive and national – rather than cross-national – political cleavages would emerge. Therefore, such a party system would almost certainly be a factor aiding the disintegration of the EU.[17] The fact that European elections are fought on national, normal, and common policy issues rather than on European issues is positive in this perspective.

The conclusion to be drawn from these studies is that the European parties have a chance to influence and mould public opinion if they organise competition on issues similar to national ones, collude among themselves to keep the issue of European integration off the EP political agenda, and limit the occasions for European voters to express themselves on such issues. The question is whether it will be possible to organise a Europarty system mainly based on the national isomorphic left-right alignment, while the most crucial issues agitating the EU concern problems of community definition, competence attribution, and decision rules.

Electoral representation – national and European arenas

Constitutive issues, such as membership, enlargement, democratisation, competence definition and institutional powers, refer to the definition of the European Union political community and constitutional order and, thus eventually, to its legitimacy. Within the nation state, these issues had to be resolved before the democratisation of the polity could take place and debates could concentrate on policy issues. When this did not happen, and a polity was democratised without legitimising its community and constitutional order, democratisation was likely to challenge the same territorial and constitutional bases of the polity. A polity cannot have at the same time a system of representation that concerns, on the one hand, its territorial and functional boundaries and, on the other hand, its internal differentiation of opinions and interests. The two alignments de-legitimise each other.

National parties regroup into families at the European level in a European 'party system' made up of vertical and horizontal coordination between national arenas and the European arena. They seem to be able to do so thanks to the low politico-ideological visibility of EP activities, the decisive support of the EU institutions, the concentration on national isomorphic policy issues, and the capacity to avoid taking stands on constitutive EU issues. At the same time, both national and Europarties stay silent and collude as much as they can on those constitutive EU issues where their respective divisions appear insurmountable and would undermine their effective existence.

The European political elites – which are indeed national party political elites – seem to believe that the more integration encompasses broader areas of delegation to the supranational centre, the more the traditional form of electoral legitimacy is needed, and the more a 'Europarty system' becomes necessary. There is an interest to 'engineer' a European party system that can work as a source of popular legitimacy to compensate the divisions that prevail at the intergovernmental level in the relationships among member countries. However, this must stop short of further institutional 'democratisation' of the EU. In the light of the analysis above, it is very doubtful that the European party system could perform an effective representation and channelling role if the institutional framework of the EU was to allow and require this. Party families are so inconsistent and divided on EU constitutive issues and on issues of boundary control versus openness that they would find it very difficult to select or even simply sustain an EU executive forced to take a clear stand on these types of issues.

If we cross-tabulate the nature of the issues concerning integration (functional issues isomorphic to the national ones versus EU constitutive issues) and the arenas where they can be politicised (national and European), we can describe a set of potential developments (see Table 10.1). If national type policy issues prevail in both arenas, we have the maximum likelihood of the structuring of a European party system that is isomorphic to the national ones. That is, the structuring of a European party system along dimensions of competition, partisan alignments and therefore party families, which are similar and consistent with those prevailing at the national level (*isomorphic structuring*).

If EU constitutive issues politicise in the national arenas while the European arena continues to structure along national type issues, we will witness the development of a *split party system*, with the two levels dealing with different kinds of issues and characterised by different kinds of alignments by the same parties. National alignments would suffer considerable strains as a result of the new issue dimension. However, the politicisation of EU constitutive issues in the national arenas of the member states could be controlled thanks to the considerable flexibility of the intergovernmental component of the EU system. This includes matters such as: treaty ratification and implementation can be postponed; integration may be slowed down in certain fields; countries may opt out of specific regimes; and legislative incorporations may be delayed.

Table 10.1: Type of predominant issues, arenas and type of party system

	National Arena	**Type of party system structuring**	**EU Arena**
National isomorphic functional issues*	Domestic politicisation of functional issues	ISOMORPHIC STRUCTURING ←————————————→ SPLIT PARTY SYSTEM	EU politicisation of functional issues
EU constitutive issues**	Domestic politicisation of constitutive issues	←————————————→ EUROPEAN MASS POLITICS	EU politicisation of constitutive issues

Notes:

*Issues related to market regulation, welfare and social policy, environment, ...

**Issues related to membership, competences, institutional design, ...

A split party system results also if national elections continue to be fought around national functional issues while EU constitutive issues are politicised in the European arena. This scenario would, however, be more problematic. As showed above, EU issues concerning membership, competences and institutional design tend to split European party families along national lines. Therefore, the politicisation of such issues in the European arena would have disruptive consequences for the autonomy and legitimacy of the European Parliament as a supranational body (different from the intergovernmental Council). The 'unified' EP does not allow the same flexibility as the multiple national arenas, whose differences are mediated by intergovernmental negotiations. Salient divisions concerning the EU 'constitution' would hardly be manageable by the current party families in the EP.

Finally, in the situation in which constitutive issues would be politicised both at the national and European level, we will witness the development of a true type of *European mass politics*, with de-structuring effects for the prevailing alignment at both levels: a party system in which left-right alignments are de-structured by territorial and EU constitutive issue alignments, and EU constitutive issue alignments are de-structured by left-right ideological families. In this latter case, the emergence of a new cleavage grounded on EU-specific polarisations is more likely. The aspects of this potential cleavage are not for discussion here.

In the present situation, Europarties perform only one role among the many played in national politics: they organise the infrastructure of the workings of the European Parliament, structuring the elections' outcomes into a small set of options; and they organise MPs in parliamentary groups and in legislative coalitions, disciplining their members' behaviour in the chamber, committees and agenda-setting processes. Europarties do not bring up, solicit, channel, aggregate citizens' and groups' demands; they do not identify and voice a political demand that is wanting. Europarties do not compete – arguing over differences, trying to embarrass each other, seeking places and leadership positions, selecting policy stands and political tactics – *in view of electoral rewards*. Europarties do not assure political *responsibility* by selecting the top political personnel and therefore ultimately conferring, either directly or indirectly, a decision-making power. The mentioned incipient party competition refers to policy differentiation and voting behaviour, but none of what is done in the EP has a bearing on the electoral fortunes of national parties and Europarties.

Although the Europarties receive considerable institutional assistance, their emergence as real structures of representation is still problematic. The issues generated by the integration process cannot easily be reconciled with nation state-based cleavage as they redefine the basic interests and identities on which those cleavages were built. These difficulties stem from the objective alien nature of those issues that pertain to territorial expansion and integration with respect to those issues that pertain to the domestic differentiation of interests and opinions.

If we aim at building Europarties as effective organisations for the representation and resolution of non-territorial conflicts, we should start by recognising that, at the moment, they are far from having achieved this status. We should shield them from tensions and burdens that they cannot currently bear. We should carefully and slowly foster their organisational strengths and their capacity to deal effectively with those socio-economic issues on which their domestic stands are compatible with the European ones.

Notes

1 L. Hooghe, G. Marks and C. Wilson, 'Does left/right structure party positions on European integration?', in G. Marks and M. R. Steenbergen (eds), *European Integration and Political Conflict*, Cambridge, Cambridge University Press, 2004, pp. 120–140.

2 J. Detlef, 'Der Einfluss von Cleavage-Strukturen auf die Standpunkteder scandinavischen Parteien üder der Beitritt zur Europäischen Union', *Politische Vierteljahresschrift*, 1999, vol. 40, pp. 565–90.

3 L. Bardi, 'Transnational party federations, European parliamentary party groups and the building of Europarties', in R. Katz and P. Mair (eds), *How Parties Organize: Change and Adaptation in Western Democracies*, London, Sage, 1994, pp. 357–72. See also M. N. Pedersen, 'Euro-parties and European parties: new arenas, new challenges and new strategies', in S. S. Andersen and K. A. Eliassen (eds), *The European Union: How Democratic Is It?*, London, Sage, 1996, pp. 15–40.

4 S. Hix and A. Kreppel, 'From grand coalition to left-right confrontation: explaining the shifting structure of party competition in the European Parliament', *Comparative Political Studies*, 2003, vol. 36, pp. 75–96.

5 K.-M. Johansson, *Transnational Party Alliances: Analysing the Hard-Won Alliance between Conservatives and Christian Democrats in the European Parliament*, Lund, Lund University Press, 1997.

6 Bardi, 'Transnational party federations, pp. 357–72.

7 Regulation (EC) No. 2004/2003 of the European Parliament and of the Council of 4 November 2003 on the regulation governing political parties at European level and the rules regarding their funding, *Official Journal of the European Union*, 15.11.2003, L297/1.

8 E. Külahci, 'Le statuts et le financement des fédérations européennes de partis: vers un renforcement du phénomène partisan européen?', Brussels: Paper presented at the Conference of the 'Association Belge de science politique', 14–15 March 2002.

9 M. R. Steenbergen and D. J. Scott, 'Contesting Europe? The salience of European integration as a party issue', in G. Marks and M. R. Steenbergen (eds), *European Integration and Political Conflict*, Cambridge, Cambridge University Press, 2004, pp. 165–93.

10 M. N. Franklin, C. Van der Eijk and M. Marsh, 'Referendum Outcomes and Trust in Government: Public Support for Europe in the Wake of Maastricht', *West European Politics*, 1995, vol. 18, pp. 101–17.

11 H. Schmitt, *National Party Systems and the Policies of the European Union. First Results from the 1994 European Election Study*, XVIth World Congress of IPSA, Berlin, 1994, August 21–25.

12 C. Van der Eijk and M. N. Franklin, 'Potential for contestation on European matters at national elections in Europe', in G. Marks and M. R. Steenbergen (eds), *European Integration...* pp. 32–50.

13 H. Schmitt and J. Thomassen, 'Dynamic representation: the case of European integration', *European Union Politics*, 2000, vol. 1, pp. 318–39.

14 G. Marks and C. Wilson, 'The past and the present: a cleavage theory of party

responses to European integration', *British Journal of Political Science*, 2000, vol. 30, pp. 433–59. See also S. Hix, 'Dimensions and alignments in European Union politics: cognitive constraints and partisan responses', *European Journal of Political Research*, 1999, vol. 35, pp. 69–106.

15 Schmitt and Thomassen, 'Dynamic representation...', pp. 318–39.

16 J. Thomassen, A. G. Noury and E. Voeten, 'Political competition in the European Parliament: evidence from Roll Call and Survey Analyses', in Marks and Steenbergen (eds), *European Integration...*, pp. 141–64.

17 Marks and Steenbergen, *European Integration...*, p. 164.

chapter eleven | conclusion: country comparison[1]
Erol Külahci

In Chapter One, I raised the question of the effect of the European integration process on the party system (political cleavages and political competition, including the format and the mechanics) and on political parties (policy stances). In the preceding chapters, we have seen how domestic party systems and political parties in eight member states have adapted (or not) to the European Union (EU), as well as the prospect offered by European party federations and party groups. Some party systems and political parties have barely changed at all, while France has changed significantly. We have seen detailed accounts of the ways in which continuity and change have occurred and some of the consequences. After pulling the work together with regard to what is really happening on the ground, it is now time to compare the country studies[2] at both the level of the party system (macro) and individual parties (micro). The issues discussed include the experiences in post-communist EU member states. We need to look at whether the variations follow identifiable cross-national patterns.

Comparing cases

Which factors are accountable for the Europeanisation of the party system and individual parties? Country-level factors or 'non-country'-level explanations such as the interaction between ideologies and political parties? These factors are described as *intervening variables*. A reminder: the *dependent variables*, those varying outcomes that we wish to explain, are the (non) Europeanisation of the party systems and the domestic parties; the *independent variable* is the European integration (including the European parliamentary elections and the Europarties) whose effect is mediated by the intervening variables.

Our analysis approaches the basic hypotheses through concentrating on several distinct indicators that capture key aspects of our dependent variables. These were defined in Chapter One for the party system and the political parties. Regarding the intervening variables, it is important to state those that are central to the project's hypotheses. On the one hand, the main *country-specific variables* are:

- the institutional framework;
- the geopolitical model;
- the overall level of EU scepticism of the voters/public opinion;
- the existence (or not) of a Eurosceptic party; and
- the popular referendum.

On the other hand, the key *'non-country'-specific variables* that we consider are important to the project's hypotheses are:

- the institutional model (government/opposition);
- the partisan model including the ideology on various dimensions such as left-right or libertarian-authoritarian;
- the structure of cleavages;
- the level of internal party consensus or division over EU-related issues;
- the political parties' strategic responses;
- the incentives/disincentives in electoral, socio-economic and/or socio-political terms; and
- the electoral system.

Last but not least, there are also *external factors* such as economic and financial globalisation.

Disjunction between 'non-Europeanised' party systems and Europeanised political parties

In Chapter One, two main hypotheses were advanced. Which country case confirms which hypothesis?

Hypothesis I proposes that European integration has not resulted in a shift of party system. However, it has led to a shift in the policies of individual parties. In other words, there is a disjunction between a 'non-Europeanised party system' and 'Europeanised political parties'. Strong cases confirming the Mair/Ladrech paradox (see page 3) are: Italy, Germany, the United Kingdom (UK), Greece, Spain, Poland and Romania. Regarding the format, there is no change except the superficial one in the UK with the strengthening of the UK Independence Party (UKIP). European integration seems to have a limited impact on the mechanics of the party system in Germany, Greece and Spain even though the German and Spanish cases show a pro-European stance. In Italy, European integration seems to have reinforced the Eurosceptics; in the UK, it boosted the cleavage between the Eurosceptics and the integrationists.

In terms of policy stance, domestic political parties are rather 'Europeanised' (pro- and anti-Europe), while in Romania, political parties have silently been pro-European. Perhaps, this is because Romania has only been a member state since 2007.

All in all, the great majority of cases support *hypothesis I*. Moreover, these cases indicate that the European dimension is more absorbed and exploited by a pre-existing dimension of competition, rather than constituting a new dimension.

Inspired by Przeworski and Teune[3], Theodore Meckstroth points out: 'if sub-groups of the population derived from different systems do not differ with regard to the dependent variable, the differences among systems are not important in explaining this variable'.[4] In our specific analysis, the case studies show no significant variation with regard to the dependent variable. This implies that the differences among country systems (Italy, Germany, UK, Greece, Spain, Poland

and Romania) are not important in explaining the non-Europeanisation of party systems and the Europeanisation of individual parties (Mair/Ladrech paradox).

In Germany, there is a *grundkonsens* (basic consensus) in favour of European integration – except for Turkey's membership to the EU. Recently, the elite consensus had to take into consideration German public opinion and emphasise the benefits of European integration for Germany. As a result, Germany witnessed a move from Kohl's 'exaggerated' multilateralism to Schröder's 'pragmatic' multilateralism and, then, Merkel's 'self-assured modesty'. It could be expected that Chancellor Merkel's 'modesty' will continue despite some turmoil with its new liberal partner (FDP) in government.

In Italy, the Christian Democrats adopted the 'don't complain, don't explain' mode of communication with the voters. After the ratification of the Maastricht Treaty (1992), Italian party elites took explicit positions. However, Europe has not disrupted the party system nor created a cleavage. Competition over Europe has even reinforced the established patterns of competition.

In the UK, the main parties managed to control the effects of Europeanisation to a high degree with regard to the nature of British party system competition. They made concessions only for the European elections: some degree of proportionality applies to the European parliamentary arena and this allowed the emergence of UKIP. In the domestic arena, the 'first-past-the-post' system remains as it secures electoral advantages for the Conservatives and Labour. Following the May 2010 elections, one could expect the new coalition between the Conservative Party and the Liberal Democrats to continue controlling the effects of Europeanisation.

In Greece, Europe has not significantly affected the party system. At the micro level, EU membership has shaped both ruling parties' (PASOK and ND) policy options, which had been justified by and referred to the widely acceptable European framework of 'doing business'. In parallel, Eurosceptic parties have also taken to the floor (KKE, SYRIZA, LAOS). The social democratic PASOK, back in power since October 2010, has experienced tremendous socio-economic challenges in the context of the global financial and economic crisis. On November 2011, the PASOK has constituted a 'National Utility' government headed by Lucas Papademos with the ND and LAOS (which withdrew in February 2012). This government as well as the previous ones asked for support to the important Greek debt and international and European institutions agreed to help under strict austerity packages. With the 2012 elections, the results of the splinter parties (All Greek Citizen's Chariot, Democratic Left, Social Deal, Democratic Alliance, Independent Greeks) and the already existing radical left (KKE, SYRIZ) and right parties (LAOS, *Hrisi Avgi*) will be important. Indeed, the 2012 elections may be highly significant for the Greek party system to the extent that Greece might confirm hypothesis 2. In other words, experiencing the consequences of the subprimes' crisis, European integration (in conjunction with international institutions and important domestic EU member states) has resulted in a shift both of Greek individual parties and party system.

In Spain, there has been a consensus in favour of European integration close to the German *grundkonsens*. Since its accession to the EU, the popular support for

European integration has been high, although still not as strong as that of the elites.

In central and eastern Europe, the Polish and Romanian party systems experienced a normalisation of the European debate. The Romanian party system looks more committed to the EU than the Polish system and European integration was even a favourable factor for the stabilisation of the Romanian party system.

What about relevant intervening variables? Drawing on the findings of the contributions, this volume emphasises two variables that mediate the impact of European integration:

1. There is a lack of perceived added value in debating Europe at domestic level, which reinforces Hooghe and Marks. European integration is not really politicised because mainstream party elites do not see an electoral advantage in doing so.[5] Thus, our findings on these seven country studies also strengthen Mair's observation according to which this elites' attitude and behaviour serve the interests of political parties as they are insulated from electoral constraints with due exception to referendum and direct democracy.[6]

2. We can quote a country-level intervening variable, namely the role of domestic public opinion. This public support has a limited impact on the extent of Europeanisation as long as the political elites do not politicise and debate European issues. Relevant also to European ex-communist states, public opinion in central and eastern European countries visualised and associated freedom with membership to EU institutions. More particularly for the Romanian case, Europarties (a third variable) contributed to diminishing ideological distance, allowing collaboration between the centre-right government and the Hungarian regionalist UDMR.

Table 11.1 presents an overview of the impact of European integration on the format and mechanics of party systems and the policy stances of individual parties.

Table 11.1: Impact of European integration on party systems and individual parties

	Party systems		**Political parties**
	Format	*Mechanics*	*Policies*
Italy	No	Yes (reinforcing the mechanics)	Yes
Germany	No	No (pro-European)	Yes
United Kingdom	No (superficial change)	Yes (European cleavage)	Yes
Greece	No	No	Yes (weak)
Spain	No	No (pro-European)	Yes
Poland	No	No	Yes (partially)
Romania	No	No	Yes (partially)

Conjunction of Europeanised party system and political parties

Hypothesis II points out that European integration has resulted in a shift not only of individual parties, but also of the party system. In other words, a conjunction emerges of a 'Europeanised party system' and 'Europeanised political parties'. Among the country cases, France confirms this hypothesis since it has experienced an important European cleavage between Eurosceptics and integrationists.

Indeed, Europe is a significant factor – but it is not a 'new' dimension of domestic political competition. In the 1990s, the format of the French party system was affected by parties strongly opposed to European integration: the *Mouvement des Citoyens* (MDC) of the former Minister Chevènement and the *Mouvement pour la France* (MPF) emerged respectively on the left and right sides of the political spectrum.

The European issue divides French public opinion. As Bell pointed out, (Chapter Two) the European cleavage cuts across political alliances and political families. European integration is politicised because mainstream party elites probably see an electoral advantage in doing so.[7] In particular, French candidates of mainstream parties for presidential election embrace Europe and, accordingly, this has opened up competition between pro- and anti-European parties.

What about the independent variable? The EP elections provided the basis for a significant challenge to the dominance of French domestic actors. It introduced an anti-European undertow. In 1984, it allowed the expression of the *Front National* (FN) which, in turn, contributed to ending the French bipolar system, the resignation of Minister Mauroy and the opening up of the fragmentation process. On the eve of the 1999 European elections, a new conservative party emerged namely *Chasse, Nature, Pêche, Tradition* (CNPT). At the same time, these elections reinforced the extreme left parties, *Ligue Communiste Révolutionnaire* (LCR) and *Lutte Ouvrière* (LO). In the 2004 European elections, Bayrou's UDF (then called 'Modem') was rewarded with 12 per cent of the votes, contributing to the party's emergence as a component player in French politics.

With regard to the intervening variables, these can be pointed out. First, the strategic interaction among political parties proves to be decisive. In France, de Gaulle's clash with the European Commission reinforced the image that Gaullism was the defender of national interests. Such a positioning created difficulties for the Socialist Party in relation to the national interest and threatened the Socialist's alliance with the Communist Party.

Secondly, the 1979 EP elections (see page 20)'were conducted on a proportional list system and used the country as a "constituency" unlike the Fifth Republic (except 1986) of two round constituencies'. This confirms the relevance of the electoral system, which plays a part as an intervening variable.[8]

Thirdly, country-level factors influenced the outcome of the Europeanisation of the party system. European integration was associated with peace after World War II. French public opinion is generally in favour of European integration, but there are opponents to integration located predominantly among the working class. With the exception of Bayrou's *Modem*, each political party has its Eurosceptic voters. During the 2005 referendum, the content of the European Treaty was badly explained and this led to the rejection of the Constitution. As Bell writes, (see page 25) this was 'the "non" of the insecure, of the middle professions, agriculture, small businesses and labour'.

Table 11.2 summarises the impact of European integration on the French party system and individual parties.

Table 11.2: Impact of European integration on the French party system and individual parties

	Party systems		Political parties
	Format	*Mechanics*	*Policies*
France	Yes (MDC, MPF)	Yes	Yes

European socio-economic policy positions of domestic political parties

Regarding the European policy positions of domestic parties, I will present our main findings with respect to the contribution of Hooghe, Marks and Wilson. In addition to their analysis and to Bartolini's comment,[9] I review the domestic parties' socio-economic positions from our eight country studies and point out the main factors in the Europeanisation context (impact of European integration on political parties and party systems) stressed by the respective authors of this edited volume. Accordingly, I will first focus on the four major political families.

The main political families

Social democratic parties

Considering class cleavage, Marks and Wilson point out that a series of intervening variables explain variations within the social democratic family. It 'is a function of the achievements of social democracy at the national level, the costs imposed by European economic integration, and the prospects for Euro-Keynesianism'.[10] Accordingly, they identify the following important variables:

- the strength of national social democracy – weak (PS in France, PASOK in Greece, PSI and PDS in Italy, and PSOE in Spain) *versus* strong (Labour in the UK, and SPD in Germany); and
- the distinction between founding (SPD in Germany) and subsequent (Labour in the UK) member states when considering strong national social democracy.

Moreover, Hooghe, Marks and Wilson expect that 'the social democratic parties have become distinctly more pro-integration as regulated capitalism has come on to the European agenda'.[11] Confirming this line of analysis regarding, for instance, cleavages and party organisation and public opinion,[12] Delwit proposes to distinguish between external conditions (such as geopolitics and the impact of the international economy) and internal conditions (such as the domestic history and culture, political system and the electoral system).[13] Most cases tend to confirm these observations, such as the Romanian PSD and PC. The Italian People's Party/ *Margherita* developed the traditional commitment of the Christian Democrats towards the idea of a united Europe and the Left Democrats are also pro-integration. Both parties merged into the Democratic Party, being a member of the Party of European Socialists (PES). In the UK, the main influence on the return to Europe of the British Labour Party, observe Hanley and Loughlin, (see page 81) 'was probably the awareness, among union leaders and politicians alike, that Europe offered a more promising field for the promotion of a progressive social agenda than was possible in Thatcherite Britain'. In Spain, the PSOE has been very enthusiastic about European integration because Europe is considered as part of the solution to Spain's historical problems in economic and political terms. In Romania, the ex-communist PSD seems to be in favour of further integration in socio-economic fields (social, education, research, health and economic development). Other social democratic parties show signs of considerable division. Even if the French social democratic party became more pro-integration, it retains anti-European factions (*Nouveau Monde, Nouveau Parti Socialiste*) that rose following the increase of Euroscepticism in the mid-1990s.

Furthermore, the positions of the German SPD and the Polish SLD were dependent on the opposition/government variable. In opposition, and in the context of the Maastricht Treaty negotiation, the SPD threatened to reject the Treaty. It espoused programmatic pluralism, which echoed the views of various ideological streams (traditional left, post-materialist left and modernising centre), probably to catch the attention of the voters. In government, the SPD developed a vision of Europe that was more coherent and nuanced. After the fall of the Berlin wall, the European issue was marginal for the Polish SLD in opposition. In power from 1993 to 1997, the SLD confirmed Poland's commitment to EU integration. To be precise, it shunned the 'communist' model for the 'social market economy' model. Clearly, the incentives were the socio-economic transformations and domestic democratic credentials.

In brief, we emphasise two intervening variables. We confirm the importance of class cleavage and related socio-economic ideology as a mediator of European integration's influence on the social democratic parties' positions: the socio-economic advantage of Europe for the Labour Party during the period of the Thatcher government; the socio-economic and socio-political advantages of Europe in post-Franco Spain; and the Polish socio-economic transition. Social democratic parties' positions are also affected by the opposition/government dynamics (Germany, Poland and the UK) – they are important factors regarding the strategic responses of this political family.

Christian democratic parties

The impact of religious cleavages on European party systems presents two different outcomes. On the one hand, parties identifying themselves mainly with the national character of Protestant churches may be quite sceptical regarding European integration.[14] In Northern Ireland, the UUP (aligned with the Tories) and the (more extreme) DUP are against the Euro and are critical of European social policies. On the other hand, Catholic countries and/or regions are likely to be pro-European integration since this is 'consistent with the supranational aspirations of the Catholic Church and the anti-national bias of the Catholic parties that arose from their historical battles with national state-builders'.[15] Accordingly, Marks and Wilson distinguish on the Catholic side between social Christian democratic parties (French MRG and UDF-CDS, German CDU and Italian DC/PP) and right-wing Christian democratic parties such as the German CSU.

Moreover, the German CDU/CSU position was also dependent on the opposition/government variable. Under Kohl's leadership, the CDU/CSU in government pursued two main goals: the unification of Europe and German unity. Once in opposition, the CSU leader, Stoïber, contested the German contribution to the EU budget and the EMU.

To synthesise, we emphasise two intervening variables. The positions of the Christian democratic parties are largely influenced by ideology and related social cleavages; these are coupled with the opposition/government dynamics in Germany.

Liberal parties

The liberal family is the most ideologically-diverse major party family; it has been influenced by the main social cleavages.[16] There are three variants of liberal parties. First, liberal-radicalism 'is strongly pro-European integration'. This stance is against aggressive nationalism and points out the EU democratic deficit.[17] In Britain, the Liberal Democrats are strong advocates of European integration. They are also in favour of some kind of regulation with firmer fiscal incentives/disincentives 'to make polluters pay or encourage the use of energy-conserving materials' (see page 81). In France, the *Modem* (Bayrou transformed the UDF into the *Modem*) constitutes a good example of an exception to the general opposition of right-wing parties to regulated capitalism.

Secondly, liberal-conservatism 'advocates European (economic) integration as a means to lower trade barriers and institutionalize free markets'.[18] In power, the German liberal FDP favours a liberal and market-oriented perspective. In Romania, the Liberal National Party (PNL) supports economic competitiveness at the European level to which EU social standards should be subordinated.

Thirdly, agrarian or centre parties 'are distinguished by their agrarian roots and their defence of the periphery in opposition to national (and European) establishment(s)'.[19] The Polish Peasant Party – the former communist United Peasant Party – is rather Eurosceptic and had doubts about the membership of

Poland to the EU and suggested that there should be a 'partnership' with EU. The main disincentive was the socio-economic interest of the Polish farmers in relation to a 'hostile' EU Common Agricultural Policy.

Regarding our intervening variable, the position of liberal parties seem to be determined mainly by ideology and related social cleavages, as well as economic interests.

Conservative parties

In addition to the Scandinavian economic conservative parties, Marks and Wilson distinguish between national conservative parties (France's RPR, the UK's Conservative Party) and post-authoritarian conservative parties (Spain's AP/PP and Greece's ND).[20] Regarding national conservative parties, the French conservative Gaullist party (RPR/UMP) adopted a clear nationalist stance, starting with de Gaulle. Similarly, Chirac used the 'anti-European tack' to win the battle against Balladur to lead the French conservatives during the 1995 presidential election. In turn, Sarkozy was the main competitor of Chirac and declared being against Turkey's membership application to the EU. In Italy, *Forza Italia* showed hints of Euroscepticism (the lowest level of programmatic commitment in Italy). It has also to be remembered that the National Alliance (Italy) merged with *Forza Italia* to form The People of Freedom under the presidency of Berlusconi.

As far as post-authoritarian conservative parties are concerned, the Spanish *Partido Popular* (PP) has stressed that the EU should stay as a union of national states. The PP clearly has a nationalist and pragmatic orientation. It supported the convergence criteria of EMU because this would serve as a justification for cuts in domestic public expenditure.

Hooghe, Marks and Wilson have observed: 'Conservative parties with a TAN (traditional/authoritarian/nationalist) inclination tend to be Eurosceptic. The new politics dimension efficiently distinguishes between anti- and pro-integration mainstream party families'.[21] In the UK, the Conservative Party was not totally in favour of the neo-liberal approach under Thatcher as some pro-European Tory factions supported economic and political integration. Major's defeat in 1997 has lead to some decantation within the Conservative Party. In addition, the Tory response (under Howard) to the emerging UK Independence Party was to reinforce Tory Euroscepticism. In Poland, the conservative Law and Justice (*Prawo i Sprawiedliwość* – PiS) is largely Eurosceptic. It came together with the British Conservative Party and they created the European Conservatives and Reformists (ECR) in the European Parliament.

Briefly, we emphasise one intervening variable. The position of conservative parties is largely influenced by ideology: defence of the national interest is prominent in their strategies and policy choices.

The other political families

Radical left parties

Hooghe, Marks and Wilson note that 'radical left parties are highly Eurosceptical and this accounts for the inverted U-shape describing all parties on the left/right dimension'.[22] The Italian and Greek cases strengthen their expectations. The Italian *Rifondazione Comunista* shows strong opposition to European integration and the Greek KKE (communists) perceives the EU as dependent on the economic and military priorities of the United States. In addition, a new coalition party operates in the Greek party system: the SYRIZA, which is opposed to neo-liberalism and thus is critical of the EU policies and the Lisbon Treaty.

Yet, the German and Spanish cases show that not all radical left parties are highly Eurosceptic. The German Left Party supports the principle of European integration, but is against its neo-liberal content. Its leader, Oskar Lafontaine (the SPD's ex-leader), is convinced that the EU is central to attain socialist goals. The Communist Party of Spain has been in favour of EU membership. In 1986, it became the *Izquierda Unida* (IU), a 'federalist' rather than Eurosceptic party, which criticised the Maastricht Treaty and the project of the EU Constitution. This was a strategic response in relation to the PSOE. The IU is in favour of EU intervention in the majority of public policies, except in employment and social areas.

Other radical left parties seem to be rather pragmatic. The anti-Europeanism of the French communist party (see page 27) 'conformed to the interests of the world communist movement in Moscow'. It was ambiguous since it appealed to voters with its anti-European discourse while its alliance with the Socialist Party constrained the party to show a 'credible' profile. In particular, Bell observes that (see page 27) 'anti-Europeanism enabled the PCF to grab the nationalist, not to say xenophobic, high ground and mobilised its activists also on a note of strident patriotism'. However, its support for the 1997 Jospin government opened up the left anti-European space to Trotskyite parties. In addition, communist supporters left the PCF to join socialist and Trotskyite parties (*Mouvement pour un parti des travailleurs*, LO, LCR).

In summary, we emphasise four intervening variables. We confirm the importance of socio-economic ideology with regard to the policies of radical left parties. In addition, geopolitical considerations feed policy stances, such as the opposition to US hegemony. The radical left parties' strategy in the domestic competition with social democratic parties as well as access to power are important intervening variables that mediate the impact of European integration on their policies.

Regionalist parties

Considering party systems animated by a centre-periphery cleavage, Marks and Wilson have distinguished between political parties representing territorially-dispersed peripheral minorities (such as Scandinavian farmers and Lutheran fundamentalists) and political parties representing territorially-concentrated peripheral minorities (Catalonia, Basque country, Scotland, Wales). The former is:

likely to oppose all efforts to centralize authority, whether it is in the central state or at the European level. From their standpoint, European integration is, if anything, more threatening because it shifts decision making even further away from their control and is yet more alien to their cultural milieu.[23]

The latter type of regionalist party considers that 'European integration can facilitate decentralization of authority from the central state to their region or ethno-territorial nation'.[24] According to Hanley and Loughlin, (see pages 84–8) peripheral parties were initially against European integration for different combined reasons. Europe was perceived as a threat to achieving statehood and/or a capitalist programme and a rich man's club. In the 1990s, their position changed as Europe was considered 'an opportunity to by-pass their national government in a new *Europe of the Regions*' (see page 84). In the United Kingdom, the Welsh and Scottish parties of the periphery (the SNP and PC respectively) are mainly in favour of 'independence in Europe'. The Scottish Nationalist Party seems to have a clearer economic policy in favour of sovereignty in fisheries, fiscal and constitutional matters, while both parties present a more 'social democratic position' than Labour on social and environmental policies. In Northern Ireland, the fundamental cleavage 'is, whether Northern Ireland should remain part of the United Kingdom or whether it should leave the UK to join with the Irish Republic'(see page 87). Departing from this cleavage, Europe made it possible to change the parameters of Northern Ireland politics. In particular, it has led some to conceive sovereignty 'as capable of being divided and flexible rather than indivisible and rigid', (see page 85) leading to the 1998 Good Friday Agreement. The SF and SDLP endorse the Euro as well as the social policy and social rights agenda of the EU.

Hanley and Loughlin's analysis is strengthened by the experience of the Catalonian Nationalists Party (CiU), which perceives Europe as the vector of modernisation and openness against the 'rejection' and centralism of the Spanish state. In addition, the Republican Left of Catalonia (ERC) supports European integration and is in favour of a strong European government accountable to the European Parliament. Like their Scottish and Welsh counterparts, the Basque Nationalist Party (PNV) is for 'national independence within the EU' and it is in favour of European integration. In Romania, the Hungarian Democratic Alliance (UDMR) prefers to support a federal Europe. To avoid being labelled 'separatists', the UDMR has regularly used EU norms in justifying its position.

We emphasise mainly one intervening variable. The position of peripheral parties seems to be essentially determined by ideological factors linked to the centre-periphery, left-right politics and Eurosceptic integration cleavages.

Green parties

Hooghe, Marks and Wilson expect that the 'Green parties, located towards the GAL (green, alternative and libertarian) pole, have become more integrationist'.[25] The majority of cases confirm this expectation. Becoming more integrationist, the German Greens supported common regulation and common standards for environmental protection. In Greece, the *Oikologoi Prassini* is in favour of social and environmental regulations. In contrast, the British Green Party is rather Eurosceptic and prefers a principled way of conducting politics, while it recognises the merit of working with the EP.

In France, *Les Verts* support progressive integration although, as a nuance, minority factions have expressed reservations on neo-liberal Europe. Their alliance with the Socialist Party is important in the perspective of future access to government. In power and following pressure from Schröder, the *Grünen* had to withdraw German support for a car recycling directive because of its 'negative' economic effects on the German car industry.

In summary, we emphasise two intervening variables. First, we confirm the importance of ideology regarding the promotion of 'green' regulation at the European and domestic levels. The position of Green parties is also affected by the opposition-government dynamics. For example, when they were given a role in government, the Greens adapted their position and clearly followed German economic self-interests and geopolitical strategies.

Radical right and right-populist parties

Hooghe, Marks and Wilson observe that 'parties near the TAN pole, i.e. radical right and right-populist parties, are, without exception, highly Eurosceptical'.[26] All our cases confirm, to an important extent, this observation. The Italian Northern League generally opposes European integration. The German far right parties took up the social question and developed 'anti-capitalism' and 'anti-globalisation' as major themes. They perceive the EU as 'a neo-liberal tool for Anglo-Saxon or US hegemonic interests'(see page 46). In Greece, the LAOS (Popular Orthodox Rally) shares common features with other European extreme right parties on immigration-related issues and the 'nation-centred' approach.

Surprisingly, although the National Alliance (Italy) is Eurosceptic, it defended the protection of member states' economies at the European level against globalisation. The FN is highly Eurosceptic although, as an exception, Le Pen was once favourable to the Euro.

In brief, we emphasise two intervening variables. The position of the radical right and right-populist parties is largely influenced by ideology. In addition, the strategic interaction with competing parties induces a variety of positions from domestic (immigrants, anti-capitalism) to international (US hegemony) issues.

Summarising the key factors

In addition to the impact of European integration and to the various relevant distinctions and variations within party families provided by Marks and Wilson, Table 11.3 relates party families to the main factors (ideology, participation in government, strategic competition and geopolitics). Our findings strengthen the expectation of Hooghe, Marks and Wilson about the explanatory power of intervening variables such as ideology and strategic responses. Analysing the 'weight' of the various factors can be very difficult. However, this crucial methodological question cannot be ignored.[27] In this respect, Marks, Wilson and Ray have concluded in a previous study that the ideological location of a party is 'a stronger influence than strategic competition, national location, participation in government, or the position of a party's supporter'.[28] Our findings from the eight countries under study strengthen their analysis and point out, in particular, that the ideological location of a party is 'a stronger influence than' strategic competition and participation in government. On a more tentative note, our findings bring out some elements to answer Hooghe and Marks' question on the role of geopolitics.[29] Our comparative analysis found that geopolitics is explicitly important for radical left parties and constraining for the Greens. All in all, our eight country studies point out that ideological location is stronger than participation in government, strategic competition and geopolitics.

Table 11.3: Political families, domestic socio-economic party positions and main factors (eight country studies)

Political families	Social cleavages and ideology	Participation in government	Strategic competition	Geopolitics
Social democracy	X	X	X	X
Liberal	X	X		
Christian Democrat	X	X		
Conservative	X		X	
Radical left	X	X	X	X
Radical right	X		X	
Green	X	X	X	X
Regionalist	X			

Patterns of opposition/co-operation over European integration in party systems

Another central claim of this volume is that three patterns of opposition/co-operation in party systems are present in the EU countries – confirming the 'potentially' coherent and structured nature of the debate over Europe.[30] As opposed to our previous findings on the Europeanisation of party systems and individual parties, the differences between the national systems are important to explain the patterns of co-operation/competition in party systems over European integration issues. First, an important country-level factor that mediates the process of Europeanisation is the weight of a Eurosceptic party (or parties) in a given EU member state. According to Sartori, the power of a party is the strength of the parliamentary party, which 'is indicated by its percentage of seats in the lower chamber'.[31] In addition, I will refer when necessary to this electoral strength. Therefore, I distinguish different types of political party on the basis of their seats and political weight in the domestic assembly:

- the 'major' party: more than 40 per cent of the seats (X>40%);
- the 'very important' party: between 30 and 40 per cent (30%<X<40%);
- the 'big' party: between 20 and 30 per cent (20%<X<30%);
- the 'middle-range' party: between 10 and 20 per cent (10%<X<20%);
- the 'small' party: between 5 and 10 per cent (5%<X<10%);
- the 'very small' party: less than 5 per cent (5%<X).

Secondly, other factors intervene, such as the similarities/differences in terms of political parties' policy stances. As previously shown, for each political party family there are various factors in relation to these stances, such as social cleavages and ideology, participation in government, strategic competition and geopolitics.

Accordingly, I have singled out three patterns of co-operation/competition in party systems over European integration issues: the Europhile party system (EPS); the divided party system (DPS); and the party system with significant Eurosceptic parties (PSEP).

In addition to the comparative conclusions from the in-depth studies, I take into account countries that were not analysed in this book. I classify them following the different types of patterns of co-operation/competition in party systems. To do so, I consider the national election results in terms of the distribution of seats in the lower chamber, per party, up to July 2010. In that respect, I used the *PARLINE database of the Inter-Parliamentary Union* (IPU).[32] This was backed up by academic literature to analyse the domestic parties' positions on the European integration issue. This allowed me to approximate the patterns of domestic party systems in relation to European integration issues. These countries may also deserve in-depth analysis.

The Europhile party systems

The EPS is not characterised by significant opposition between pro- and anti-Europe mainstream domestic parties. In this setting, the mainstream parties are rather Europhile. However, the Eurosceptic parties are not necessarily absent, but their political weight is limited since they win less than 10 per cent of the seats in the national assemblies (10%<X). France, Germany, Spain and Romania, as well as Italy, are examples of this pattern of party competition/co-operation. However, referendums and/or European elections might change the party system for a short period. In this group, France is an unusual case as, in the past, it developed as a divided party system (DPS) with two strong anti-European parties, the Communists and the neo-Gaullists. For the European parliamentary elections (since 1979) and the presidential elections (2002), France has developed as a party system with significant Eurosceptic parties (PSEP). The 2005 referendum divided French voters

when the majority rejected the EU Constitution project, indicating that France was close to a divided party system. Nowadays and during national elections, France has moved to a more Europhile party system – although a party such as the FN of Le Pen has struggled hard to achieving significant representation in the French National Assembly.

Four additional cases, which are not among the selected country studies, also fit the pattern of the EPS: Luxembourg, Finland, Slovenia and Cyprus. In Luxembourg, political parties are rather Europhile. Following the June 2009 elections, the Christian Social Party (PCS) confirmed its status as the main domestic party. It was followed by middle-ranged parties such as the Socialist Workers' Party (POSL), the Liberal Democrat Party (PD) and the Greens. There is also the 'small' Alternative Democratic Reform Party (ADR).[33] During the referendum, Luxembourg voted in favour of the EU Constitutional Treaty.

After the March 2007 election in Finland, the three major parties were, in order of importance, the Centre Party (KESK), the National Coalition Party (KOK) and the Social Democratic Party (SDP). They have supported Finland's European integration. They were followed by 'small' parties such as the Left Alliance, the Green League, the Swedish People's Party (SFP) and the Christian Democrats (KD).[34] The principal Eurosceptic party, the True Finns,[35] was a 'very small' party (five seats). This has changed following the April 2011 elections: the radical right True Finns realised an important breakthrough by winning almost 20 per cent of the seats in the Parliament. Since then, the Finish party system could be considered as pro-European with one significant Eurosceptic party.

Following the September 2008 election, Slovenia has two main parties: the Social Democrats and the Slovenian Democrat Party (SDP). They are followed by the 'middle-range' For Real-New Politics Party (ZARES) and by 'small' parties such as the Democratic Party of Pensioners of Slovenia (DeSUS), the Slovenian National Party (SNS), the Slovenian People's Party-Youth Party of Slovenia (SLS-SMS), the Liberal Democracy of Slovenia (LDS) and representatives of ethnic minorities.[36] They all showed a very broad consensus regarding the EU, except the SNS.[37]

Long before its accession to the EU, the party system in Cyprus was divided – the main Eurosceptic party was the Progressive Party of the Working People (AKEL). At the prospect of the membership of Cyprus to EU, the AKEL changed and adapted to the EU context.[38] Nowadays, it is the 'big' party in the government coalition.[39] The Democratic Rally (DISY), a conservative party, is its big competitor. The remaining political parties are also pro-European: the 'middle-range' and centre-right Democratic Party (DIKO) and the 'small' Movement of Social Democrats (EDEK).[40] There are also the small European Party (EK) and the Ecologists-Environmentalist Movement.

The divided party system

The DPS is animated by the European cleavage between the Eurosceptics and the integrationists. It is in opposition to the pro- and anti-Europe mainstream parties on isomorphic and constitutive issues as well as on the EU orientation. In this setting, the Eurosceptic parties are necessarily present. Their political weight is very significant since they win more than 30 per cent (X>30%) of the seats in the national assemblies. The UK and Poland confirm this pattern of co-operation/ competition in party systems. In some cases, Eurosceptic parties are even governing the country, such as in Hungary, the UK and Poland.[41] However, Poland has very recently experienced a presidential election that showed the pro-European Bronislaw Komorowski with a very slight edge over the Eurosceptic Jaroslaw Kaczyński.

Four additional cases that are not among the selected country studies would also fit the pattern of the DPS: Sweden, Slovakia, Malta and Hungary.

The Swedish party system is animated by the European cleavage between and within political parties.[42] Following the September 2006 elections, the Social Democrat Party (SAP) passed from the status of major party to a very important one. The loss of almost 5 per cent was enough to allow the switch in favour of the 'Alliance for Sweden'[43] (M, CP, FP and Kd). The SAP is followed by its 'big' rival, the Moderate Party (M). Other 'small' parties are also present in the national arena: the Centre Party (CP), the Liberal Party (FP), the Christian Democratic Party (Kd), the Left Party (VP) and the Green Party (Mpg). The Kd is divided among factions defending various positions on Europe, while the Greens present Eurosceptic positions.[44] On the other hand, the FP and the M are Europhile.[45] Two referendums took place in Sweden: membership to the EU (1994: Yes) and Economic and Monetary Union (2003: No).

The Slovak Republic is characterised by strong Euroscepticism.[46] After the June 2010 elections,[47] opposition to Europe seems prominent with most of the parties being Eurosceptic. On the 'soft' side of Euroscepticism, there are two parties that are moderately opposed to Europe: the 'major' left SMER (Direction) and the 'small' Christian Democratic Union (KDU). On the 'hard' side of Euroscepticism, there is the middle-range Slovak National Party (SNS). An additional party in 'hard' opposition to Europe is the declining 'very small' Communist Party of Slovakia. Moreover, non-Eurosceptic 'middle-range' parties include among others the Slovak Democratic and Christian Union Democratic Party (SDKU-DS).[48]

The European cleavage is also present in the Maltese two-party system.[49] The Maltese Labour Party (MLP) presents a Eurosceptic position while the Nationalist Party (NP) is rather Europhile. During the 2003 EU membership referendum to the EU, the MLP confirmed its Euroscepticism while the NP favoured EU accession. The Maltese electors voted 'yes' to membership and, accordingly, the NP in government dissolved Parliament and called a general election for five weeks' time and won.[50] A few years later, on the occasion of the March 2008 election, the NP again won the majority of the seats in the House of Representatives, leaving its 'major' competitor, the MLP in the opposition – with the difference of just one seat.[51]

In Hungary, the European cleavage animates the two 'major' political parties (April 2006 elections).[52] The Socialist Party (MSzP) looks to be rather pro-European while its competitor, the Hungarian Civic Union – Christian Democratic People's Party (FIDESz–KDNP), seemed to be a soft Eurosceptic party – note that the KDNP party ran on the lists of the FIDESz. The pro-European side is slightly reinforced by 'small' parties such as the Hungarian Democratic Forum (MDF) and the Alliance of Free Democrats (SzDSz). In addition, Hungary experienced the referendum for membership to the EU with a low turnout (2003: Yes). EU salience has remained low although at some point there were intense inter-party debates.[53] The April 2010 elections gave an outstanding legitimacy to the FIDESz–KDNP (262 seats, 67.8 per cent), being the first non-coalition and very Eurosceptic government of post-communist Hungary.

The party systems with significant Eurosceptic parties

Most domestic European party systems are pro-European with significant Eurosceptic parties. This pattern of co-operation/competition brings into opposition pro-Europe mainstream parties against anti-Europe 'non-mainstream' parties debating EU orientation as well as constitutive or isomorphic issues. The former type represents 'governing' parties; the latter type is given opposition parties. Some of them have the potential to support the government (the Netherlands) or to be part of a governmental coalition. Referendums could be very destabilising for the EU orientation. In one or another country, referendums on European integration issues might reinforce Eurosceptic parties and Eurosceptic voters (X>50%). In this setting, a Eurosceptic party is necessarily present and its political weight is significant since it wins between 10 and 30 per cent (10%<X<30%) of the seats in Parliament. The analysis by Botetzagias and Vernardakis of Greece (Chapter Six) confirms this third pattern.

Eleven additional cases, which are not among the selected country studies, would also fit the pattern of the *party system with significant Eurosceptic parties* (PSEP): Belgium, the Netherlands, Ireland, Denmark, Portugal, Austria, Czech Republic, Estonia, Lithuania, Latvia and Bulgaria. One may also distinguish countries with very significant Eurosceptic parties (20%<X<30%), such as the Netherlands, Denmark, Portugal, Austria, Czech Republic and Latvia.

Belgium is animated by the cleavage between the Francophone and the Flemish (Dutch) speaking communities.[54] The political families are divided by this cleavage, which has created corresponding political parties at the linguistic level.[55] Following the June 2010 Belgian elections, the core of the party system is a collection of middle-range political parties: the right-wing Flemish Eurosceptic[56] party (*Nieuw-Vlaamse Alliantie* – N-VA) with 18 per cent of the seats, the Francophone *Parti socialiste* (PS), the liberal Francophone *Mouvement Réformateur* (MR) and the Flemish Christian Democrats (*Christen-Democratisch en Vlaams* – CD&V). They are followed by small parties such as the Flemish Social Democratic Party (*Sociaal Progressief Alternatief* – sp.a), the Flemish liberal *Open Vlaamse Liberalen en Democraten* (Open VLD), the Francophone Christian Democrats (*Centre démocrate humaniste* – CDH) and the Francophone greens (*Ecolo*), as well as the very small Flemish green (*Groen*). In addition to the N-VA, which is the strongest party in Belgium, there are also other Eurosceptic parties, such as the radical right Flemish *Vlaams Belang*, and very small parties, such as the right populist lead by Jean-Marie Dedecker (*Lijst Dedecker*), and the Francophone extreme-right party (*Front national* – FN).[57] Following the June 13, 2010 election, the President of the Francophone Socialist Party, Elio Di Rupo, was the latest politician trying to form a new government. On Wednesday 14th September 2011, he made an outstanding breakthrough towards the formation of the Belgian government as 8 political parties (Flemish and Francophone Liberal, Christian-Democrat, Green and Socialist families) have agreed mainly to 'split' the electoral district of Brussels-Halle-Vilvoorde.

In the Netherlands, the 2005 referendum on the EU Constitutional Treaty indicates the existence of an important pro- and anti-Europe divide, both between political parties and between voters. On the one hand, most of the parties in government (the Christian Democrats – CDA, the Liberal Party – VVD and the 'small' Progressive Democrats – D66) and in opposition (the Labour Party – PvdA and the 'small' Green Left – GL) were in favour of the treaty. On the other hand, the 'middle-range' Socialist Party (SP) and the right-wing Party for Freedom (*Group Wilders/Partij voor de Vrijheid*) were among the main anti-treaty parties. They represent more than 22 per cent of the Dutch voters. They campaigned respectively against the Economic and Monetary Union and the Euro, and against Turkish membership. It ended up with the 'Nee' of the Dutch voters. European issues are still a secondary concern for the Dutch voters[58] and the early elections on 13th June 2010 confirmed the relative strength of Eurosceptic parties in the Netherlands. The Party for Freedom is the third party (16 per cent) while the SP is the fifth party (10 per cent) in terms of seats in the Dutch House of Representatives.[59]

The core of the Irish party system is not really characterised by Euroscepticism. Following the May 2007 elections and in order of importance, the system is composed of the 'major' party *Fianna Fail* (FF), the 'big' *Fine Gael* (FG) and the 'middle-range' Labour Party (LP).[60] Euroscepticism is rather confined in the 'very small' parties such as the nationalist *Sinn Féin Party* (SF) and in the Green Party.[61] The referendum is a key feature of Irish European politics and there have been several of these: the EC membership (1972: Yes), the Single European Act (1987: Yes), the Maastricht Treaty (1992: Yes), the Amsterdam Treaty (1998: Yes), the Nice Treaty (2001: No; 2002: Yes), and the Lisbon Treaty (2008: No; 2009: Yes).

In Denmark, the core of the party system is not affected by Euroscepticism. Subsequent to the November 2007 elections,[62] the two big parties are the Liberal Party (*Venstre*) and the Social Democratic Party. The pro-European ideology is reinforced by the 'middle-range' Conservative People's Party and the 'small' Radical Liberal Party. However, Euroscepticism has increased in strength and characterises the positions of two 'middle-ranged' parties: the Danish People's Party and the Socialist People's Party. As in the Irish case, Denmark experienced various referendums: the EC membership (1972: Yes), the Single European Act (1986: Yes), the Maastricht Treaty (1992: No), the Maastricht Treaty with the Edinburgh Agreement (1993: Yes), the Amsterdam Treaty (1998: Yes) and the Euro (2000: No).[63]

The two core Portuguese parties are not affected by Euroscepticism. Following the February 2005 elections, the Socialist Party (PS) scored an outstanding electoral result allowing the PS to become the 'major' Portuguese party, while the centre-right Social-Democratic Party (PSD) was reduced from a 'very important' party to a 'big' party. Subsequent to the September 2009 elections,[64] the PS confirmed its leading position as a 'very important' party, while the PSD changed by presenting the score of a very important party. At the margin, three 'small' parties present a Eurosceptic profile and total more than 20 per cent of the votes: the Unitarian Democratic Coalition (CDU), which brings in the Communist and the Greens, the Popular Party (CDS-PP) and the Left Bloc (BE). In Portugal, the left-right cleavage is bisected by the pro- and anti-EU cleavage; the latter cleavage, of course, carries less weight than the former.[65]

Following the September 2008 elections, the Austrian party system is characterised by two 'big' pro-European parties, although with decreasing electoral performance: the Social Democratic Party (SPÖ) and the People's Party (ÖVP).[66] They are followed by 'middle-range' political parties. By order of importance, there are two far-right parties which are by definition Eurosceptic and which both aggregate more than 28 per cent: the Freedom Party (FPÖ) and the Alliance for the Future of Austria (BZÖ) created by Jörg Haider. They are followed by the Greens (10.43 per cent). The salience of 'Europe' is low with regard to inter-party competition.[67]

The European cleavage seems to operate also in Czech politics. The conservative and Eurosceptic Civic Democrat Party (ODS) was created by Vaclav Klaus. Before the 2010 elections, the Czech party system could be considered as a 'divided party system' in view of the ODS's strength and was a very important party. Klaus and the ODS showed some reluctance to give their blessing to the Lisbon Treaty. Yet, the May 2010 elections indicated that the ODS is a big party (26.5 per cent).[68] This implies that the Czech party is no longer a divided party system on European issues according to our criteria. Following the 2010 elections, the Czech Social Democrat Party (CSSD) is the first 'big' Czech party followed by the 'middle-range' Communist Party of Bohemia and Moravia (KSCM).

Following the 2007 Estonian elections,[69] the 'big' political parties are Euro-enthusiasts: the Reform Party and the Centre Party. They are joined by the 'small' People's Union (R). At the Eurosceptic end of the spectrum, there is mainly the 'middle-range' Social Democratic Party (SDE).[70] Estonian politics are also animated by, on the one hand, 'newcomers' such as the 'middle-range' *Pro Patria and Res Publica Union* (IRL) and the 'small' Greens and, on the other hand, the 'very small' parties representing the Russian minority.

Subsequent to the October 2008 Lithuanian elections, the Homeland Union-Lithuanian Christian Democrats (TS-LKD) became a 'very important' party. It was followed by two 'middle-range' parties: the Social Democratic Party (LSDP) and the Rising National Party (RNP). Two 'small' parties are present in the national political arena: the 'Labour Party + Youth Coalition' and the Liberal Movement of the Republic of Lithuania.[71] On the Eurosceptic side, Lithuanian politics seemed to witness the emergence of the nationalist and middle-range Order and Justice Party and the 'very small' Union of Lithuanian Peasants and Peoples.[72]

On the occasion of the October 2006 Latvian elections, the People's Party (TP) confirmed its position as a 'big party'. Accordingly, the coalition continued with the Union of Greens and Farmers (ZZS), the Electoral Union of Latvia First Party (LPP) and the Latvian Way Party (LC).[73] This centre-right coalition looks rather pro-European. In addition, there are two 'middle-range' political parties: the Christian Democratic party New Era (JL) and the Russian minority Concord Centre (SC). They are followed by two small parties: the Russian minority party entitled For Human Rights in United Latvia (PCTLV) and the Conservative Union for Fatherland and Freedom (TB/LNNK). It 'seems' that the PCTLV, the TB/ LNNK and the SC flirted with Euroscepticism[74] – all together, they aggregate 29 per cent of the seats.

Europe was not a salient issue in the 2005 election, when the Bulgarian Socialist Party, part of the Coalition for Bulgaria, scored 34.17 per cent, and the National Movement Simeon II reached 19.9 per cent. It was followed by the Movement for Rights and Freedoms (PDS), a Turkish community-based party.[75] Subsequent to the July 2009 Bulgarian elections,[76] the major political party is the centre-right Citizens for European Development of Bulgaria Party (GERB). It is followed by middle-range political parties: the Coalition for Bulgaria (CB), the DPS and the ATAKA party, an ultra-nationalist party that campaigned on an anti-EU platform. Small parties follow, such as the Blue Coalition (BC) and the Order, Lawfulness, Justice Party (RZS).

Table 11.4 presents a snapshot of the typology of member countries in relation to the three patterns of co-operation/competition in party systems.

Table 11.4: Three patterns of co-operation/competition in party systems

Europhile party systems	Divided party systems	Party systems with significant Eurosceptic parties
France	United Kingdom	Belgium
Germany	Sweden	The Netherlands
Italy	Poland	Ireland
Luxembourg	Slovakia	Denmark
Spain	Malta	Greece
Slovenia	Hungary	Portugal
Cyprus		Austria
Romania		Finland
		Czech Republic
		Estonia
		Lithuania
		Latvia
		Bulgaria

European integration as a source of domestic depoliticisation?

Peter Mair argues that European integration contributes to the reinforcement of the general trend of 'depoliticisation' in domestic politics (see page 3). Certainly, more in-depth studies are needed to explore Mair's hypothesis. The country studies in this book suggest that European integration may in some cases reinforce depoliticisation (the United Kingdom, Greece, Spain and Poland) while in other cases it seems unrelated (see Table 11.5).

Confirming depoliticisation

In the British case, the EU has probably encouraged depoliticisation 'as the majority of British voters see it [the EU] as making politics even less attractive than national issues'. In addition, and to a certain extent, even more important than the EU's influence, other internal and external factors enhance depoliticisation. In domestic terms, partisan politics present more and more an elite-driven nature that marginalises citizens. An additional source of depoliticisation is represented by the negative images and representations of the EU that the tabloid press presents. Last but not least, the party system of the UK is affected by various external factors such as pressures induced by globalisation. In contrast with Mair and taking into account these internal and external factors of depoliticisation, Hanley and Loughlin (Chapter Five) do not consider the British case a prime example of overcoming the problems of depoliticisation.

Table 11.5: Country studies confirming/questioning Mair's hypotheses

	Confirmation	Questioning
France		X
Italy		X
Germany		X
UK	X	
Greece	X	
Spain	X	
Poland	X	
Romania		X

The cases of Spain, Poland and Greece seem to confirm the reinforcement of depoliticisation by European integration. For example, Botetzagis and Vernardakis conclude (Chapter Six):

> that the issue of 'Europe' does not figure in national elections, as one would have expected due to either a 'realistic/traditional' or to a 'strategic' (i.e. aiming at 'depoliticising' the voters) course of action by individual parties. Yet *neither* does it figure in the European election.

Disconfirming depoliticisation

Two types of negative cases can be distinguished. There are cases characterised by an effect opposite to the one expected by Mair – the politicisation. The French case shows an impressive politicisation of national rather than European issues. In other words, Europeanisation is boosting the internal debate about domestic issues much more than supranational ones. This situation results from an array of aspects. First, the mainstream parties are not able to contain the extreme parties of the right and the left that use anti-integration rhetoric. Secondly, some factions within parties are equally out of control. These intra-partisan oppositions have a favourable echo next to citizens because they make use of the already existing anti-European undertow in French society. In addition, the Italian case does not show trends of depoliticisation induced by European integration, as the Italian parties' positions over the European issue seem to be quite structured as well as diverse. This may indicate that European issues are debated and politicised in the Italian political arena.

However, the second type of negative cases shows that European integration has no – or limited – effect on domestic depoliticisation. In presenting the German case, Hertner and Sloam (page 46) consider that 'even though the policy space, repertoire, and instruments available to German parties have been limited due to the process of European integration, political competition has not become depoliticised'. In her chapter on Romania, Soare claims (Chapter Nine):

> that, although there is evidence for the Romanian domestic politics depoliticisation, [the] EU is neither a cause nor a consequence since it has never been an internalised framework, a channel through which political debates were triggered and public concerns represented.

Europeanisation, party politics and supranational representation

Taking account of cross-national similarities and differences in the study of the Europeanisation of party systems and political parties, we subscribe to the line of cross-national research that 'is valuable, even indispensable, for establishing the generality of findings and the validity of interpretations derived from single-nation studies'.[77]

The test of the research assumptions shows that the differences among national systems are not important in explaining the Europeanisation or non-Europeanisation of party systems and of individual parties.

The outcome of the Europeanisation or non-Europeanisation of party systems can be explained by a conjunction of independent (European integration, including the EP elections in France) and intervening variables (the strategic interaction among political parties and the role of public opinion). On the one hand, the *non*-Europeanisation of party systems (identified in most of the country cases) is explained by the party elites' unwillingness to bring Europe into national debates. Thus, the party system is not really Europeanised. This confirms the analysis from the literature that the elites prefer to be insulated from electoral constraints and public opinion as they perceive no electoral advantage in politicising Europe at the domestic level, except in case of a referendum and direct democracy.[78] On the other hand, the Europeanisation of party systems is explained by the influence of European integration mediated by strategic party interactions and electoral incentives, public opinion and referendums. One example is the French case, which can be considered according to the literature as a 'deviant' case. Arend Lijphart has defined deviant case analyses as 'studies of single cases that are known to deviate from established generalizations. They are selected in order to reveal why the cases are deviant – that is, to uncover relevant additional variables that were not considered previously'.[79] Further research would be interesting in order to analyse if other countries in Europe confirm, refine or sharpen the findings derived from the analysis of the French case.

The outcome of the Europeanisation or non-Europeanisation of individual parties is also explained by a conjunction of an independent variable (European integration) and intervening variables (cleavage structures and political families as well as relevant variations, distinctions and characteristics within party families[80]; strategic competition, participation in government and geopolitics). In addition to the independent variable (European integration and in addtion to Bartolini's comments), our findings on the eight countries studied strengthen the analysis of Marks, Wilson and Ray, who conclude that the ideological location of a party is stronger than strategic competition and participation in government.[81] More tentatively, our findings respond to the question posed by Hooghe and Marks about the role of geopolitics,[82] which proves to be explicitly important for social-democracy, radical left parties and constraining for the green family.

Regarding the geopolitical model, Delwit points out appropriately that it 'was' an important explanation during the East-West polarisation for understanding the social-democratic family.[83] Since the end of communism in Europe, geopolitical incentives/disincentives seem to have been less important for western European political parties while parties in the post-communist EU (central and eastern Europe) are/may be concerned much more by Russia. We point out that ideological location is stronger than participation in government, strategic competition and geopolitics. In other words, and referring to Bartolini's distinction,[84] the country studies show that the genetic model (cleavage and ideology) is stronger than the partisan model (strategic competition), the institutional model (participation in government) and the geopolitical model.

However, the differences among domestic systems are important in explaining the patterns of co-operation/competition in the party systems on European integration issues. These differences are related mainly to the weight of the Eurosceptic party (or parties) in a given EU member state. In addition, the evidence shows the importance of factors such as the similarities/differences in terms of political parties' policy stances. Drawing on the findings of this book, the impact of European integration on the patterns of co-operation/competition lead to three distinct structured types of domestic party systems:

1. The *Europhile party systems* (EPS): France, Germany, Italy, Spain, Romania and, perhaps, Luxembourg, Slovenia, Cyprus.
2. The *divided party systems* (DPS): UK, Poland and, perhaps, Sweden, Slovakia, Malta and Hungary.
3. The *party systems with significant Eurosceptic parties* (PSEP): Greece and, perhaps, Belgium (after June 2010 elections), the Netherlands, Ireland, Denmark, Portugal, Austria, Finland (after April 2011 elections), Czech Republic (after May 2010 elections), Estonia, Lithuania, Latvia and Bulgaria.

In the context of the current financial and economic globalisation crisis, one can observe the reinforcement and the breakthrough of Eurosceptic right-wing populist or radical right parties,[85] which are weakening the EPS while strengthening the PSEP in the EU countries. The 2008 global financial crisis has radically worsened the domestic socio-economic situation by inducing significant austerity policies. Shifts in the wider world economy and pressures of the global economy on the EU and its member states, including party systems and political parties, has not yet produced all the dramatic socio-economic and socio-political effects.[86]

It is important to link these findings on the domestic party politics of Europeanisation with the issue of EU representation and democracy.[87] Accordingly, Fritz Scharpf, puts forward a dichotomy between input-oriented authenticity (government by the people) and output-oriented effectiveness (government for the people).[88] He argues that the main problem in terms of Europe's democratic deficit is the 'government for the people' and, in particular, the lack of substantial socio-economic policies to face an unemployment crisis and social policy issues, and to answer to the demands of the people.

Agreeing with Scharpf, I also consider that the challenge is to think of a new equilibrium between the 'government by the people' and 'the government for the people' in the context of European integration. Improvement has occurred in terms of Europarty regulation.[89] However, European party federations are still underdeveloped in organisational and functional terms.[90] In parallel, the European Parliament has emerged as one of the major actors of European politics since the first European elections in 1979, making a significant contribution to the development of political representation at the European level.[91] As a complementary solution, the European Ombudsman considers that the Lisbon Treaty opens up opportunities both for people and political elites to better interact on European issues, although the risk of 'renationalisation' remains.[92] However, this has not been sufficient to reinforce European political parties as structures of representation and conflict resolution. Accordingly, Bartolini (Chapter Ten) has developed the peculiarities of European political parties by combining the genetic, morphological and representation perspectives.

In principle, the politicisation of European integration issues may reinforce the input-oriented authenticity. In practice, and in the context of each of the twenty-seven member states (and more in the future), the reinforcement of the use of referendums and/or of critical opinion polls of national citizens and anti-Europe political parties may lead to serious problems concerning the progress of European integration. One conclusive example is the experience of referendums on the European Constitution Treaty.[93] In this configuration, the participation of 'anti-Europe' in both public opinion and political parties in European politics may lead to very weak or 'no' progress in European integration, especially within the six countries with divided party systems (United Kingdom, Sweden, Poland, Slovakia, Malta and Hungary) and the thirteen party systems of those with significant Eurosceptic parties (Belgium, the Netherlands, Ireland, Denmark, Greece, Portugal, Austria, Finland, Czech Republic, Estonia, Lithuania, Latvia and Bulgaria). Accordingly, the paradox is that reinforcing only the domestic democracies of member states in relation to European issues can actually block effective progress in European integration. It is a significant political consequence of people and political elites' domestic preferences on European politics and policy. Therefore, one may expect that 'controversial referendums are likely to be suppressed by repackaging reform into smaller and therefore less referendum-prone, bundles'.[94] However, governing Europe on a technocratic or elitist basis may seem to be a suitable solution for the development of European integration.

Nevertheless, as suitable as it may be, it is problematic in the light of democratic standards. In theory, it is expected that 'national elections should be more and more about Europe; whereas European elections should be more and more about questions of day-to-day policy making'.[95] However, Mair observes on the ground that this is not happening as national elections are more about conflicts over policy alternatives, which are constrained by the EU, while European elections are dominated by debates over the direction of EU, which are constrained by national governments.[96] This is what Bartolini considers to be a split party system. In particular, Bartolini (see pages 166–7) presents the following disadvantages of this system: European party families are split along national lines on EU issues (membership, institutional design, competences) while the autonomy and the legitimacy of the EP is questioned as a supranational body.

Regarding the role of Europarties, Mair is sceptical about the existence of the European party system.[97] The degree of scepticism is less for Bartolini, who points out that Europarties play a minor role as they try contributing when setting the agenda, disciplining their party members' behaviour within EU institutions, organising coalitions between political families and in structuring the European elections. However, Bartolini also notes that European party federations and party groups do not assure political responsibility in relation to the elite political personnel, the conception of electoral strategy and tactics. Nevertheless, he points out the key role of European party federations and parliamentary parties in providing potential direction from this split party system towards European mass politics (see page 167). In the words of Richard Katz:

> the greatest change in the European party system would be the replacement of the current national party systems by a single system of Europe-wide parties contesting national and sub-national elections, in the same way that the current national parties contest sub-national elections.[98]

Nonetheless, Bartolini's chapter considers Europarties becoming real structures of representation as problematic. He points out that the Europarties are under-organised and not dealing effectively with socio-economic issues. Accordingly, he notes that Europarties can become 'effective organisations for the representation and for the resolution of non-territorial conflicts' by focusing on the strengthening of their organisation and 'their capacity to deal effectively with those socio-economic issues on which their domestic stands are compatible with the European ones' (see page 168).

Confirming the identified peculiarities of European political parties, the country studies point out that there are factors that present the potential to complicate reaching socio-economic consensus and compromise between domestic parties within Europarties such as ideology, participation in government, strategic competition and geopolitics. Additional country-specific variables are worth exploring such as culture, history and symbols,[99] as well as economic dependence/interdependence and domestic economic interests.[100]

My co-authors and I have focused on the impact of European integration on party systems (political cleavages and political competition, including the format and the mechanics as well as politicisation/depoliticalisation and national patterns) and on political parties (policy stances). Accordingly, the methodological and theoretical approach, as well as the conclusion of this book, provides a useful observation of the variety of systems and parties in different European countries and the development of Europarties.

Following our analysis of the Europeanisation of party systems and political parties, there is much more to ascertain. Suggestions that the politicisation of Europe may be good for democracy and representation must continue taking into account the (potential) role of national political parties, the party systems and the Europarties.

First, regarding democracy, would an innovative equilibrium between input-oriented authenticity and output-oriented effectiveness emerge in the multilevel European governance and politics?

Second, it is useful to observe why, how and when the debate over Europe affects other European countries' party systems and political parties. Thus it is important to carry out additional country studies based on Luxembourg, Slovenia or Cyprus (EPS); Sweden, Slovakia, Malta or Hungary (DPS); Belgium, the Netherlands, Ireland, Denmark, Portugal, Austria, Finland, Czech Republic, Estonia, Lithuania, Latvia or Bulgaria (PSEP); on candidate countries (Croatia, Iceland, The former Yugoslav Republic of Macedonia, Montenegro and Turkey) and potential candidate countries (Albania, Bosnia and Herzegovina, Kosovo and Serbia).

Third, would the nature and the role of Europarties evolve and move from their underdeveloped state to take into account input from *society* and deal effectively with socio-economic issues?

Notes

1 I especially thank Lect. Ana Maria Dobre for excellent exchanges on comparative method and for proofreading this chapter. For their suggestions, I thank also Prof. David Hanley, Senior Lect. Simon Lightfoot and Prof. John Loughlin.

2 For an initial impression, see E. Külahci, 'European integration, party systems and individual parties: comparative politics approach and the assumption of variations', *Revue d'études européennes*, 2007, no. 1, pp. 8–11.

3 A. Przeworski and H. Teune, *The Logic of Comparative Social Inquiry*, New York, Wiley, 1970, p. 35.

4 T. W. Meckstroth, '"Most different systems" and "most similar systems": a study in the logic of comparative inquiry', *Comparative Political Studies*, 1975, vol. 8 (2), p. 137.

5 L. Hooghe and G. Marks, 'A postfunctionalist theory of European integration: from permissive consensus to constraining dissensus', *British Journal of Political Science*, 2009, vol. 39, p. 19.

6 P. Mair, 'The limited impact of Europe on national party systems', *West European Politics*, 2000, vol.23 (4), pp. 47–8; J.-M. De Waele (ed.), *European Union Accession Referendums*, Brussels, Editions de l'Université de Bruxelles, 2005.

7 Hooghe and Marks,'A postfunctionalist theory...', p. 19.

8 E. Külahci, 'EU political conditionality and parties in government: human rights and the quest for Turkish transformation', in I. Botetzagias (ed.), 'Europeanising Southern Europe', *Journal of Southern Europe and the Balkans*, 2005, vol.7 (3), pp. 387–402.

9 See Chapter Ten in this volume.

10 G. Marks and C. J. Wilson, 'The past in the present: a cleavage theory of party response to European integration', *British Journal of Political Science*, 2000, vol.30 (3), p. 443.

11 L. Hooghe, G. Marks and C. J. Wilson, 'Does left/right structure party positions on European integration', in G. Marks and M. R. Steenbergen (eds), *European Integration and Political Conflict,* Cambridge, Cambridge University Press, 2004, p. 129.

12 P. Delwit, *Les partis socialistes et l'intégration européenne: France, Grande-Bretagne, Belgique*, Brussels, Editions de l'Université de Bruxelles, 1995, pp. 17–54, pp. 255–7, pp. 261–76.

13 *ibid.*, pp. 253–61.

14 Marks and Wilson, 'The past in the present...', p. 438.

15 *ibid.*

16 *ibid.*, pp. 448–51.

17 *ibid.*, pp. 448–9.

18 *ibid.*, p. 449.

19 *ibid.*

20 *ibid.* p. 456.

21 Hooghe, Marks and Wilson, 'Does left/right structure ...', p.135

22 *ibid.*, p. 128.

23 Marks and Wilson, 'The past in the present...', p. 438.

24 *ibid.*

25 Hooghe, Marks and Wilson, 'Does left/right structure...', p.137.

26 *ibid.*, p. 133.

27 G. Marks, C. Wilson and L. Ray, 'National political parties and European integration', *American Journal of Political Science*, 2002, vol. 46 (3), p. 592.

28 *ibid.*, p. 585.

29 Hooghe and Marks, 'A postfunctionalist theory...', p. 23.

30 The distinction proposed by this book differs in crucial respects from the three patterns of party competition of Aleks Szczerbiak and Paul Taggart. Indeed, the present typology is different from the one proposed by Taggart and Szczerbiak who focus mainly on Eurosceptic parties:

   - limited contestation grouping instances of limited Euroscepticism (France, Germany, Italy, Belgium, The Netherlands, Luxembourg, Spain, Portugal, Finland, Ireland, Slovenia);
   - the open contestation characterised by the spectacular nature of Euroscepticism (UK, Greece, Sweden, Austria, Malta, Czech Republic, Denmark and Norway); and
   - the constrained contestation bringing together sensitive post-communist candidate states (Poland, Hungary, Slovakia, Latvia, Lithuania, Estonia).

   See A. Szczerbiak and P. Taggart, 'Conclusion: opposing Europe? three patterns of party competition over Europe', in A. Szczerbiak and P. Taggart (eds), *Opposing Europe? The Comparative Party Politics of Euroscepticism, Volume 1: Case Studies and Country Surveys,* Oxford, Oxford University Press, 2008, p. 350, p. 354, and p. 358.

31 G. Sartori, *Parties and Party Systems: A Framework for Analysis*, Colchester, ECPR Press, Classic Series, 2005, p. 107.

32 The electoral strength of the political parties in each of these countries was found in the database of the Inter-Parliamentary Union – the Parline database http://www.ipu.org/parline-e/parlinesearch.asp.

33 'Luxembourg Chambre des Députés (Chamber of Deputies). Last elections', see the Parline database.

34 'Finland, Eduskunta-Riksdagen (Parliament): Last elections', see the Parline database.

35 R. Tapio, 'Finish party politics of Euroscepticism', in Taggart and Szczerbiak (eds), *Opposing Europe?* pp. 168–80.

36 'Slovenia Drzavni Zbor (National Assembly) Last elections', see the the Parline database.

37 A. Krasovec and S. K. Lipicier, 'Euroscepticism and Slovenian political parties: a case of weak party-based Euroscepticism', in Taggart and Szczerbiak (eds), *Opposing Europe?,* pp. 314–27.

38 I. Katsourides, 'Europeanization and Political Parties in Accession Countries: The Political Parties of Cyprus', Paper prepared for the EpsNet 2003 Plenary Conference.

39 'Cyprus Vouli Antiprosopon (House of Representatives) Last elections', see the the Parline database.

40 Katsourides, 'Europeanization and Political Parties... '.
41 This was also the case, to a lesser extent, of Greece in the 1980s and the Italian 1st Republic (first term).
42 N. Aylott, 'Softer but strong: Euroscepticism and party politics in Sweden', in Taggart and Szczerbiak (eds), *Opposing Europe?*, pp. 181–200.
43 'Sweden Riksdagen (Parliament) Last elections', see the the Parline database.
44 Aylott, 'Softer but strong...', pp. 181–200.
45 *ibid.*
46 K. Henderson, 'The Slovak republic: Eurosceptics and phoney Europhiles', in Taggart and Szczerbiak (eds), *Opposing Europe?*, pp. 277–94.
47 'Slovakia Národná rada (National Council) Last elections', see the the Parline database.
48 Henderson, 'The Slovak republic...', pp. 277–94.
49 Taggart and Szczerbiak, (eds), *Opposing Europe?* p. 355.
50 D. Fenech, 'The 2003 Maltese EU Referendum and General Election', *West European Politics*, 2003, vol. 26 (3), pp. 163–70.
51 'Malta Il-Kamra Tad-Deputati (House of Representatives) Last elections', see the the Parline database.
52 *ibid.*
53 A. Batory, 'Euroscepticism in the Hungarian party system: voices from the wilderness?', in Taggart and Szczerbiak (eds), *Opposing Europe?*, pp. 263–76.
54 P. Delwit, J-M. De Waele and P. Magnette (eds), *Gouverner la Belgique: Clivage et Compromis dans une Société Complexe*, Paris, PUF, 1999; P. Delwit, *La vie politique en Belgique de 1830 à nos jours*, Brussels, Editions de l'Université de Bruxelles, 2009, pp. 342–9; M. Brans, L. De Winter and W. Swenden (eds), *The Politics of Belgium: Institutions and Policy under Bipolar and Centrifugal Federalism*, London, Routledge, 2009.
55 Delwit, *La vie politique..*, pp. 151–319.
56 K. Deschouwer and M. Van Assche, 'Party-based Euroscepticism in Belgium', in Taggart and Szczerbiak (eds), *Opposing Europe?*, p. 89.
57 P. Delwit, E. Külahci, B. Hellings, J.-B. Pilet and E. Van Haute, 'L'Européanisation de la représentation communautaire: Le cas des partis francophones belges', in C. Belot and B. Cautrès (eds), 'Vers une européanisation des partis politiques?', *Politique européenne*, 2005, no. 16, pp. 83–102.
58 C. De Vries, 'The impact of EU referanda on national electoral politics: the Dutch Case', *West European Politics*, 2009, vol. 32 (1), pp. 149–50 and p. 163.
59 'Netherlands Tweede Kamer der Staten-Generaal (House of Representatives), Last elections', see the Paline database.
60 'Ireland Dáil Éireann (House of Representatives) Last elections', see the the Parline database.
61 K. Gilland, 'Shades of green: Euroscpeticisim in Irish political parties', in Taggart and Szczerbiak (eds), *Opposing Europe?* pp. 117–33.
62 'Denmark Folketinget (The Danish Parliament) Last elections', see the the Parline database.

63 A.-C. L. Knudsen, 'Euroscepticism in Denmark' in Taggart and Szczerbiak (eds), *Opposing Europe?*, pp. 152–67.

64 'Portugal Assembleia da Republica (Assembly of the Republic) Last elections', see the the Parline database.

65 M. C. Lobo, 'Portuguese attitudes towards EU Membership: social and political perspectives', in S. Royo and P. C. Manuel (eds), *Spain and Portugal in the European Union: The First Fifteen Years*, London and Portland, Frank Cass, 2003, pp. 106–15.

66 'Austria Nationalrat (National Council) Last elections', see the the Parline database.

67 F. Felland, 'Euroscepticism in Austrian political parties: ideologically rooted or strategically motivated?', in Taggart and Szczerbiak (eds), *Opposing Europe?*, pp. 201–20.

68 'Czech Republic Poslanecka Snemovna (Chamber of Deputies) Last elections', see the the Parline database.

69 'Estonia Riigikogu (The Estonian Parliament) Last elections', see the the Parline database.

70 E. Mikkel and A. Kasekamp, 'Emerging party-based Euroscepticism in Estonia', in Taggart and Szczerbiak (eds), *Opposing Europe?*, pp. 295–313.

71 'Lithuania Seimas (Parliament) Last elections', see the the Parline database.

72 I. Matonytè and V. Gaidys, 'Euroreferendum in Lithuania', in De Waele (ed.), *European Union Accession Referendums*, pp. 65–77.

73 'Latvia Saeima (Parliament)' Last elections, see the the Parline database.

74 J. Ikstens, 'EU referendum in Latvia', in De Waele (ed.), *European Union Accession Referendums,* pp. 65–77.

75 See also Lyubka Savkova, 'Europe and the Parliamentary Election in Bulgaria', *EPERN (European Parties Elections and Referendums Network)*, Sussex University, 25 June 2005.

76 'Bulgaria Narodno Sabranie (National Assembly)', see the the Parline database.

77 M. L. Kohn, 'Cross-national research as an analytical strategy', *American Sociological Review*, 1987, vol. 52 (6), p. 713.

78 Mair, 'The limited impact...', pp. 47–8.

79 A. Lijphart, 'Comparative politics and the comparative method', *American Political Science Review*, 1971, vol. 65 (3), p. 65.

80 Marks and Wilson, 'The past in the present...'; Hooghe, Marks and Wilson, 'Does left/right structure...'.

81 *ibid.*, p. 585.

82 Hooghe and Marks, 'A postfunctionalist theory...', p. 23.

83 Delwit, *Les partis socialistes...*, pp. 294–7.

84 S. Bartolini, *Restructuring Europe: Centre Formation, System Building, and Political Structuring Between the Nation State and the European Union*, Oxford, Oxford University Press, 2005, p. 321.

85 P. Delwit, J.-M. De Waele and A. Rea (eds), *L'extrême droite en France et en Belgique*, Brussels, Editions Complexe, 1998; P. Ignazi, *Extreme Right Parties in Western Europe*, Oxford, Oxford University Press, 2006; P. Delwit

and P. Poirier (eds), *Extrême droite et pouvoir en Europe: The extreme right parties and power in Europe*, Brussels, Editions de l'Université de Bruxelles, 2007.

86 D. Hanley, 'Christian Democracy and the Paradoxes of Europeanization: Flexibility, Competition and Collusion', *Party Politics*, 2002, vol. 8, no. 4, p. 467.

87 D. Castiglione, 'We the citizens? Representation and participation in EU constitutional politics', in R. Bellamy, D. Castiglione and J. Shaw (eds), *Making European Citizens: Civic Inclusion in a Transnational Context*, New York, Palgrave Macmillan, 2006; D. Beetham and C. Lord, *Legitimacy and the EU*, London and New York, Longman, 1998: they analysed three dimensions of the EU legitimacy deficit (identity, representation and output); H. Schmitt and J. Thomassen (eds), *Political Representation and Legitimacy in the European Union*, Oxford, Oxford University Press, 1999; E. Külahci, 'European party federations (EPFs) and the EU legitimacy deficit: conceptualising the horizontal pathway', in N. Winn and E. Harris (eds), 'Europeanisation: Regulation and Identity in the New Europe', Perspectives on European Politics and Society, Journal of Intra-European Dialogue, vol. 4 (1), 2003, pp. 117–45; E. Külahci, *La social-démocratie et le chômage*, Brussels, Editions de l'Université de Bruxelles, 2008, pp. 8–14 and pp. 168–78.

88 F. Scharpf, *Governing in Europe: Effective and Democratic?*, Oxford, Oxford University Press, 1999.

89 E. Külahci, 'Le statuts et le financement des fédérations européennes de partis: vers un renforcement du phénomène partisan européen?', Brussels: Paper presented at the Conference of the 'Association Belge de science politique', 14–15 March 2002, see also the published version of this paper at Külahci, *La social-démocratie...*, pp. 47–56.

90 Delwit, *Les partis socialistes...*, pp. 282–4; P. Delwit and J.-M. De Waele, 'Les élections européennes et l'évolution des groupes politiques au Parlement européen', in M. Telo (ed.), *Démocratie et construction européenne*, Brussels, Editions de l'Université de Bruxelles, 1995, p. 278; S. Hix 'Parties at the European Level and the legitimacy of EU socioeconomic policy', *Journal of Common Market Studies*, 1995, vol. 33 (4), pp. 527–54; P. Delwit, J.-M. De Waele, E. Külahci and C. Van de Walle, 'Les fédérations européennes de partis: des partis dans le processus décisionnel européen?', in P. Magnette and E. Remacle (eds), *Le nouveau modèle européen. Vol.1. Institution et gouvernance*, Brussels, Editions de l'Université de Bruxelles, 2000; P. Delwit, 'Les fédérations européennes et les groupes politiques au Parlement européen: vecteurs de la représentation dans l'Union européenne?', in S. Saurugger (ed.), *Les modes de représentation dans l'Union européenne*, Paris, L'Harmattan, 2003, pp. 97–112; Külahci, *La social-démocratie...'*, pp. 153–78; see also the Chapter Ten in this volume by Stefano Bartolini.

91 F. Attinà, 'The voting behaviour of the European Parliament members and the problem of the Europarties', *European Journal of Political Research*, 1990, vol.18, pp. 557–79; S. Hix and C. Lord, *Political Parties in the European Union*, London, Macmillan, 1997; P. Delwit, J.-M. De Waele and P. Magnette (eds), *A quoi sert le Parlement européen?*, Brussels, Editions Complexe, 1999.

92 Discourse of Nikiforos Diamandouros (European Ombudsman) during the

round table 'Identity and Citizenship in a Supranational Polity' in the frame of the Intune Project (http://www.intune.it/) financed by Framework Programme 6 and coordinated by Prof. Maurizio Cotta (Siena University), Brussels, 12 November 2009.

93 D. Castiglione, J. Schönlau, C. Longman, E. Lombardo, N. Pérez-Solórzano and M. Aziz, *Constitutional Politics in the European Union. The Convention Moment and its Aftermath*, Basingstoke and New York, Palgrave Macmillan, 2007.

94 Hooghe and Marks, 'A postfunctionalist theory...', p. 20.

95 Mair, 'The limited impact...', p. 46.

96 *ibid.*

97 *ibid.*, pp. 38–9.

98 R. Katz, 'Parties in Europe and Parties of Europe', conference organised by Stefano Bartolini, *Multi-level Party Systems: Europeanization and the Reshaping of National Political Representation*, Florence, European University Institute, 16–18 December 1999, p. 32.

99 Delwit, *Les partis socialistes...*, pp. 257–8.

100 E. Külahci, 'Europarties: agenda-setter or agenda-follower? Social democracy and the disincentives for tax harmonization', *Journal of Common Market Studies*, 2010, vol. 48 (5), pp. 1283–306.

index

www.ingramcontent.com/pod-product-compliance
Lightning Source LLC
Chambersburg PA
CBHW072120020426
42334CB00018B/1660